LEO STRAUSS

ON THE BORDERS OF JUDAISM, PHILOSOPHY, AND HISTORY

SUNY series in the Thought and Legacy of Leo Strauss

Kenneth Hart Green, editor

LEO STRAUSS
ON THE BORDERS OF JUDAISM, PHILOSOPHY, AND HISTORY

Jeffrey A. Bernstein

SUNY PRESS

Cover art: oil painting by Giorgio di Chirico entitled Turin Spring (1914).

Published by State University of New York Press, Albany

© 2015 State University of New York

All rights reserved

Printed in the United States of America

No part of this book may be used or reproduced in any manner whatsoever without written permission. No part of this book may be stored in a retrieval system or transmitted in any form or by any means including electronic, electrostatic, magnetic tape, mechanical, photocopying, recording, or otherwise without the prior permission in writing of the publisher.

For information, contact State University of New York Press, Albany, NY
www.sunypress.edu

Production, Diane Ganeles
Marketing, Fran Keneston

Library of Congress Cataloging-in-Publication Data

Bernstein, Jeffrey Alan, author.
Leo Strauss on the borders of Judaism, philosophy, and history / Jeffrey A. Bernstein.
pages cm. — (SUNY series in the thought and legacy of Leo Strauss)
Includes bibliographical references and index.
ISBN 978-1-4384-5651-5 (hc : alk. paper)—978-1-4384-5652-2 (pb : alk. paper)
ISBN 978-1-4384-5653-9 (e-book)
1. Strauss, Leo. 2. Jewish philosophy. 3. Judaism and politics. I. Title.
BM755.S75B47 2015
181'.06—dc23
2014027592

10 9 8 7 6 5 4 3 2 1

To my parents—Judith and Stephen Bernstein
To my children—Zachary and Nathaniel Bernstein
To my wife—Ingrid Rasmussen
Jerusalem and Athens one and all

CONTENTS

Acknowledgments ix

Abbreviations xv

Introduction xvii

Part I. On the Way to Jerusalem and Athens

Chapter One: The Theological-Political Problem, Strauss's Critique of Modern "Jewish Philosophy," and the Legacy of Kant 3

Chapter Two: Strauss's Maimonides 33

Part II. Jerusalem and Athens *in Deed*

Chapter Three: Philosophy as a Platonic Dialogue, or Jerusalem and Athens *in Jerusalem* 63

Chapter Four: The Theological-Political Significance of "What Is Political Philosophy?" 89

Part III. Conclusion

Chapter Five: The Transmission of Philosophy as a Way of Life: Maimonides Viewed Through a Spinozan Lens 135

Notes 165

Bibliography 207

Index 223

ACKNOWLEDGMENTS

A book is a thing about which it can justifiably be said, "You didn't build that on your own." This does not, to my mind, amount to a refusal to take credit or responsibility for the contents in this volume. It is, rather, an admission that writing and thinking, while in one sense irreducible to context, nonetheless happens as a response to other irreducible individuals. I have many such individuals to thank for their help throughout the process of conceiving, thinking, and composing this book.

I wasn't originally going to write a book on Strauss. My dissertation (written during my years at Vanderbilt University) was on Spinoza, Schelling, and Heidegger on the question of human freedom. Coming to the conclusion that the question of human freedom requires taking a stance on the question of what Karl Löwith referred to as meaning in history, my project mutated into one involving Spinoza, Kant, and Schelling (my interest in Heidegger having waned somewhat over the years) on the question of a nonteleological conception of history. That many of these "chapters" came out in article form indicated to me that I was ambivalent about the project. That ambivalence can be articulated as follows: if I was writing a book about Spinoza, Kant, and Schelling and I knew that Spinoza would "win," why was I writing a book about Spinoza, Kant and Schelling? While my initial project stalled, my interest in freedom, history, and, ultimately, the order that history seemed to imply, did not. Continuing to think long and deeply about these issues led me to undertake the project, the results of which you are about to read. Simply stated, Strauss is the only philosopher I could think of who uses the entire history of philosophy as a lens through which to illustrate order and freedom as modes of the human soul. This would be the most basic way of expressing the dialectical relationship that Strauss calls "Jerusalem and Athens."

I began reading Strauss's *What Is Political Philosophy?* during my undergraduate years at Clark University. I found the thinking and questioning contained therein to be compelling without yet quite understanding why it was thus so. But I saw enough, and had enough support from my first philosophy professors, Walter Wright, Gary Overvold, and Steven Gardner, to know that Strauss was a figure worth pursuing. For this (among other things) I thank them. It was during my time at Vanderbilt that I received content and context that gave my interest direct focus. My dissertation adviser, teacher, and friend, Idit Dobbs-Weinstein, provided two important narratives about Leo Strauss's books. When I was in graduate school, she told her students to "read Strauss in moderation, but avoid reading the Straussians—because you don't know what their agendas are, in what ways they are presenting their material, or what they are hiding from you—except for David Lachterman (which also means read Jacob Klein)." And so, I religiously read Strauss in moderation and avoided his students and friends, except for Klein and Lachterman. Years later, when I returned to Strauss, I asked Idit what her problems with "the Straussians" really were. Her answer: "Oh, they're alright—it's just that some of their writings are a bit derivative at times." In thinking about the two different statements, I saw her desire to inoculate her students against mimetic adherence to authority (a desire evident in all the courses I took with her and in all her dissertation instruction) come to light again. As I look back on it, I realize now that, while she was teaching us Aristotle, Ibn Rushd, Maimonides, Gersonides, Leone Ebreo, Spinoza, Adorno, and Benjamin, she was also silently teaching us Strauss the entire time. I thank her not only for the trajectory of my philosophical education and development in general but also for giving me the resources for approaching Strauss when the time was right.

The more proximate cause for returning to Strauss has been my friendship with Alan Udoff. During dinner at a *glatt kosher* Moroccan restaurant, during *Pesach*, in the context of an invited talk at his institution (St. Francis College), I asked him which modern Jewish thinker he believed would "stand the test of time." His answer was so compelling to me (and the dinner ended so late) that I forgot his actual words. Upon asking him to repeat his statement, Alan sent me the following e-mail message: "If we allow that Leo Strauss is a Jewish thinker, then, among the moderns that could be spoken of in that way, he more than anyone else will stand the test of time. Strauss has earned this distinction by recovering the Jerusalem/Athens question as a living question. So long as Athens remained within the boundaries of a tradition and its handbooks, that recovery could not have taken place. It was through Heidegger that Strauss would find a way to break through those boundaries. One cannot but conclude then, that the deepest Jewish thinker of modern times owes a debt that current Jewish thought, as if acting on principle, cannot acknowledge, to say nothing of repay." In intimating that Strauss's relation to other modern Jewish thinkers involved (1) a progress precisely insofar as his own thought did not simply assume the historicity of modern thought to be itself progressive and (2) a progress precisely insofar as it involved a (free) *return* to earlier sources, Alan crystallized my interests in freedom and history and brought these interests into a new setting. That Strauss owed the "Athens" part of this relation to his early study with Heidegger (which I do not greatly pursue in the present context), illuminates, perhaps, the ambiguous, ambivalent, yet vital character of what it means to engage in Jewish thought. I can honestly say that, were it not for Alan's conversation, feedback, and friendship, this book would not have been written.

At Holy Cross, I have been fortunate enough to be the recipient of nearly unending opportunities for dialogue concerning my work on Strauss with colleagues both past and present. My first thanks goes to Dustin Gish, who, during the period when my work assumed its initial form as an essay, tirelessly provided compelling feedback. Thanks also go to Denise Schaeffer who, as a result of a single reading session on "What Is Political Philosophy?" generated my compulsion to turn my work into a book. If my colleagues have grown tired of my Strauss-talk, they should (affectionately) direct their complaints to Dustin and Denise. In lieu of such complaints, I would like to express my gratitude to the following colleagues for enduring, and extending, my ongoing research: Alan Avery-Peck, Lawrence Cahoone, Robert Cording, Matthew Dinan, Thomas Doughton, Christopher Dustin, Mark Freeman, Robert Garvey, James Kee, Daniel Klinghard, Joseph Lawrence, William Morse, Lee Oser, and David Schaefer. Unbeknownst to them, they all bear some of the responsibility for the contents of this book. Without the support of the year long Faculty Fellowship grant that I received during the 2012–2013 academic year, this book might never have actually come to fruition. I would like to thank Charles Weiss, the Committee on Research and Publication, the Philosophy Department, and the College of the Holy Cross for awarding me this grant and thus making my research possible.

My work on Strauss also owes a great debt to the wider academic community. Friends and colleagues near and far gave crucial feedback and support during the composition of this book. Thanks go to Nasser Behnegar, Timothy Burns, Roland Danil, Warren Zev Harvey, Kenneth Hart Green, Robert Howse, Julie Klein, Nitzan Lebovic, Daniel Libenson, Damon Linker, Thomas Meyer, Svetozar Minkov, Joshua Parens, Benjamin Sax, Steven Smith, Richard Velkley, Philipp von Wussow, Hardwig Wiedebach, and Martin Yaffe for their sustained guidance and help. With respect to Strauss's trip to Jerusalem in 1954–55, I wish to thank Ofer Tzemach of the Hebrew University archives and Eva Schorr, editor of the journal *Iyyun*, for their help in locating relevant materials. During the faculty fellowship year, I benefited immensely from a trip to the University of Chicago. There I was given the opportunity not only to speak with Nathan Tarcov, Heinrich Meier, Ralph Lerner, and George Anastaplo (RIP), but also to conduct research at the Leo Strauss archives in the Regenstein Library. I thus owe a special debt of gratitude to Tarcov, Meier, Lerner, Anastaplo, and to the archive staff at Regenstein for their generosity. The situation is similar with respect to Ken Green (editor of the SUNY series on the Thought and Legacy of Leo Strauss), who enthusiastically supported my project from its inception and Michael Rinella and Diane Ganeles who saw it through to its conclusion.

My parents Stephen and Judith Bernstein never failed to encourage me to follow my compulsions in the philosophical life while simultaneously showing me how a life of questioning, criticism, and even "wandering far from home" is also part and parcel of a Jewish life. Their continued love and support is something for which I am forever grateful. My children, Zachary and Nathaniel, have both taught me the necessity of sustained reflection on the relationship between order and freedom. By example, they have also demonstrated sustained toleration for their father's philosophical compulsions. Finally, I would like to thank my wife, Ingrid Rasmussen, for her love, support, and extreme patience with what must have seemed like endless hacking away at a project that, while always pleasant, was never convenient and often sequestering. My debt to her is one that—while perhaps capable of being reciprocated—cannot in principle be repaid.

ABBREVIATIONS

Texts by Leo Strauss

EW: Early Writings
FP: "Farabi's Plato"
FPP: *Faith and Political Philosophy*
GS: *Gesammelte Schriften*
JPCM: *Jewish Philosophy and the Crisis of Modernity*
LAM: *Liberalism Ancient and Modern*
LSM: *Leo Strauss on Maimonides*
LSMM: *Leo Strauss on Moses Mendelssohn*
MEW: "More Early Writings"
NIPPP: "On a New Interpretation of Plato's Political Philosophy"
OT: *On Tyranny*
NRH: *Natural Right and History*
PAW: *Persecution and the Art of Writing*
PL: *Philosophy and Law*
SA: *Socrates and Aristophanes*
SCR: *Spinoza's Critique of Religion*
TM: *Thoughts On Machiavelli*
RCPR: *The Rebirth of Classical Political Rationalism*
WIPP: *What Is Political Philosophy? And Other Studies*

Other Texts

CPM: A Commentary on Plato's Meno, Jacob Klein
JMW: *The Jew in the Modern World*, edited by Paul Mendes-Flohr and Jehudah Reinharz
LSTPPP: *Leo Strauss and the Theological-Political Problem*, Heinrich Meier
OTB: *On the Bible: Eighteen Studies*, Martin Buber

INTRODUCTION

> I sent the club a wire stating, "Please accept my resignation. I don't want to belong to any club that will accept me as a member."
>
> —Groucho Marx

It is an irony of history that a figure whose entire philosophical career is defined by a nondogmatic approach to philosophy should continue to be the object of such heated polemical and dogmatic battles—both affirmative and critical. For some, Leo Strauss is a beacon of wisdom in a sea of relativism; for others, he is the figure who most vigorously jettisons the search for wisdom in favor of the pursuit of power. The situation is not made clearer by the more substantive differences that remain in attempting to find the central distinction around which his work gravitates: Was Strauss most interested in the quarrel between the Ancients and the Moderns? Was he ultimately attempting to draw our attention to the distinction between philosophy and poetry? The philosopher and the city? The philosopher and the gentleman? Jerusalem and Athens? The esoteric versus the exoteric? Finally, there is disagreement as to which "methodology" is best suited to gain access to his work: Is Strauss "writing between the lines" to his readership? If so, does this mean that there is there a "code" to be followed, or rather that his readers need to undergo the experience of working through problems presented in his texts? And ought one attempt to read Strauss systematically—that is, with an eye toward presenting a "whole" of his work; by deemphasizing the chronological order in which he presents his statements in favor of the continuity of ideas expressed in his work? Or ought one to read him from the vantage point of a historian, taking his early years—prior to the formation of a Straussian "school"—as formative and informative with respect to his later writings?

Paradoxically, it may be that Strauss's own nondogmatic approach created the vacuum that both his disciples and critics have attempted to fill. By "nondogmatic" I mean his adopting a philosophical stance while simultaneously showing the limitations of that stance.[1] In so doing, careful readers are able to see the alternative that Strauss presents, in however moderate a manner. While I take my own project to illustrate Strauss's nondogmatic approach to philosophy and Judaism, I do not by any means wish to cast aspersions on other presentations of his work. I believe that the abovementioned debates have facilitated readers' comprehension of key alternatives opened up by Strauss's thought. In Aristotelian parlance, we ought to be grateful to earlier Strauss commentators for having handed down to us the practice and manner of thinking. These discussions also serve to show how wide the gap between any particular interpretation and the wealth of material that exists (and that continues to be discovered) in Strauss's oeuvre.

I begin with these "process" considerations not simply for purposes of presenting a caveat, but rather because they get to the heart of my interpretation of Strauss. Strauss was, in no way, a neutral thinker—that is, he did not present different positions as if he were outside of them or disengaged from them. Yet he also did not let the differences become a stumbling block or limitation with respect to his own ability to present in the strongest light what he took to be the fundamental problems. Put differently, Strauss's thought is continuously located on one side of the distinction in question, but it remains on the border of that distinction. In this respect, Strauss's thought is indeed radical; it gets to the root of a given problem (i.e., an alternative expressed in the form of a distinction), shows that root for what it is (either fundamental or derivative), and shows what life looks like from each side of that distinction. His own positions remain understated but by no means neutral.

What, on my account, is the fundamental distinction in which this "Strauss on the border" comes to light? Strauss himself gives us a now well-known statement of it in "Progress or Return?"

> The very life of Western civilization is the life between two codes, a fundamental tension. There is, therefore, no reason

> inherent in the Western civilization itself, in its fundamental constitution, why it should give up on life. But this comforting thought is justified only if we live that life, if we live that conflict, that is. No one can be both a philosopher and a theologian, or for that matter, a third which is beyond the conflict between philosophy and theology, or a synthesis of both. But every one of us can be and ought to be either the one or the other, the philosopher open to the challenge of theology, or the theologian open to the challenge of philosophy. (JPCM, 117)

I deal more specifically with this passage in chapter 1; this much, however, can be said now: to my knowledge, this is the only place where Strauss speaks about a fundamental distinction that gives rise to, and continues the perseverance of, both philosophical and extraphilosophical characteristics of an entire civilization. Put differently, the distinction between the philosopher and the city is one that impacts philosophy as a way of life ("nonphilosophy" being too diffuse and ephemeral to be classified, in Strauss's terms, as such a way). Similarly, the distinction between the Ancients and the Moderns concerns two very different accounts of the activity of philosophy—the former as a way of life, and the latter as a school.[2] The philosophy/poetry and philosopher/gentleman distinctions both involve alternatives that, on closer inspection, provide more limited accounts of the "whole" than philosophy does—that is, the poet presents nondemonstrative images and the gentleman provides inaccurate, if still reasoned, accounts of the "whole" that the philosopher more rationally and accurately describes.[3] Finally, the distinction between the esoteric and the exoteric, in Strauss's account, applies to different styles of philosophy only. All the distinctions, save one, relate first and foremost to philosophical activity.

It is only the distinction between Jerusalem and Athens that simultaneously includes and transcends philosophy as a way of life. Without rendering chapter 1 superfluous, one can say that this distinction refers to two different and competing responses to the same question: what is the best or most just life? This problem, insofar as it involves not simply individuals but also communities, is a political problem. And insofar as both "cities," in Strauss's terms, acknowledge that the only way to provide an absolute foundation for law and politics is by reference to divine authority, it is a theological problem. Therefore, Jerusalem and Athens are two responses to what Strauss calls the "theological-political problem." Jerusalem refers to the way of life based on obedience to divine law, while Athens refers to the way of life based on the human search for wisdom. While there are overlapping features, these two responses are, for Strauss, exclusive: one cannot have "dual citizenship," as it were. Most remarkable, perhaps, is that the above passage indicates that this problem, and therefore the distinction between Jerusalem and Athens, has no solution—it is a fundamental problem.

If the distinction between Jerusalem and Athens is a fundamental problem, this has enormous consequences for what it means to be human. First, a great deal of human life is a manifestation of either intellectual freedom or the search for order and peace. From a practical point of view, many (if not most) desire some mean between these two needs. This, however, in no way obviates the theoretical problem as to which city (in each case) prevails over the other. For Strauss, the entire thrust of modern philosophy attempted to either mock Jerusalem out of existence or render it innocuous (either by rationally demonstrating its irrationality, or by constructing a synthesis of the two, which leads to a third, ultimate position). In Strauss's account, these attempts failed because, in presupposing that there was a worldly way to theoretically dissolve the distinction, they obscured the theological-political problem and forgot that the desire for order is a fundamental desire of human life. Strauss's most important philosophical gesture, in my reading, is to reawaken this problem *as a problem to be contemplated.* What makes his philosophy so unique, I claim, is his approach to this problem: *he uses the entire history of philosophy as a lens or optic through which to explore and illustrate these two competing ways of life.* In so doing, Strauss provides a forum for his reflective readers to engage with, and undergo, the competing claims of these different ways of life.

Strauss does not use all the figures in this history equally, however. There is one figure that stands at the intersection between the search for human wisdom and the desire for peace and order that occupies a visibly privileged place in Strauss's thought. That figure is Maimonides. Despite the fact that—at different points in his career—Strauss gains a heightened interest in the thought of Nietzsche, Spinoza, Hobbes, Machiavelli, Plato, Aristotle, and Xenophon, Maimonides remains a companion to Strauss from beginning to end. At least one reason for this is that Maimonides (writing at the height of exposure to, and tension between, Jerusalem and Athens), attempted to do justice to both the contemplative needs of potential philosophers and the practical needs of nonphilosophers; he wrote his texts with different audiences in mind. Maimonides, in other words, exemplified (for Strauss) the transhistorical fact that "wisdom [is] not separated from moderation."[4]

If this were only a matter of Strauss and his reading of Maimonides, the general issues I have raised would not be shown in their full complexity. My point is not simply that Maimonides is the thinker of choice for Strauss, but that Strauss's choice of Maimonides illustrates a lifelong commitment to be engaged with the religion into which Strauss was born and which he himself would, early on, practically reject: Judaism. Strauss comes to appreciate Maimonides after intense youthful engagements with different philosophical and religious outlooks available in the context of Weimar Germany—that is, Nietzschean thought, neo-Kantianism, neo-Orthodoxy, the "new thinking" of Rosenzweig and Heidegger, and Zionism. Once he discovers Maimonides's philosophical/Athenian political philosophy, he not only begins to write about the twelfth century Andalusian Jew, but he lets Maimonides's thought shape and inform his own writing; this is particularly true with respect to the issue of writing/speaking to difference audiences. Thus, Maimonides's presence becomes apparent even in places where Strauss does not mention him. This characteristic of Strauss's thought is exemplified, for me, in the essay "What is Political Philosophy?" In addition to being a consideration of classical and modern political philosophy, it also fulfills the Maimonidean task of (1) delivering a practical message of moderation to nonphilosophers, while allowing the potential philosophers to view the theological-political problem and its responses in Jerusalem and Athens, and (2) silently indicating the importance of Maimonides within the discussion of classical and modern political philosophy. Because of this, I claim that "What Is Political Philosophy?" stands as a high-water mark in Strauss's oeuvre, expressing in philosophical form the journey and results of Strauss's move away from modern philosophy and modern Jewish thought toward the premodern philosophy of Maimonides.

Advocating premodern political philosophy, reading Maimonides as a citizen of Athens—these are, to be sure, controversial positions. They were controversial in Strauss's day, and they remain so for anyone writing about them today. During Strauss's youth, the controversies became manifest in the form of polemics about the Enlightenment heritage of liberalism and, in a Jewish context, the concern over what effect an "Athenian Maimonides" might have on the Jewish people.[5] Now that Strauss has become a legitimate topic of philosophical inquiry, the controversies express themselves in terms of how one conceptually and methodologically approaches him with respect to issues such as these. Because of this, it behooves me to make explicit my manner of reading Strauss in relation to some of the current debates.

It used to be that the largest conceptual distinction in Strauss circles was between "East Coast Straussianism"—that is, that Jerusalem and Athens were absolutely incompatible—and "West Coast Straussianism"[6]—that is, that Jerusalem and Athens could be, if not simply synthesized, then at least reconciled. The classic representatives of these schools were, respectively, Allan Bloom and Harry Jaffa. While this distinction, in its early form, occurred largely in the context of political science departments, it has now transformed in content and widened in institutional scope to include the disciplines of religious studies and philosophy as well. Heinrich Meier (whom I discuss in chapter 5) has taken the "East Coast" position beyond its classical form in holding that, for Strauss, Athens (i.e., philosophy as a way of life) needs the continued existence of Jerusalem for purposes of self-recognition through engagement with the fundamental alternative. For Meier, Strauss was a philosopher who (in addition to finally refuting revelation) was only concerned with Jerusalem insofar as it aided the self-recognition of philosophy.[7] Leora Batnitzky (who also understands Strauss's affirmation of both Judaism and philosophy) believes that Strauss construed Jerusalem and Athens by means of "the analytic separation and subsequent practical coordination of philosophy and revelation."[8] As with Meier's extension of the classical "East Coast" position, Batnitzky's view is not identical to its "West Coast" progenitor—Jerusalem and Athens cannot be synthesized but "practically coordinated" in order to maintain peace and order (both practical virtues) while allowing the philosophical life to flourish as well.

Both readings, in my account, are strong. They both contain a clear understanding that philosophy, as originally understood, is not one academic discipline among others, but rather a way of life. For Meier, this way of life is exclusive to its alternative except insofar as that alternative (unintentionally) aids philosophy in its self-understanding. For Batnitzky, the two can be coordinated toward something like (to employ a term I do not believe she uses) *peaceful coexistence*. I agree with both Meier and Batnitzky that (1) Strauss was not a "believing Jew" (i.e., he was a philosopher) and (2) he recognized the significance of Jerusalem. My reading is distinct from their readings in the following manner: I hold that Strauss's engagement with Jerusalem *is itself an aspect of philosophy as a contemplative way of life*. To say that Jerusalem helps Athens understand its own activity is to, perhaps unwittingly, subordinate Jerusalem as an alternative to philosophy. Similarly, to say that there needs to be a practical coordination of Jerusalem and Athens is to deemphasize the possibility that Jerusalem may, *in some respect*, constitute an important moment of contemplation for Athens. I hold the following: First, given that Jerusalem is a fundamental alternative to Athens, it must, for Strauss, be illuminated *on its own terms* as an alternative to Athens in responding to the theological-political problem. This means that Strauss has the *pedagogical* aim of showing his readers what kind of person becomes a citizen of either Jerusalem or Athens in order to show them what kind of persons they are. Second, given that Strauss is a philosopher, a citizen of Athens, he approaches this issue nondogmatically. While he is clear about his own orientation, he does not for a moment "moralize" about philosophy over revelation. Strauss is, first and foremost, a teacher—he brings questions to sight.

Moreover, if, as Strauss claims, philosophy and revelation are both unsuccessful in refuting each other because neither accepts the others' basic premise, then Strauss has an additional concern: the tendentious pushing of an agenda at the expense of the other side is a manifestation of fanaticism. Scholastic sectarianism is just as toxic for the philosophical life as it is for the religious life. While Strauss does believe that the "snobbish silence and whispering of the sect" is preferable to "the savage noise of the loudspeakers of the mass party,"[9] he views the activity of philosophy—"nothing but genuine awareness of the problems, i.e., of the fundamental and comprehensive problems" (WIPP, 116)—to be preferable to both. This entails adopting a stance that is not only (1) affirmative of the strengths of Jerusalem and Athens, and (2) critical of Jerusalem as a fundamental alternative to Athens, but also *and most importantly* (3) exhibitive of the *limitations* of both Jerusalem and Athens. Although I make this aspect of Strauss explicit only briefly at the end of chapter 5, it runs through my entire study: Insofar as Jerusalem and Athens are responses to a theological-*political* problem, the fanatical adherence to one metaphorical city risks producing political fanaticism of one sort or another. Strauss's construal of Jerusalem and Athens seeks to exhibit the limits of each city so as to offset this fanatical adherence to either city—his presentation of Jerusalem and Athens is, in large measure, *a critique of political idolatry.* In this respect, despite their political differences and philosophical approaches, Strauss's thought exhibits a notable kinship with Theodor Adorno's political-philosophical adaptation of the Judaic ban on images.[10] This, to my mind, is the most radical philosophical move Strauss makes—he *philosophically* illustrates *both* ways of life *as they are.*

This, by now well-known conceptual disagreement has had to compete with a more recent methodological disagreement largely as a result of the interest in Strauss by intellectual historians. At stake is the question concerning the correct way to approach Strauss's intellectual corpus. Traditionally speaking, Strauss has been approached in a *synchronic* manner—that is, there has been a deemphasis on chronology (given Strauss's critiques of historicism) in favor of focusing on the continuity of themes and ideas that compelled Strauss throughout his life. Methodologically speaking, this means taking account of Strauss's late autobiographical pieces as an important orienting feature of presenting the "whole" Strauss.[11] The much more recent alternative approach has been *diachronic* in character. It is adequately stated in the following passage of a review-essay concerning David Janssens' book on Strauss: "Janssens takes two points for granted, namely, that Strauss's writings reveal his convictions as he formed them in the process of writing and that his own later autobiographical statements about his earlier development are accurate and may serve as authoritative guides to the interpretation of his earlier writings. Strauss is taken as the authoritative guide to Strauss."[12] Rather, practitioners of the diachronic approach believe that more authority ought to be given to early correspondence and youthful writings—within the larger context of Weimar culture and politics—in order to show how Strauss's views evolved prior to his discovery of esotericism and the formation of a "Straussian" school. For this reason, materials such as the now widely available audio files for Strauss's course lectures (provided by the Leo Strauss Center) have been of little interest to diachronic practitioners. In keeping with this, the diachronic approach considers early archival materials to be of equal, if not greater, value than interpretation of Strauss's published work.[13]

I believe that both approaches have contributions to make concerning the understanding of Strauss. I believe that they are not, in fact, exclusive. A lot depends on the type of inquiry in which one is involved. Newly found materials in archives aid research into the life and development of a thinker's context. Gaining a view of one's development before they became the major figure (by means of correspondence, events, accounts from friends and associates) can only widen the scope and increase the view of the person in question. However, these materials are no *more* authoritative than Strauss's own statements. If the reliance on Strauss's autobiographical accounts is open to the charge of naïveté toward the possibility of revision, the analogous use of archival materials is open to the charge of potential irrelevancy. The former approach risks neglecting aspects of Strauss's context to which he was responding; the latter approach risks instating a determinist frame that reduces philosophical thought to political views/events and personal encounters. Consideration of these things can be quite appropriate for biographical or historical inquiries. I believe that its appropriateness for philosophical inquiries is more limited. However, this does not mean that it is simply unimportant—rather, it is ministerial to philosophical concerns. It would be dogmatically synchronic to disallow reasoned speculation and reference to relevant materials simply because one does not have complete access to the thinker's mind—one never does. Insofar as there will always be a space between the interpretive account of Strauss and Strauss's own thought, I believe that a combination of approaches is preferable. Put differently, while interpretation is always "ministerial to the text," it also exhibits an "irretrievably occasional character"[14]—it is an imitation of the true whole.[15]

As a result, I have made use of both approaches when the occasion calls for them. The two chapters in part I proceed from considerations in intellectual history, to matters in Strauss's intellectual biography, finally ascending to properly philosophical interpretation of Strauss's texts. I have made use of early (and late) correspondence (to be found in the *Gesammelte Schriften*), materials from the Strauss archives in Chicago as well as the Hebrew University archives in Jerusalem. I have drawn from unpublished lectures and courses as well as unpublished correspondence. And I have made reasonable speculation about what Strauss *may have intended* when he made certain statements. None of these should be understood as an attempt to bestow a Cartesian-like certainty on my interpretation of Strauss. They are all intended to be supportive of—ministerial to—tracing an arc of the "whole" of Strauss's thought with respect to the Jerusalem/Athens distinction. And this arc can *only* come to rest in the published essays, lectures, and books of Strauss that provoked so much interest in the first place. In claiming that Strauss is a citizen of Athens on the border of Jerusalem, my approach has been one of synchrony on the border of diachrony.

Part I of my study—"On the Way to Jerusalem and Athens"—charts the path Strauss took in coming to the Jerusalem/Athens distinction. In chapter 1, I distinguish Strauss's understanding of Jerusalem and Athens from previous iterations of the Hebrew/Greek dichotomy—that is, Tertullian, Augustine, Matthew Arnold, Lev Shestov, Hans Kohn, and Erich Auerbach. I then proceed to show that, far from being a manifestation of the early "Weimar" years, Strauss's preoccupation with Judaism was something that traveled with him—sometimes explicitly, sometimes implicitly—from the beginning to the end of his philosophical journey. Indeed, it is as a result of this confrontation that he comes to discover the theological-political problem with Jerusalem and Athens as its responses. Finally, I show the conceptual contours of his critique of both modern Jewish thought and modern philosophy. Insofar as modern Jewish thought and philosophy (here represented by Hermann Cohen and Martin Buber) is Kantian in character, it misses the fundamentality of the theological-political problem and views Jerusalem and Athens as a distinction open to a practical solution.

In chapter 2, I discuss Strauss's turn toward Maimonides as the exemplar of premodern rationalism. It is in Maimonides's thought that Strauss finds an understanding of the theological-political problem and the Jerusalem/Athens distinction. Given that Strauss's "Athenian" Maimonides was an unconventional reading, as he began to formulate it, I begin with more accepted—"modern" readings of Maimonides occurring in Strauss's early Weimar context—that is, those provided by Hermann Cohen, Isaac Husik, Julius Guttmann, Harry Austryn Wolfson, Salo Baron, Alexander Altmann, and Simon Rawidowicz. From Strauss's perspective, all of these commentators mistakenly assume some modern premise in their interpretations of Maimonides (e.g., that Maimonides genuinely wanted to harmonize the Bible and Greek philosophy, or that Maimonides considered the contemplative life only as it occurs in a practical context). I then begin to illustrate the development of Strauss's own interpretation through his correspondence with Gerhard Krüger, Karl Löwith, Gershom Scholem, Jacob Klein, and Seth Benardete. What Strauss's correspondence reveals is that, as a result of his "reorientation" in the 1930s, he discovers a Maimonides who is theoretically uncompromising in his advocacy of philosophy and who also wrote exoterically in order not to upset the community in which he lived. This parallels Strauss's own situation with respect to his interpretation of Maimonides. Insofar as correspondence helps to corroborate views rather than establish them *ex nihilo*, I have used them to lead into my philosophical discussion concerning Strauss's Maimonides—the thinker who most stringently recovered Platonic political philosophy within the context of the disputes between Jerusalem and Athens, and, therefore, most deeply understood the need to speak to different audiences.

Part II of my study—"Jerusalem and Athens *in Deed*"—focuses on Strauss's deed at the Hebrew University of Jerusalem in 1954–55, and subsequently in "What Is Political Philosophy?",[16] where he simultaneously recollects classical political philosophy, recovers the theological-political problem, and reoriginates the Jerusalem/Athens distinction for the potential philosophers in hearing/reading distance of his words. Chapter 3 first explores Strauss's twofold relation to the State of Israel—that is, that it needed to be affirmed as a practical solution for the Jewish people, but that it was not a *Jewish* solution for Judaism. This ambivalence makes his trip to the Hebrew University even more remarkable, as it entails bringing the Jerusalem/Athens distinction *to Jerusalem*. Readers should note that, while Strauss's seminal essay derives from his 1954-1955 Judah Magnes Lectures given at the Hebrew University of Jerusalem, it is not simply identical to those lectures. First, the essay (understandably) contains revisions and additions not given in the lectures. Second, it appears that the third lecture (which corresponds to the third section of Strauss's essay) was never actually given at the Hebrew University.[17] For this reason, my comparison between what Strauss gave to his listening audience and what he gave to his readership in posterity is limited. However, I believe that Strauss's written additions in the final version[18] of his essay constitute both a continuation in the same direction taken, and a sharpening of the points made, in his lectures. Nevertheless, I will address the differences between the formulations in the lectures and the essay when they bear on the points I make.[19] I then explore the "literary character" of his Hebrew University lectures and essay insofar as they are structured in the manner of a Platonic dialogue, as Strauss conceives it. In beginning with a prologue that sets the context in which the argument, action, and argument of the action can be seen by potential philosophers, Strauss is able to communicate both to nonphilosophers and to philosophers at the same time. Finally, I evaluate Strauss's prologue (i.e., the first paragraph of his lectures) in order to show his reticent announcement of the entire contents of the lectures at the beginning. In so doing, Strauss allows the potential philosophical members of his audience to eventually see the "whole" of the Jerusalem/Athens distinction.

Chapter 4 consists of a close reading of "What Is Political Philosophy?," in order to show the moments in the essay where Strauss hints and indicates to his potential philosophers that he is, in fact, addressing Jerusalem even while "remaining silent" about it. This chapter ends with a restatement of Strauss's account of the history of political philosophy in order to show the silent presence of Maimonides's thought in the essay. In this way, "What Is Political Philosophy?" can be understood as expressing in deed, the very path that Strauss traveled to Jerusalem and Athens (as described in chapters 1 and 2). And the Strauss that emerges from this performance is (like his Maimonides) a citizen of Athens on the border of Jerusalem.

Chapter 5 deals with the question of whether premodern philosophy is accessible to those living in modernity. This question is identical with the question as to whether the contemplative life is possible anymore? For Strauss, I claim the answer is yes. Paradoxically (despite Strauss's apparent interpretation to the contrary), the transmission of Maimonidean philosophy occurs through the medium of Spinoza. *I do not argue that Strauss is a Spinozist.* There is as yet no reason to assume that he had any truck with Spinoza's monism, nominalism, or materialism. Instead I claim that, through his careful readings in *Persecution and the Art of Writing* (the collection of essays that most deeply engages Jewish medieval thought, as well as Spinoza), Strauss quietly sets up a parallel between the premodern (and Spinozan) forms of knowing (i.e., imagination, reason, and intellect/understanding) with the triadic structure of the Platonic dialogue (i.e., argument, action, argument of the action). In tracing this parallel through the essays dealing with Maimonides, Judah Halevi, and Spinoza, I claim that Strauss indicates that Spinoza is the mode of transmission through which Maimonidean philosophy is brought, however imperfectly, to modernity. In this way, Strauss shows himself to be on the borders of Judaism, philosophy, and history. I draw this reading of Strauss out more fully in my consideration of two contemporary Strauss-interpretations (Heinrich Meier's and Miguel Vatter's, respectively) that do not view Strauss as a "thinker of (or on) the border." I contrast my own reading with Meier's conception of Strauss as a political philosopher who has quietly refuted revelation (on the one hand) and Vatter's conception of Strauss as a political theologian who views Platonic philosophy as possible only in the context of the historical event of revelation (on the other hand). I conclude this chapter, and the book, with two brief suggestions as to what I believe Strauss's "being on the border" contributes to our understanding of the philosophical life. For me, Strauss serves as a clear example of what a nondogmatic orientation within the philosophical way of life looks like. It is an orientation in which both its own limitations as well as the alternatives are allowed to show themselves as they really are. Differently stated, it is the attempted subordination of the love of one's own in favor of the love of the good.

PART I

On the Way to Jerusalem and Athens

CHAPTER ONE

The Theological-Political Problem, Strauss's Critique of Modern "Jewish Philosophy," and the Legacy of Kant

In a provocative reading of his teacher, Stanley Rosen has this to say about Strauss's "exoteric flirtation with Hebraic tradition":[1] "Strauss identifies as coeval with philosophy the question *quid sit deus*? But he never suggests that the philosopher, the archetypical citizen of Athens, is also a resident of Jerusalem . . . No competent student of Leo Strauss was ever in doubt as to his teacher's choice . . . At the same time, it does not follow that there was not for Strauss a real problem in choosing between Jerusalem and Athens. Neither does it follow that Strauss was an unmitigated 'ancient' or resident of Athens."[2] For Rosen, Strauss's investigation into the political rhetoric and esoteric teachings of classical philosophers shows that he was at bottom a modern.[3] This means that Strauss understood philosophy and religion "to rest upon an act of the will."[4] He deduces support for this view from Strauss's 1967 lecture "Jerusalem and Athens: Some Preliminary Reflections," where Strauss holds that "We are . . . compelled from the very beginning to make a choice, to take a stand"[5] in the matter of Jerusalem and Athens. The decisive quality of our inhabiting one or another city therefore suggests (what Rosen argues at great length earlier in the book) that Strauss's "return" to the ancients is itself an exoteric doctrine concealing the fact that our allegiance is ultimately premised on a conception of "will" deriving from Kant (and "set free" by Nietzsche).[6] The names "Jerusalem" and "Athens" would therefore refer to arbitrary choices indexed to nothing other than one's own faculty of decision making. Seen in this light, the choice between Jerusalem and Athens, whatever else one might say about it, is less significant than the fact that it is a willful choice.

If I take issue with this reading of Strauss, it is certainly not because of Rosen's contention that Strauss is a modern. Rather, I believe that the manner of Strauss's "modernity" and the status of Jerusalem and Athens in his thought need to be reexamined. I agree, for instance, that Strauss was a citizen of Athens. However, Rosen's rhetorical posture (that is, Strauss's "competent students" recognized this fact), situates the discussion within the context of ancestral authority rather than conceptual analysis; differently stated, Rosen's claim is a species of religious rather than philosophical argument. One must, instead, leave "the closed and charmed circle of the 'initiated'" and deal with Strauss's thought as it comes to sight (WIPP, 114). I further contend that Strauss's citizenship in Athens in no way relegates his relationship with Jerusalem to a merely exoteric status. That Strauss was not himself a believer does not mean that he took the possibility of Jerusalem to be philosophically insubstantial.

Again, I agree that Strauss's thinking is deeply informed by the modern, German tradition of philosophy, beginning with Kant; the very fact that he seeks to make a *return* to classical philosophy and the Hebraic tradition situates his thinking in the German philosophical tradition from Kant to Heidegger.[7] However, that Strauss's thought originates in a modern horizon in no way means that it is reducible to the modernity of willful subjectivity; the philosopher, for Strauss, is precisely *compelled* by the philosophical life: "The philosopher therefore has the urge to educate potential philosophers simply because *he cannot help* loving well-ordered souls" (WIPP, 121; my emphasis).[8] What is it that draws the philosopher to the philosophical life and the believer to religion? Far from being the product of an arbitrary and capricious will, the choice between Jerusalem and Athens is characterized by human *desire*. In elucidating what Strauss understands by Jerusalem and Athens, therefore, one also gains for oneself a sense of what fundamental "things" human beings desire. Strauss's return from modern thought to Jerusalem and Athens can ultimately be understood as a return to the fundamental question concerning the form of life humans desire to live.

In order to show the importance of this return in Strauss's thought, this chapter will discuss (1) his usage of the distinction between Jerusalem and Athens; (2) his lifelong genuine interest in the theological-political problem (a problem to which the choice between Jerusalem and Athens serves as its proper response); and (3) how the Kantian character of modern "Jewish philosophy" (in its Cohenian and Buberian iterations) simultaneously occludes and necessitates a return to (and recovery of) this distinction. The first section can be characterized as intellectual history, the second as intellectual biography, and the third as philosophy. My contention is that this movement through the first two is necessary *for us* in order to begin to see Strauss's properly philosophical position.

Insofar as Strauss is not the first thinker to refer to the mutual relation of, and difference between, Judaism and Hellenism (nor even the first thinker to employ the specific terms *Jerusalem* and *Athens*), it is necessary to provide a brief discussion of some major prior formulations of this distinction.

Jerusalem and Athens

"Jerusalem and Athens" refers, in the first instance, to Tertullian's famous statement "What indeed has Athens to do with Jerusalem? What concord is there between the Academy and the Church? What between heretics and Christians?"[9] In this polemical context, the distinction functions primarily theologically. For Tertullian, there can simply be no relation (save oppositional) between the human search for wisdom embodied in the name "Athens" and the revealed word of Christ embodied in "Jerusalem." While Strauss denies that there can be simple concord (let alone synthesis) between the two, he does not unqualifiedly privilege one over the other as Tertullian apparently does.

One might be tempted to understand Augustine's distinction between the City of God and the city of man as analogous terms to Jerusalem and Athens. In *City of God*, perhaps responding to the fall of the Roman Empire, he writes: "I classify the human race into two branches: the one consists of those who live by human standards, the other of those who live according to God's will. I also call these two classes the two cities, speaking allegorically. By two cities, I mean two societies of human beings, one of which is predestined to reign with God for all eternity, the other doomed to undergo eternal punishment with the Devil."[10] The immediate difference with Strauss's treatment lies in the allegorical usage that Augustine makes of the two cities—that is, they not only refer to different ways of living but to different historical, teleological, and eschatological trajectories. To the extent that the two cities are (for Augustine) analogous to Jerusalem and Athens, we might say that (as for Tertullian) the distinction between the two has already been decided in favor of the City of God.

When one considers Augustine's account concerning the origin and development of the two cities, it becomes immediately clear why the historical, teleological, and eschatological character of his discussion both (1) essentially determine his account and (2) cannot be analogous to the Jerusalem/Athens distinction. Augustine's account takes its departure from the scriptural narrative of Cain and Abel: "Now Cain was the first son born to those two parents of mankind [i.e., Adam and Eve], and he belonged to the city of man; the later son, Abel, belonged to the City of God. It is our own experience that in the individual man, to use the words of the Apostle [Paul], 'it is not the spiritual element which comes first, but the animal; and afterwards comes the spiritual,' and so it is that everyone, since he takes his origin from a condemned stock, is inevitably evil and carnal to begin with, by derivation from Adam; but if he is reborn into Christ, and makes progress, he will afterwards be good and spiritual. The same holds true of the whole human race. When those two cities started on their course through the succession of birth and death, the first to be born was a citizen of this world, and later appeared the one who was a pilgrim and stranger in the world, belonging as he did to the City of God."[11] Augustine's account is essentially historical, teleological, and eschatological because it comes essentially from a Biblical context; just as, according to Strauss, there is no word for *nature* in the Hebrew Bible (JPCM, 119), there is also no great emphasis on *historical* teleology or *historical* eschatology in classical philosophy.[12] While Augustine's scriptural interpretation is clearly a *doctrinally* Christian one (e.g., the Pauline relation between *carnality* and *spirituality*), the pure categories used in his interpretation have a deeper kinship with the Hebrew Bible than with Greek philosophy.

A closer analogue to Jerusalem and Athens is provided in Augustine's *Confessions* (the account of his conversion to Christianity).

In the words of Hannah Arendt, Augustine was "the first man of thought who turned to religion because of philosophical perplexities,"[13] and nowhere, in his work, is the tension between Greek philosophy and Christian faith (as based in scripture) more clearly focused than in Book 7. Augustine's reception of Plato is Neo-Platonic in the same measure and to the same extent that his interpretation of scripture is Christian—that is, he understands the one/good that gives rise to the ideas in symmetry with the Father and the Son. Nonetheless, the distinction between Greek philosophy and the Bible comes through clearly. Athens is "where the books [of the Platonists] came from";[14] this is true, for Augustine in more than simply a geographical sense—"By the Platonic books, I was admonished to return into myself . . . I entered and with my soul's eye, such as it was, saw above that same eye of my soul the immutable light higher than my mind."[15] This self-examination and access of the light of the one/good, however, lacks a *crucial*[16] element—what Augustine did not find in the Platonic books was, quite simply, God's self-emptying revelation in human form and sacrifice for the sins of humanity.[17] Again, that Augustine's account is *doctrinally* Christian is less significant for the present discussion than the conceptuality undergirding that particular doctrine: what the Platonic books lack is a divinity who is historically active and compels humans toward obedient love[18]—in short, there is no *relationship* between humans and a divine persona in "Athens." Again, Augustine's conception (like Tertullian's) is decided on theological grounds.

In 1869 (*arguably* just past the high point of European Enlightenment culture), the English poet and essayist Matthew Arnold articulated the relationship between "Hebraism" and "Hellenism" in a far more similar manner (save one decisive respect) to Strauss. In *Culture and Anarchy*, Arnold describes Hebraism and Hellenism as two civilizational "instincts" or "currents," which "the more we go into the matter . . . seem to converge, and together to bear us along towards culture."[19] For Arnold, these two forces exert a dialectical tension that produces the resources available for education and promoting cultivation—that is, "com[ing] as near as we can to the firm intelligible law of things, and thus . . . get[ting] a basis for a less confused action and a more complete perfection than we have at present."[20] There are, in fact, some passages in which one can *almost* hear pre-echoes of Strauss: "Hebraism and Hellenism,—between these two points of influence moves our world . . . The final aim of both Hebraism and Hellenism, as of all great spiritual disciplines, is no doubt the same: man's perfection or salvation."[21] "The governing idea of Hellenism is *spontaneity of consciousness*; that of Hebraism, *strictness of conscience*."[22] Intellect, therefore, properly belongs to the realm of Hellenism, while ethics or morality belongs to the realm of Hebraism. The decisive qualification, in the comparison with Strauss, is Arnold's emphasis on culture. The modern concern with culture, for Strauss, is brought about by the occlusion of the fundamental human situation that finds its highest expression in Jerusalem and Athens.[23] For now, one can say that this situation involves the irremediably political character of human life; for Strauss, Jerusalem and Athens are two responses to this political character. Therefore, while (1) Hebraism resembles Jerusalem (to the extent that both involve moral considerations), (2) Hellenism resembles Athens (to the extent that both involve the use of intellect), (3) both together resemble Jerusalem and Athens in their "productive" effects on civilization, and (4) one discerns a preference in Arnold for Hellenism (as one does in Strauss for Athens), Arnold's distinction, in Strauss's account, operates at a derivative and "post-political" level. In a well-known footnote to the first nonintroductory essay to *Philosophy and Law*, Strauss writes that: "If 'religion' and 'politics' are *the* facts that transcend 'culture,' or, to speak more precisely, the *original* facts, then the radical critique of the concept of 'culture' is possible only in the form of a 'theologico-political treatise,'—which of course, if it is not to lead back again to the foundation of 'culture,' must take exactly the opposite direction from the theologico-political treatises of the seventeenth-century, especially those of Hobbes and Spinoza."[24] Whereas Arnold finds Hebraism and Hellenism as modes of culture arising from culture (thus continuing the arc of thought initiated by Hobbes and Spinoza), Strauss seeks to trace culture back to its origins in the dual relation that religion and philosophy have to the political. One might say, therefore, that Strauss's project *largely* takes up the *content* of Arnold's distinction but radically recasts the *horizon* in which it occurs.

Closer to Strauss's own time, Lev Shestov, Hans Kohn, and Erich Auerbach have all made analogous distinctions. Shestov's *Athens and Jerusalem* (1937),[25] Kohn's *The Idea of Nationalism: A Study in Its Origins and Background* (1944)[26] and Auerbach's *Mimesis: The*

Representation of Reality in Western Literature (1946)[27]—written on the eve, during, or in the aftermath of the Second World War—all attempt to recover the origins of Western civilization in the aftermath of massive destruction and the perceived failure of Enlightenment conceptions of progress. Each of their descriptions of (what for Strauss will be formulated as) the Jerusalem/Athens distinction is therefore accompanied by a sobering aura of uncertainty.

For Shestov, the distinction is an actual opposition that manifests itself simply as the difference between rational thought and revealed, prophetic faith: "The fundamental opposition of biblical prophecy to speculative philosophy shows itself in particularly striking fashion when we set Socrates' words. 'The greatest good of man is to discourse daily about virtue' (or Spinoza's *gaudere vera contemplatione*—'to rejoice in true contemplation') opposite St. Paul's words, 'Whatsoever is not of faith is sin.'"[28] This opposition is, for Shestov, irreconcilable. His "answer," in the light of his backward glance, is to cease tarrying with the past; Shestov maintains (in Nietzschean fashion) that an excessive backward-looking philosophy is unhealthy for thought—it is "the end of all philosophy."[29] One needs, instead to forge ahead and (in Kierkegaardian fashion) take the leap of faith into the radically unknown—"Philosophy is . . . struggle. And this struggle has no end and will have no end. The kingdom of God, as it is written, is attained through violence."[30] At first blush, Shestov's statement appears to be a precursor to Strauss's oft-quoted remark that humans must "live th[e] conflict" between philosophy and theology (JPCM, 117). I will return to this.

For Kohn and Auerbach, the distinction between reason and faith becomes manifest as the distinction between space and time. Kohn's statements are of a programmatic nature in the service of elucidating the origins of the tribal (Hebraic) and universal (Hellenic) civilization-forming impulses: "For the Greek, the stone with which he built was a symbol of space and perception; for the Jew, the stream into which he dipped was a symbol of time and becoming . . . Thus God personified himself to the Jews, not in the image, but in the call . . . Sight is the sense of space; hearing, the sense of time."[31] Auerbach makes a similar point from the perspective of the history of literary representation: "[There are] two kinds of style [present in] the representation of reality in European culture. The two styles, in their opposition, represent basic types: on the one hand [i.e., the

Homeric, exemplified by Odysseus] fully externalized description, uniform illumination, uninterrupted connection, free expression, all events in the foreground, displaying unmistakable meanings, few elements of historical development and of psychological perspective; on the other hand [i.e., the Old Testamentary, exemplified by Abraham], certain parts brought into high relief, others left obscure, abruptness, suggestive influence of the unexpressed, 'background' quality, multiplicity of meanings and the need for interpretation . . . [and] development of the historically becoming."[32]

Common to Kohn's and Auerbach's accounts is an emphasis on the *difference* between (as it were) the illuminating spatiality characteristic of Greek philosophy and the opaque historicity characteristic of the Hebrew Bible. Differently stated, Greek philosophy emphasizes seeing what is in front of you, whereas Biblical thought emphasizes listening for the historic(al) call from the Wholly Other. The former is accessible through a combination of reason and intellect, the latter by faith alone. For Kohn, and Auerbach, both impulses (or "styles", or "types") have together formed the essential historical trajectory of the European West. I can, at this point, summarize these two accounts by invoking Kohn's words: "All the great turning points in the history of Western humanity started by, and expressed themselves in, a reinterpretation of the inheritance from Hellas and Judea."[33] At first blush, this sounds suspiciously like the opening words to Strauss's 1967 lecture: "All the hopes that we entertain in the midst of the confusions and the dangers of the present are founded positively or negatively, directly or indirectly on the experiences of the past. Of these experiences the broadest and deepest, as far as Western men are concerned, are indicated by the names of the two cities Jerusalem and Athens" (JPCM, 377).

The purpose of this review is neither to reduce Strauss's account to a historical trajectory nor to argue that it "fell from the sky" perfect and fully formed. Rather, it is to give a conceptual introduction to Strauss's account by viewing it within a community of like-minded thinkers. Historically speaking (i.e., from his own references), we can assert without qualification that Strauss was familiar with Arnold.[34] Given Strauss's deep and abiding knowledge of the history of philosophy, it is difficult to believe that Strauss had only a cursory familiarity with Augustine.[35] Given Strauss's ordering of the two terms in his distinction, it is reasonable to suppose that he had some familiarity with Tertullian (at least with chapter 7 of

The Prescription Against Heretics).[36] Given the cultural connections between Auerbach, Kohn, and Strauss (all German Jews), it is not unreasonable to assume that Strauss was most likely familiar with their thought. Whether Strauss was familiar with Shestov remains an open question[37]—he was at least familiar with Shestov's sources, including particularly the late modern writings of Nietzsche and Kierkegaard. Philosophically speaking, this is all somewhat beside the point. If, as Strauss claims, truth is "necessarily anonymous," then these thinkers form a community simply by virtue of the proximity of their accounts of what Strauss refers to as Jerusalem and Athens.[38] In clarifying this relation, one begins to see the uniqueness and significance of Strauss's own account.

Strauss conceives of the relation between Jerusalem and Athens in terms of (1) exclusive citizenship concerning reason and revelation (like Tertullian, Augustine, and Shestov), (2) a dialectical relationship between "natural" impulses (like Arnold), and (3) a sensory distinction—that is, between hearing the historical call of revelation (WIPP, 186) and seeing nature[39] (like Kohn and Auerbach). Yet he *simultaneously* rejects (1) the *complete and utter* exclusivity of *all aspects* of the two cities (as purported by Tertullian and Shestov), (2) the grounding of both cities in culture (as in Arnold and, to an extent, Auerbach), and (3) the fundamentally historical-geographical or theological *topos* of the cities (as in Kohn in the first case, and as in Augustine and Tertullian in the second). For Strauss, Jerusalem/Athens is not essentially a historical or geographical distinction but refers rather to a "fundamental tension" (JPCM, 117) that is present in civilizational life insofar as it refers to "a fundamental dualism in man" (JPCM, 120), to "alternatives or antagonists in the drama of the human soul" (JPCM, 123).[40] Whether we conceive of these alternatives in the manner of Platonic ideas or Aristotelian potentialities is, for the present discussion, not terribly important. The distinction is, for Strauss, philosophical in one respect and transphilosophical in another: it is philosophical insofar as it allows one to *view* "the drama of the human soul." Unlike Shestov, this drama need not issue in violence (although, descriptively speaking, it certainly has at times led to it). Rather, it asks the following question of human beings: Which alternative compels you? What do you desire? Stated differently, the distinction refers to a choice that issues in self-knowledge. It is transphilosophical insofar as it refers to a choice *between* the philosophical form of life and its alternative.

Finally this drama does not require a decision (contra Carl Schmitt) based on nothing other than an act of will (as Rosen claims), because (in Aristotelian terms) this drama is based in the "desiring intellect" that *is* the human soul.

In a rare moment of prescription, Strauss offers the following account of the Jerusalem/Athens relation and how humans *ought* to respond to it: "The very life of Western civilization is the life between two codes, a fundamental tension. There is, therefore, no reason inherent in the Western civilization itself, in its fundamental constitution, why it should give up life. But this comforting thought is justified only if we live that life, if we live that conflict, that is. No one can be both a philosopher and a theologian, or for that matter, a third which is beyond the conflict between philosophy and theology, or a synthesis of both. *But everyone of us can be and ought to be either the one or the other, the philosopher open to the challenge of theology, or the theologian open to the challenge of philosophy*" (JPCM, 117; my emphasis). To say that we *ought* to be one or the other is to acknowledge the possibility that we might currently be neither (thus, the prescriptive character of this statement). To say that the life of Western civilization depends on this conflict[41] (i.e., that it would be "given up" without it) is to focus the question on how this life might *continue* (which suggests that it could, effectively, die). If Western civilization is indeed based *in* this conflict, it is unclear how Shestovian violence between the two cities would enhance the life of Western civilization (if only because such violence presumably abolishes one side or another). It is also unclear how the modern tendency of occluding the difference between the two cities would enhance such life, insofar as it would obscure the different "grounds" on which the two cities are "built". The only philosophical way to maintain the conflict in its productive tension is to *understand* it, to keep it constantly in view. The search for wisdom therefore becomes central to the life of Western civilization.

The search for wisdom, in fact, serves as the proper goal of both cities (JPCM, 379). That they have radically different starting points, and therefore define this proper goal differently, points to the different desires at which they aim to satisfy. ""Jerusalem" is the name that indicates the desire to live a life based in the mercy characteristic of obedience to (divine) law (JPCM, 118)—that is, in action. Athens" is the name that indicates the desire to live a life based in free human inquiry and contemplation—that is, in thought and speech. I bracket the term *divine* for now, since both names acknowledge the import of divinity (as Rosen acknowledges), and since the question of law is as much a *political* question as it is a *theological* one. We can, however, reiterate that both Jerusalem and Athens (in the latter's specific modality as Socratic political philosophy) are responses to the same theological-political problem and both take "wisdom" to be the goal. For Strauss, the task is to keep the question—whether this wisdom comes from reason and intellect or alternatively from obedience to divine law—continually before one's eyes. Even if one can only inhabit one city, one needs to be continually open to the possibility of the other city. The choice between the two cities is thus based (contrary to Rosen's claim) in this search as it manifests itself in the particular makeup or proportion of desires comprising an individual's soul.[42]

One needs, therefore, to be on the *border* of the two cities. This is not a term that Strauss uses, but he does provide a comparable image: "the prophets . . . had run the same risks in Jerusalem as Socrates in Athens. They had shown by their actions or by their speech that the man who loves perfection and justice must leave the cities inhabited exclusively by the wicked, to search for a city inhabited by good men, and that he must prefer, if he does not know of such a city or if he is prevented from bringing one about, wandering in the desert or in caverns to the association with evil men."[43] Within the context of the present discussion, we can say that—in order to live in a manner affirmative of the life of the civilization that we inhabit—we must be located at the periphery (or border) of the city rather than its center.[44] One might even wonder whether, for Strauss, the center of the city is where evil men reside; might Strauss be saying that an overzealous patriotism toward (i.e., love of) one's own city is evil? At any rate, whether one adopts the life of hearing the divine word or of seeing intelligible objects, one must always be stationed where one can be most challenged by the other city. If we wish to refer to this position as a "battle" stance, it is clearly an intellectual (rather than a physical) one.

At this point, I am open to the charge of interpreting Strauss along Weberian lines. For Weber (on Strauss's reading), while the alternative between "human guidance and divine guidance" (NRH, 74) is fundamental and unresolvable (either by synthesis, harmonization, or victory of one side over the other), it leads ultimately to despair and the pretense of neutrality with respect to the two terms (NRH, 64–65, 74–76). Strauss directly opposes Weber's view (in "Farabi's Plato") when he asserts that Farabi's "[philosophical] suspend[ing] of judgment as to the truth of the super-rational teaching of religion" is simply exoteric (FP, 372–373). In his own name, Strauss writes that "I do not know whether there ever was a 'philosopher' whose mind was so confused as to consist of two hermetically sealed compartments" (FP, 734). If, for Strauss, Farabi and Maimonides were thoroughgoing rationalists, if "the classics demonstrated that truly human life is a life dedicated to science, knowledge, and the search for it" (FPP, 78), the philosopher cannot (and, we might say, ought not) remain neutral—that is, they must continually attempt to refute the form of life based on revealed law. What, then, can Strauss's statement about citizens of one city being "open to the challenge" of the other mean?

I will provide a more detailed treatment of this issue in chapter 5 (when I discuss the work of Heinrich Meier, the most significant proponent of this reading of Strauss). This much can be said, however: I believe that Strauss's claim regarding the challenge of Jerusalem and Athens affirms the philosopher's imperative to refute the claims of Jerusalem *as well as* affirms the philosopher's need to continually face the claims of Jerusalem. The philosopher comes to knowledge of his or her own position precisely through the engagement with the religious claims concerning divine law. Put differently, there can be no Athenian refutation of Jerusalem without an Athenian exposure to—and undergoing[45] of—the claims of Jerusalem. In this respect, Athens needs Jerusalem for the good of Athens. Moreover, the philosopher (to the extent that he or she needs to be concerned about the civilization in which philosophy occurs) needs to continue the productive tension constitutive of that civilization. In this respect, Athens needs Jerusalem for the good of Western civilization. Finally, insofar as philosophy (by virtue of its focus on the articulation of the questions and problems over the solutions) is not a sectarian enterprise (WIPP, 116), the philosopher must engage others in a nondogmatic manner; in this way, the philosopher both awakens the desire for moderate action in nonphilosophers as well as awakens the contemplative desire in potential philosophers. If Jerusalem is that "city" singularly susceptible to religious fanaticism, this engagement promises to be beneficial both to intra- and interpolitical aspects of Jerusalem. In this respect, Athens needs Jerusalem for the good of Jerusalem.

This short digression was necessary in order that I address the charge of inadvertently reading Strauss along Weberian lines. For Strauss, the citizen of Athens is neither neutral nor myopically at battle with Jerusalem. Philosophy depends on *divine* law for its own recognition; and, politically speaking, philosophy also depends on divine *law* for its own survival. The critics of my view are, however, correct in one particular respect: I have not spoken about whether Jerusalem needs Athens as much, or in the same way, as Athens needs Jerusalem. That question serves as the limit case of my investigation.[46] Insofar as he identifies himself as a citizen of Athens, we do not know how Strauss conceives of a Jerusalemite engagement with Athens. It is, one might say, a fundamental problem coeval with the thought of Strauss. All I have tried to do is to show that, *as a citizen of Athens*, Strauss is committed to both a nonneutral and nondogmatic engagement with Jerusalem. This claim ought to be substantial enough on its own; for what it highlights is nothing less than (1) the philosopher's need to attempt to refute revelation, (2) the philosopher's need to remain nondogmatic and *zetetic*, and (3) the philosopher's recognition of the fundamental need/desires of the human soul (to which Strauss gives the names "Jerusalem" and "Athens"). The first two are properly philosophical; the third is properly transphilosophical.

I return to my discussion. In between the grounds or premises and the goal of both cities, surface similarities come to sight; this is the reason why Strauss cannot simply affirm Tertullian's and Shestov's characterization. Both cities manifest the concern over justice; both cities make use of rational means in order to legitimate their ways of life;[47] finally, both cities acknowledge the need of a divine foundation for law. I can put the point as follows: When Jerusalem makes use of reason, it issues in Kalam (rational discourse justifying belief in divinity); when Athens makes reference to divine myth, it does so with the aim of producing good citizens. While Strauss certainly distinguishes the two cities, his presentations of them makes clear that he does not subscribe to the view that they are exclusive *in every respect*: "What Plato says in the tenth book of the *Laws* about man's inability to escape from divine retribution is almost literally identical with certain verses of Amos and Psalm 139. In this context, one may even mention . . . the kinship between the monotheism of the Bible and the monotheism toward which Greek philosophy is tending, and the kinship between the first chapter of Genesis and Plato's *Timaeus*" (JPCM, 106). The analogous concerns over divine retributive justice and divine creation through "fashioning" shows that the two cities are related *as alternatives to each other*. Moreover, in his 1967 lecture, Strauss shows that the Genesis narrative is approachable in a reasoned manner (if not completely from a rational horizon), while presenting Hesiod's *Theogony* (as well as the Parmenidean and Empedoclean fragments as the representative of Athens (JPCM, 382–398)! Also of relevance here, and in a reversal of what we might expect, Strauss's presentation of Genesis deals primarily with human issues while his presentation of the Greeks focuses on the divine.[48]

Finally, in the same lecture, we find the remarkable statement that "the 'pure reason' in Plato's sense is closer to the Bible than the 'pure reason' in Kant or, for that matter, Anaxagoras' or Aristotle's sense." (JPCM, 396). That Strauss, as a citizen of Athens, would prefer Anaxagoras and Aristotle (we can also add here Farabi and Averroes) to the (mythical) narratives of Plato and the Bible is clear enough—but why does he add Kant? Are we to understand Kant and Aristotle as philosophical brethren? Not without qualification. To the extent that they are both *philosophers*, the answer is yes (in which case, they would, similarly, be brethren of Plato). However, *insofar as Kant's philosophy is modern*, Strauss registers a negative answer. I will show in which ways Strauss reacts against Kant in the section of this chapter titled "The Kantian Character of 'Jewish Philosophy.'" Already one can discern the emergence of a fourfold distinction: Jerusalem, Athens, ancients, and moderns. The Ancients/Moderns distinction functions horizontally in Strauss's discourse; it is a *historical* distinction that, *as historical*, obscures the theological-political problem and its point of greatest tension—the Jerusalem/Athens distinction. In contrast, Jerusalem and Athens is properly (trans)philosophical insofar as it names permanent and fundamental forms of life as they originate in the human soul. A major aspect to Strauss's project of recovering Jerusalem and Athens is to work back through the distinction between the ancients and the moderns. Far from according modern philosophy and modern Jewish thought a subordinate status, however, Strauss holds that it is precisely by taking one's point of departure from modern thought that one might, in some sense, *depart* from modern thought. This will, again, become clear in the section below titled "The Kantian Character of 'Jewish Philosophy.'"

If the Jerusalem/Athens distinction ultimately amounts to alternative responses to the theological-political problem, Strauss cannot simply take one term as primary or esoteric and the other as derivative or exoteric. To do so would amount not simply to a rejection of one of the cities but rather to a rejection of the distinction as *a genuine problem at all.* Even a brief consideration of Strauss's intellectual trajectory suggests a different narrative. Differently stated, Strauss's engagement with Jewish texts and thought is coextensive with his entire philosophical path—from beginning to end.

Strauss's Path to the Theological-Political Problem

The wealth of recent scholarship concerning the young Strauss makes possible the brevity of my discussion.[49] I do need, however, to sketch the contours of Strauss's path to the theological-political problem, in order both to establish Strauss's lifelong engagement with Judaism and then to proceed to the main discussion concerning Strauss's critique of modern "Jewish philosophy."

Strauss's early years illustrate a story of conflicts that arose for a young Orthodox Jew first discovering philosophy (in the form of Plato, Schopenhauer, and Nietzsche) at gymnasium, and subsequently being swept up into the whirlwind both of neo-Orthodox discussions of religion (involving the works of Rudolf Otto, Karl Barth, and Franz Rosenzweig), and political Zionism.[50] Does Strauss's youthful embrace of the three signal an inability to simply inhabit Jerusalem (to the extent that an Orthodox upbringing comes to be seen as one modality of that city)? Rémi Brague is, I believe, correct when he holds that "the only question we have to face is the Jewish nature of Strauss's enterprise."[51] His writings of the time (engaging with figures as diverse as Jacobi, Otto, Max Nordau, Theodor Herzl, Paul de Lagarde, Hermann Cohen, Sigmund Freud, Franz Rosenzweig, and Julian Ebbinghaus) certainly suggest such tension regarding Jewish thought. This tension, though, did not prevent Strauss from engaging with Jewish thought on the highest level. He joined Franz Rosenzweig's Fries Jüdisches Lehrhaus during the 1925–26 academic year, and led a reading group on Cohen's *Religion of Reason Out of the Sources of Judaism*;[52] at the same time, Strauss was appointed to the Akademie für die Wissenschaft des Judentums, where he studied medieval Jewish texts with Julius Guttman (in particular, Joseph Albo's *Book of Roots* and Maimonides's *Guide of the Perplexed*).[53] Finally, new documentation discovered by Thomas Meyer shows that, during his appointment to the Akademie, Strauss was sent to Kassel during a seven-month period in 1925, where he offered courses in Biblical Hebrew and a seminar on German Judaism since Moses Mendelssohn.[54] This basic information tells us that the Weimar years saw a struggle and conflict for Strauss about Jewish thought, but not an unqualified rejection.

Ultimately, however, this struggle and conflict does show that Strauss understood his thought to inhabit Athens rather than Jerusalem. In his correspondence with Gerhard Krüger (December 27, 1932 draft) appears Strauss's now well-known statement, "Our difference has its ground in this—that I cannot believe, that I must search for a possibility where I can *live* without belief."[55] For Strauss, this raises the question as to whether the ancients or the moderns provide the resources for such a life.[56] Moreover, Strauss's emphasis on the word *live* appears to support the claim that an engagement with the Ancients/Moderns distinction is necessary, in Strauss's thought, in order to recover the more fundamental distinction between Jerusalem and Athens. This is not to suggest that, at such an early stage, Strauss was already working with a definitive and fully formed conception of this distinction (and the recovery of it). It is reasonable to suggest, however, that these statements are early articulations of the problematic. Regarding his engagement with neo-Orthodoxy, this is confirmed, in large measure, by Strauss's 1962 retrospective account: "The reawakening of theology, which for me is marked by the names Karl Barth and Franz Rosenzweig, appeared to make it necessary to investigate how far the critique of orthodox theology—Jewish and Christian—deserved to be victorious. Since then the theological-political problem has remained *the* theme of my investigations" (JPCM, 453). Regarding his engagement with political Zionism, one only has to turn to his 1962 Chicago Hillel lecture, "Why We Remain Jews," where he recalls an early meeting with the revisionist Zionist leader Ze'ev Jabotinsky: "He asked me, 'what are you doing?' I said, 'Well, we read the Bible, we study Jewish history, Zionist theory, and, of course, we keep abreast of developments, and so on.' He replied, 'And rifle practice?' And I had to say 'no'" (JPCM, 319).

If one considers information about Strauss's early work together with his later reflections, one finds that his struggle consists in the discovery of a form of life supple and subtle enough to simultaneously affirm philosophy as well as the challenge to it from revelation in general and revealed law in particular. Strauss's ultimate turning away from modern Jewish figures like Rosenzweig and Cohen, if construed as a wholesale rejection of Judaism, is as misunderstood as his answer to Jabotinsky is if construed merely as a retreat from the necessity of bearing arms. Both his movement away from neo-Orthodoxy and Zionism are aspects of Strauss's philosophical critique of modernity. Insofar as neo-Orthodoxy ultimately ties religion to personal experience, it derives from the same modern emphasis on individualism one finds in thinkers such as, in Strauss's account, Hobbes and Spinoza. Similarly, insofar as Zionism amounts to an advocacy of a practical, historical, and worldly solution to the so-called Jewish problem, it is a continuation of the Enlightenment project of progress through historical teleology. Both avenues, for Strauss, amount to an occlusion of the theological-political problem by ideologies of modern individualism and historical progress. *These* are the impulses that are the source of conflict for Strauss. While neo-Orthodoxy might provide a phenomenology of subjective religious experience, it does not address the question of the religious *way of life*. And while a state of Israel might very well be a *modern political* answer to the Jewish problem, it is neither a *philosophical* nor a *Jewish* answer to the Jewish problem. What Strauss says explicitly about the state of Israel holds for neo-Orthodox Judaism: "[it] is . . . a modification of the *galut* . . . but it is not the end of the *galut*. In the religious sense, and perhaps not only in the religious sense . . . [it] is part of the *galut*. Finite, relative problems can be solved; infinite, absolute problems cannot be solved . . . From every point of view, it looks as if the Jewish people were the chosen people, at least in the sense that the Jewish problem is the most manifest symbol of the human problem insofar as it is a social or political problem" (JPCM, 143).

This "social or political problem," which admits of no worldly solution, is (for Strauss) the theological-political problem—the problem concerning human association. This problem concerns the most just form of life for humans. However, given the manifest plurality of individuals and groups, this form of life needs laws for its organization, arrangement, and continuity. Given the fallibility and plurality of human opinions, human laws continually run the risk of being either apparently or actually unjust. This noncoincidence of law and justice leads to what Strauss calls "the problem of justice" (NRH, 150–151). This points to the conclusion that "there cannot be true justice if there is no divine rule or providence" (NRH, 150n24). That this conclusion, for Strauss, points beyond the realm of politics leads to the further implication that "the justice which is possible within the city, can be only imperfect or cannot be unquestionably good" (NRH, 151). The problem of the noncoincidence of law and justice within the city constitutes the problem of divine law, which is, paradoxically, "the common ground between the Bible and Greek philosophy . . . They solve that problem in a diametrically opposed manner" (JPCM, 107). This problem is philosophical insofar as it seeks a view of "the whole" problem of human association (with its center of gravity in the problem of justice). It is theological insofar as it acknowledges that divine law constitutes the only authority powerful enough to bring "true justice" to individuals and groups living in proximity to each other. It is political insofar as it refers to question over how human differences can be justly negotiated at the individual and group level. And it is a fundamental problem insofar as (according to Heinrich Meier), it amounts to an "existential challenge" between philosophy and revealed law which "does not [simply] concern the question of whether philosophy or religion should rule . . . [but rather] the question: *What is the right life?*"[57] If neo-Orthodoxy and Zionism obscure the theological-political question, they do so because they fail to recognize the permanence of the problem *as a problem.* In both cases, Judaism manifests "spiritual dependence" (JPCM, 140) on the Enlightenment.

In his introduction to Moses Mendelssohn's *Morning Hours* and *To the Friends of Lessing* (finished in 1937 for the Jubilee Edition of Mendelssohn's *Collected Writings*, but published only posthumously in 1974), Strauss provides an eloquent, if sobering, testimony to this spiritual dependence. The context for this testimony concerns the heated and fiercely polemical debate between Mendelssohn and Friedrich Jacobi over whether their mutual friend Gotthold Ephraim Lessing was or was not a Spinozist. Mendelssohn argued that he was not (or at least not in an unqualified sense), while Jacobi argued that he was. Further, Jacobi mentioned that Lessing had confided in him to the effect that he had never told Mendelssohn his true views (insofar as he perceived Mendelssohn to be overly rigid and dogmatic). Strauss derives transbiographical significance from the hurt and betrayal that Mendelssohn felt.[58] The relevance of this account to the present discussion makes Strauss's passage worth quoting at length:

> The pure expressions of the pain of the friend are more perceptible to our ear than the strained outbreaks of the annoyances of the outsmarted whose carefully devised tactic has come to naught. The pain over the barrier that separated [Mendelssohn] from Lessing, of which he had only now become aware, was so deep that words failed him for properly describing the brutality with which Jacobi had brought this barrier to his awareness. Not merely had there fallen on his friendship, which was the greatest happiness of his life, a shadow that, in a truly forgivable manner, crushed his self-esteem. Together with this, his trust toward the non-Jewish world had been shaken: after all, unreserved friendship with Lessing was at the same time also the oldest and most trustworthy bridge that connected him with that world at all, the testimony most precious to him of the possibility of complete understanding between men of the opposite background. One can appreciate again by now how great the hurdles must have been, despite which Mendelssohn kept working on his trust in non-Jewish friends—he who was as free of pathological sensitivities as a mere human can be, who bore no greater distrust than what is justified sufficiently by the experiences of the Jews at all times. Without assuming such a justified distrust toward the non-Jewish world, one cannot, as things stand, understand his behavior in the quarrel with Jacobi, nor for that matter, his behavior

> toward Bonnet in the quarrel with Lavater. To be sure, the same natural hatred against the Jews did not then yet have the principle of nationalism at its disposal; but even so, the anti-Jewish theory and practice of the Christian Churches supplied it with weapons scarcely less effective . . . For the proper understanding of his reaction to Jacobi's public communication, . . . one has to keep in mind Mendelssohn's experience of the distrust of the non-Jewish world toward the Jews, no less than his own distrust as a Jew toward the non-Jewish world. (LSMM, 104–105).

In this passage, Strauss understands Mendelssohn's experience as a sort of archive or registry containing insight into the problem of "spiritual dependence" from which Enlightenment Judaism suffers. Put differently, the reason that Mendelssohn felt so betrayed is because he harbored the hopes that hatred of Jews admits of a modern political or modern religious solution;[59] Strauss does not harbor similar hopes. This in no way signals despair or cynicism on Strauss's part; rather, it suggests that one needs to keep the theological-political problem (as well as its inadequate "solutions") ever before one's eyes in order to understand the way things are. That Strauss's project does not claim to provide an answer to this question simply means that he rejects the modern emphasis of practicality over contemplation. If we look ahead to the introductory paragraph of "What Is Political Philosophy," however, we see that this rejection of the modern solution is not a wholesale rejection of the theological-political problem in general, let alone of Jerusalem in particular: "But while being compelled, or compelling myself, to wander far away from our sacred heritage, or to be silent about it, *I shall not for a moment forget what Jerusalem stands for*"(WIPP, 10; my emphasis). While Strauss critiques the modern character of Enlightenment Judaism, he does so in the service of recollecting Jerusalem as one possible response to the theological-political problem (insofar as it is one possible response to the problem of justice). In other words, he remains open to the challenge of Jerusalem even when he speaks from the standpoint of Athens.

One sees this recollective process at work in Strauss's abovementioned 1962 Hillel lecture "Why We Remain Jews." In his introduction, Joseph Cropsey notes the strangeness of the title (JPCM,

311). Strauss acknowledges that when the title was suggested to him, he "was repelled by it, not to say shocked by it" (JPCM, 312). Readers might wonder why Strauss is repelled at such a title. Might he be repelled precisely because he does not want to remain a Jew? He does, after all, say in this lecture that Judaism is a "heroic delusion" (JPCM, 327); but he qualifies this almost immediately: "What is a delusion? We also say a 'dream.' No nobler dream was ever dreamt" (JPCM, 328). Is he suggesting that his listeners/readers be open to such a heroic delusion/dream? But why would he suggest this if he is, in fact, repelled by Judaism? Two further statements are of help here: "I draw the following conclusion. It is impossible not to remain a Jew. It is impossible to run away from one's origins. It is impossible to get rid of one's past simply by wishing it away" (JPCM, 317); "It is surely nobler to be a victim of the most noble dream than to profit from a sordid reality and to wallow in it" (JPCM, 328). I note first that Strauss holds the possibility of an unqualified rejection of one's formative past to be another delusion; in that sense, it is impossible to not remain a Jew. However, if the choice is between (1) a sordid reality based on said delusion or (2) a noble delusion, Strauss opts for the latter. Again (in contrast to his aforementioned moment of prescription), Strauss is not here attempting to deduce practical consequences from this situation. He is inviting (or compelling) his audience to recollect what it means to be a Jew. In a contemplative context, it makes sense to acknowledge that a complete rejection of Judaism is both impossible and undesirable.

This is not all. I have, until this moment, simply assumed that Strauss's interest in political Zionism is coeval with his interest in Zionism as such. "Why We Remain Jews" suggests otherwise. I note that, during the question-and-answer period (in response to a question of whether "a man is being dishonorable if he chooses to disagree with, or break away from, his origins, what his family believes" [JPCM, 340]), Strauss makes an interesting reference to the famous cultural Zionist Ahad Ha'am (Asher Ginsberg): "[in an effort to] give examples, of what the traditional posture was[,] I remind you of only one essay which is still worthy of being read by everyone who is interested in this. That is an essay by Ahad Ha'am . . . which he called 'In External Freedom and Internal Slavery' [i.e., 'Slavery in Freedom'], and in which he compared the situation of the Jews in the Russian ghetto to the chief rabbi of France . . . Ahad Ha'am showed . . . on the basis of what [the chief rabbi] said . . . that he was a slave, not a free man. Externally, he was free: he could vote, and do many other things, acquire property, whatever kind he liked. But in his heart he was a slave. Whereas the poorest Polish Jew . . . was externally a man without rights and in this sense a slave, but he was not a slave in his heart. And that is of crucial importance in this matter" (JPCM, 341). Is this nothing more than an impromptu response to a basic question from the audience? Might Strauss be, in this instance, giving a performance?

If one consults Ahad Ha'am's 1891 essay one finds the following passage: "Why, then, should not history allow *us* to make our exit? We have done all that we could for our mission: we have produced the Scriptures. Further, there is nothing for us to do: Why, then must we live? One of our 'missionist' thinkers, a learned preacher, deals with this question in an article titled, 'Why Do We Remain Jews?,' and tries to answer the question from another angle. We remain faithful to Judaism, he thinks, because there is no other religion for which we could change it. Every other religion contains something which we cannot accept . . . I at least know 'why I remain a Jew'—or, rather, I can find no meaning in such a question, any more than if I were asked why I remain my father's son."[60] Ha'am's raising of the same question and answering it in an analogous fashion leads to the suspicion that—while the title of Strauss's lecture was not of his choosing—the substance of the lecture (both word and deed) certainly was. By referencing Ha'am's essay, Strauss was effectively (1) gesturing to the members of his audience who knew the trajectory of Zionist literature, (2) tying his own reflections back to this literature, and (3) letting his audience/readers know (*sub speciae posteritas*, as it were) that there was at least a *moment* in the intellectual history of Zionism which was "still worth reading" and which was not simply reducible to modernity. In this context, I remind readers that Ahad Ha'am was also the author of a well-known (if polemical) tract on Maimonides.[61]

The pieces that I have attempted to put together, during this discussion of Strauss's path to the theological-political problem, constitute the beginnings of a "contemplative critique" of modern Judaism (in both its neo-Orthodox and political iterations). In what follows, I will show how Strauss extends this critique to encompass the modern formation of "Jewish philosophy" regarding the work of Martin

Buber and Hermann Cohen. This critique is indicated in the second section of Strauss's 1967 lecture (which section is titled "On Socrates and the Prophets"). Although Strauss's explicit discussion is brief, it allows careful readers to see precisely what is at stake in his response to "Jewish philosophy" and its grounding in the thought of Kant.

The Kantian Character of "Jewish Philosophy"

It might strike readers as strange to stage this exhibition of the Kantian character of both Cohenian and Buberian forms of "Jewish philosophy" in the section of Strauss's 1967 lecture entitled "Socrates and the Prophets"; Kant is mentioned only three times in that section (in an obvious reference to Cohen's influences), and Buber is nowhere mentioned. If we take a look at the references to Kant (all in one paragraph), however, they set the stage for the drama to come: "Cohen understood Plato in the light of the opposition between Plato and Aristotle—an opposition that he understood in the light of the opposition between Kant and Hegel. We, however, are more impressed than Cohen was by the kinship between Plato and Aristotle on the one hand, and the kinship between Kant and Hegel on the other. In other words, the quarrel between the Ancients and the Moderns seems to us to be more fundamental than either the quarrel between Plato and Aristotle or that between Kant and Hegel" (JPCM, 399). According to Strauss, Cohen downplays the Ancients/Moderns distinction in favor of some form of philosophical "ideal types"—that is, Plato/Kant versus Aristotle/Hegel. Cohen was deeply informed by Plato and Kant and his reading of Maimonides was deeply anti-Arisotelian.[62] Insofar as one does not need Strauss for this information, what else might he be referring to? In highlighting the import of the Ancients/Moderns distinction for his own project, in contradistinction to Cohen's, Strauss is suggesting that Cohen's thought remains circumscribed by modern premises that it subsequently obscures. If Cohen cannot properly access Athens, the same might hold true for Jerusalem. Again one sees that the Ancients/Moderns distinction would appear to be necessary for a recovery of Jerusalem and Athens.

Readers might do well, at this point, to recall some other instances where Strauss has made the connection between Kant and

Cohen. In his 1925 "The 'Jewish Writings' of Hermann Cohen," Strauss provides a narrative regarding "the development of German Judaism since Moses Mendelssohn" (MEW, 118). This development occurs in two steps: (1) "the traditional Jewish connection dissolves itself under the influence of Europe's critique" (MEW, 118–119) and (2) the new consolidation of the Jewish connection . . . [emerging as] a legitimate proceeding of the later from the earlier . . . [which in Cohen's case] led him . . . to the Kantian system" (MEW, 119). Interpolating from Strauss's other writings, we can say that the first, "dissolving" phase happened as a result of the critique of revelation in the theological-political treatises of (thinkers such as) Spinoza and Hobbes. Judaism, for Mendelssohn, was an ethical religion void of special revelation (and its political instantiation in and as law). The second "consolidating" phase—of which Cohen is (in this essay) the prime example—involves the regrounding of Judaism in the philosophy of Kant. One mode of this regrounding, for the Strauss of 1965, is certainly Cohen's Kantian conception of morality as self-legislation (JPCM, 162)—hence, Cohenian Judaism continues the ethical emphasis given to it by Mendelssohn but now grounded in Kantian moral subjectivity. Strauss elaborates on the relation between ethics and religion for Cohen in his 1972 introductory essay to Cohen's *Religion of Reason*: "while religion cannot be reduced to ethics [for Cohen], it remains dependent on 'the method of ethics.' Man's moral autonomy must not in any way be called in question" (JPCM, 269). Insofar as Cohen construes Judaism to consist of the idea of the God-human relation, Strauss holds that (for Cohen) "God is the Holy One for the sake of the holiness of man, which consists in man's sanctifying himself" (JPCM, 273). For Strauss, Cohen's adoption of Kantian moral subjectivity, insofar as it replicates the emphasis on the individual found in Mendelssohn (LSMM, 123–125), takes it both as an unquestioned starting-point and as an improvement over premodern forms of Judaism (based in revealed law). Finally, Strauss refers to this emphasis on the improvement of modern (post-Kantian) Judaism over traditional Judaism as Cohen's "idealizing" mode of interpretation: "[Cohen] interprets Jewish thought by 'idealizing' or 'spiritualizing' it, i.e., by thinking it through and by understanding it in the light of its highest possibilities" (JPCM, 269). And this is, in effect, the mode of interpretation which, in Strauss's reading, Kant formulates in the *Critique of Pure Reason* (and which Strauss critiques elsewhere): "when we compare the thoughts that an author expresses about a subject, in ordinary speech as well as in writings, it is not at all unusual to find that we understand him even better than he understood himself, since he may not have determined his concept sufficiently and hence sometimes spoke, or even thought, contrary to his own intention."[63] In short, Cohen is the name, for Strauss, that most evokes the modern construction of "Jewish philosophy" and the occlusion of Jerusalem and Athens.[64] I can now consider Cohen's dependence on Kant (in his relation to Buber) as it shows itself in Strauss's 1967 lecture.

The second section of "Jerusalem and Athens" begins with a general discussion of Cohen's "synthesis" of Plato and the Biblical by virtue of "the social ideal" as it occurs in his well-known essay, "The Social Ideal in Plato and the Prophets" (JPCM, 398). For Strauss, this utterly modern construct is the product of Cohen's thought "belong[ing] to the world preceding World War I. Accordingly he had a greater faith in the power of modern Western culture to mold the fate of mankind than seems to be warranted now" (JPCM, 399). Strauss contrasts Cohen's synthetic view of Plato and the prophets with his own conception of Jerusalem and Athens when he holds that "Catastrophes and horrors of a magnitude hitherto unknown, which we have seen and through which we have lived, were better provided for, or made intelligible, by both Plato and the prophets than by the modern belief in progress" (JPCM, 399). In stating this, Strauss affirms both Jerusalem and Athens as forms of life free from the "spiritual dependence" on the modern idea of historical progress; and insofar as his critique of modernity gravitates around the critique of historical teleology, Strauss's project has an analogous character to those of Theodor Adorno, Walter Benjamin, and Hannah Arendt. What matters in the present context is Strauss's simultaneous refusal to synthesize Plato and the prophets *while showing them to be in genuine dialectical tension with one another.*

In speaking more specifically about the prophetic mission, however, something strange occurs. Strauss introduces this discussion with the following sentence: "I cannot speak in my own words of the mission of the prophets" (JPCM, 400). Whose words, then, will Strauss be using? Given that this discussion occurs in a section dealing with Cohen's synthesis, one might at first assume the answer to be Cohen. Strauss begins by citing Isaiah 6 (i.e., where, upon being granted the prophetic vision of God on His throne flanked by six-winged seraphim, Isaiah is called to prophesy), explaining that, while Isaiah volunteered for his mission, he could not well have refused God's command (JPCM, 400). He also raises the issue of "false prophets" and cites Jeremiah 28 (where Jeremiah confronts the false prophet Hananiah) as a source text. Are these, in fact, Cohen's words? Cohen does cite Isaiah 6:3 three times in *Religion of Reason*, but only in the context of discussing either God's uniqueness (ROR, 45, 395) or God's virtues (ROR, 404)—never concerning the prophetic mission.[65] He does not discuss this passage in "The Social Ideal" essay; neither does he (as far as I can tell) discuss Jeremiah 28 anywhere.[66] Who is the absent author of the words uttered by Strauss in this lecture?

Martin Buber references Isaiah 6 explicitly, within a more general discussion of the social mission of the prophets, in his 1938 introductory lecture at the Hebrew University of Jerusalem, entitled "Plato and Isaiah." While he contrasts the prophetic outlook of Isaiah with the worldly and political outlook of Plato (in contrast to Cohen's interpretation), he nonetheless addresses the question of Isaiah's social mission: "Isaiah does not believe that spiritual man has the vocation of power. . . . To stand powerless before the power he calls to account is part of the prophet's destiny. . . . Isaiah beheld the throne and the majesty of Him who entrusted him with the message."[67] Buber similarly discusses Jeremiah 28 (as it deals with the social and political role of the true prophet) in his 1942 essay "False Prophets": "Hananiah considered himself a great politician, for he thought that in an hour of danger he had succeeded in strengthening the people's resistance. But what he actually strengthened was an illusion, which when it collapsed would cause the collapse of the people's strength. Jeremiah, on the other hand, wanted to protect the people from just that. The only way to salvation is by the steep and stony path over the recognition of reality. The feet of those who take it bleed, and there is always the threat of dizziness, but it is the one and only way" (OTB, 169). It seems that Strauss has subtracted Buber's signature and replaced it with Cohen.[68] Why?

What binds their thought together, either politically or philosophically, such that Strauss can legitimately effect this substitution?

Both Cohen and Buber were deeply concerned with the fate of the Jewish people; Cohen chose the path of a socially prophetic Jewish religion based in Germany, while Buber chose the path of cultural Zionism in Israel. As mentioned above, these issues were very much part of the intellectual and political climate in which Strauss emerged as a thinker. While Strauss does not mention it, his interest in, and knowledge about, Zionism makes extremely plausible the possibility that he was familiar with the famous debate between Buber and Cohen that took place in the pages of Buber's journal *Der Jude* during the summer of 1916.[69] In that debate, Buber argues specifically that the land of Israel amounts to an ideal for all humanity: "This, in brief, is our creed: that Zion restored will become the house of the Lord for all peoples and the center of the new world, . . . in which 'the blood-stained garment of war is burned' and the 'swords are turned into plowshares.' The new humanity needs us. However, it needs us not dispersed and working at cross-purposes, but together and united" (JMW, 654). Cohen, in contrasts, argues that "Modern Judaism is historical; through historical development it acquires self-consciousness. And, the guide to our religious development is prophetism, the high point of which is messianism. We interpret our entire history as leading toward this goal of messianism. . . . In consequence of its messianic conceptions of God, the Jewish religion is thoroughly a world religion" (JMW, 653). Despite their radically different views as to the *geographical topos* of messianic Judaism, its *philosophical topos* is clear: the Judaism of today has ideal and publically recognizable universal significance for the world. Despite Buber's Nietzschean phraseology (e.g., "the new humanity") and Cohen's Hegelian formulation (e.g., "self-consciousness" as acquired through "historical development"), both owe their modern philosophical-political stances to one thinker—Immanuel Kant.

The Kantian influence on Cohen could not be more obvious; less so is Kant's influence on Buber. Yet in his 1938 essay, "What Is Man?" Buber states that Kant's *Prolegomena to Any Future Metaphysics* saved him from committing suicide (at age 14), by showing him that the antinomies characteristic of space and time do not characterize "the inner nature of the world but [only] ... the nature of my senses."[70] In positing a noumenal realm, Kant had shown Buber a way to construe personal experience irreducible to the maddening puzzles of the phenomenal world. For our purposes, this matters insofar as it underscores Buber's reliance on a modern conception of the world (as fundamentally split between subject and object). I will return to this issue at the end of this chapter. More specifically to the present point, however, both Buber and Cohen explicitly refer to Kant's seminal essay "Perpetual Peace: A Philosophical Sketch." In the "Social Ideal of Plato and the Prophets," Cohen holds that "Judaism's social idealism is related to its Messianism. Here, the close affinity to Kant is quite obvious. Kant wrote an essay on 'Perpetual Peace,' showing that the idea of universality is basic not only to his ethics but also to his view on history. History would seem incomprehensible to him if it did not have a goal. This goal, he says, is perpetual peace."[71] In "Plato and Isaiah," Buber discusses Kant's text as a critique of the Platonic "thesis" that appropriate political leaders are either philosophers or educated by philosophers (OTB, 151): "In his memorable tractate *Perpetual Peace*, Kant opposed this thesis of Plato's without mentioning him by name. The rebuttal is part of a passage that appeared only in the second edition and that Kant designated as a 'secret article' of his outline on international law" (OTB, 152). The passage which Buber cites runs: "It is not to be expected that kings will philosophize or that philosophers will become kings; nor is it to be desired, however, since the possession of power inevitably corrupts the free judgment of reason. Kings or sovereign peoples (i.e., those governing themselves by egalitarian laws) should not, however, force the class of philosophers to disappear or to remain silent, but should allow them to speak publicly."[72] While Buber takes this article as a sign of Kant's resignation (as a result of Church history) regarding the willingness of society to tolerate philosophy (OTB, 152), he does not dispute the requirement of publicity. Put differently, what places Kant in, albeit subordinate, proximity to the prophets is precisely the publicity of their statements. It is the possibility of such publicity that gives Judaism, for both Cohen and Buber, its universal, ethical, and social-idealistic character. Judaism fulfills the Enlightenment ideal of public education in and through its own prophetic-messianic vocation.

I suggest that Strauss was, again, compelling his audience to recollect the philosophical grounds for modern "Jewish philosophy" (which philosophy amounts to the synthesis of Jerusalem and Athens in the practical-ethical form of "Plato and the Prophets") by placing two otherwise dissimilar figures (Cohen and Buber) together. Strauss's critique of modern "Jewish philosophy" can now be stated as follows: the replacement of contemplation with practical, social idealism leads to the fantasy that the fundamental human problem concerning political association can be solved solely by means of public debate (or, rather, prophecy), with the hopes of either abolishing prejudice or relegating it to the private sphere. In so doing, modern "Jewish philosophy" deprives both Judaism and philosophy of the intellectual resources needed to respond to such a problem. This is not to say that the Enlightenment has not brought a great measure of success. Viewed retrospectively, from the end of the twentieth century, however, that success has not been unqualified.

Strauss addresses the limitations of "publicity" in his 1958 Kant seminar: "you can have it the other way around, where, if an immoral prince, immoral in Kant's sense, has taken hold of a people as a whole, then the moral policy is not publicly defensible. The moral policy would become frustrated by publication."[73] Whether by means of propaganda, government control, or both, "publicity" can be corrupted. In other words, "publicity" fails as an objective standard by means of which morality can be viewed (let alone taught). The individual subject/moral self of modern philosophy cannot simply be the fundamental datum for the study of politics because individuals—*occurring as they do in public spaces not of their making or control*—can be coerced and/or deceived. On the other hand, a precise awareness of this fact *might* allow people—by means of contemplation—to intellectually resist or avoid such coercion and deception (i.e., to ascend from the "second cave" to the "first"). Although Strauss does not state this as a reason, his critique of German Judaism as spiritually dependent on German culture (JPCM, 140) suggests that such resistance is an additional factor as to why philosophy cannot simply be grounded in an act of will—at least not if philosophy retains its premodern sense of being a search for wisdom.

Through his critique of modern "Jewish philosophy," Strauss allows readers to see the fundamental problem (concerning human association and its most legitimate order) that modern philosophy and modern Judaism occlude—that is, the theological-political problem. During a December 3, 1951 University of Chicago Hillel House meeting, titled "An Evening with Martin Buber" (and in a conversation of whether one should discuss Judaism from the perspective of "science," as political and social scientists are wont to do), Strauss poses a question to Buber that both (1) raises this fundamental problem and (2) shows that Buber is, in some measure, aware of it. Strauss asks Buber how he would account for the "fluidity of human communities" (i.e., that they exhibit more plurality than unity and more disagreement than consensus). Buber responds by saying simply that there is no faith that is absolutely common to all people; the different faiths cannot be compared for the purpose of judging which ones are better and which worse: "We cannot make faith into an 'objective' being."[74] For Strauss, the recognition that Judaism cannot adequately be discussed in a scientific (i.e., "objective," "public") manner indicates the limitation of both science and the modern, Kantian, subject-object philosophy on which it is based. That limitation—that is, the legacy of Kant—is coeval with the occlusion of the theological-political problem. What we find, at the end of Strauss's critique of modern "Jewish philosophy" (as, more generally, with his critique of modern philosophy and modern Judaism) is the necessity of recovering that problem as well as the responses to it issued under the names "Jerusalem" and "Athens."

CHAPTER TWO

Strauss's Maimonides

> Come, Nathan, would you
> By suchlike subtleties completely shatter
> Her brain, already sadly overwrought?
>
> —Lessing, *Nathan the Wise*[1]

> The union of all men is not possible on the level of reason or of wisdom . . . All mental life has its roots in the things which divide men, and is at any rate connected with those things.
>
> —Leo Strauss, "Introduction to *The Guide of the Perplexed*"[2]

Although we do not possess the essay on Lessing's play, which was to end Leo Strauss's projected volume "Philosophy and the Law: Historical Essays" (a good deal of which forms the contents of *Persecution and the Art of Writing*), we do have a statement of the book's plan, which notes that "The recollection of the man Maimonides was probably one of the motives underlying Lessing's *Nathan the Wise*, the outstanding poetic monument erected in honor of Jewish medieval philosophy" (JPCM, 470). For the present purposes, the acknowledgment of "the man Moses" as "recollected" in Lessing's work is significant insofar as it suggests the possibility that the height of premodern thought is able to be transferred to a radically different context (WIPP, 82, 82n3).[3]

Lessing's epigram highlights another aspect of Strauss's Maimonides as well. I begin, therefore, with a provocation: According to Strauss's February 16, 1938 letter to Jacob Klein, Strauss formulates what will come to be the social and political problem with his interpretation of Maimonides—that is, that it will be destructive to contemporary Judaism: "If I let this bomb blow in a few years (should I live that long), a huge battle will flare up. [Nahum] Glatzer . . . said to me that for Judaism Maimonides is more important than the Bible—thus if one deprives Judaism of Maimonides, one deprives it of its root (*Grundlage*) . . . Thus, it will yield the interesting result that a merely historical observation—the observation that Maim. was absolutely not a Jew in his belief—is of extremely timely significance: the incompatibility in principle of philosophy and Judaism . . . will be demonstrated *ad oculos*."[4] To say that Maimonides was not a Jew in his belief is controversial only if one accepts traditional Judaism as a "faith-tradition" based on belief; Leo Strauss did not.[5] To be sure, this does not mean that traditional Judaism involves no belief; it *does* mean that traditional Judaism is premised neither on an existential condition called faith, nor on an adherence to doctrine (i.e., "belief"). Rather, Judaism (like Islam) is a religion based on divine law. One might state the point overgenerally for the sake of introduction: The reorientation in Leo Strauss's thinking in the 1930s involves (among other things) the recognition that premodern Judaism is not exhausted—not even primarily characterized—by the neo-Orthodox preoccupations with personal belief, subjective religious experience, and direct relationship with God; instead it is characterized by adherence to law.[6] Strauss's turn away from neo-Orthodoxy to interest in the law, however, takes a decidedly philosophical form—that is, he is not interested in a practical (re-) instantiation of divine law but, rather, in the *idea* of divine law. That interest is part and parcel of his recognition of the theological-political problem. Strauss's Maimonides, therefore, is both a recovery of Jerusalem and Athens and a direct philosophical response to, and critique of, modern Jewish thought.

In order to better appreciate the contours of this critique, I present it in a manner analogous to chapter 1: I begin with a bit of intellectual history (concerning the then-contemporary interpretations—or "modern readings"—of Maimonides against which Strauss distinguished himself), and intellectual biography (concerning the development of Strauss's reading of Maimonides), in order to present a philosophical picture regarding the "whole" of his understanding of Maimonides.

Modern Readings of Maimonides

The commentators discussed in this section—Hermann Cohen, Isaac Husik, Julius Guttmann, Harry Austryn Wolfson, Salo Baron, and Alexander Altmann, and Simon Rawidowicz form the constellation in and through which Strauss distinguishes his own reading of Maimonides. Strauss indeed was familiar with the work of every member in this constellation.[7] My concern in this section cannot be with Strauss's full engagement with these thinkers; instead I aim to briefly sketch the contours of this constellation in order to better show where Strauss's Maimonides breaks with these more modern versions of Maimonides. In order to show how this constellation functions within Jewish discourses—and in order to highlight the distinctiveness of Strauss's interpretation—one might begin with the general claim that, from the nineteenth century onward, Haskalah Judaism (i.e., Western European Enlightenment Judaism) takes two predominant intellectual forms—scientific and apologetic. The first form is, literally, exemplified in the Scientific Study of Judaism movement (i.e., *Wissenschaft des Judentums*). Relative to the present purposes, an interesting instance of the second form is the Maimonides anthology movement in 1930s Germany (spearheaded by Schocken and headed in large measure by Nahum Glatzer and Alexander Altmann).

The Scientific Study of Judaism, like its analogue in nineteenth-century Protestant circles, was in many ways an inheritor of the early modern development of Biblical criticism philosophically developed in the works of Hobbes and Spinoza. Eschewing the traditional understanding of Judaism and the Hebrew Bible as a manifestation of God's command, the *Wissenschaft* movement sought to purge Judaism of its superstitions and prejudices and replace them with a reasoned and organized canon of methodologies and interpretive practices through which Judaism could reach a mature, and somewhat secularized, understanding of itself. This description of the *Wissenschaft* movement, however, runs the risk of being taken as caricature (given that I will eventually show Strauss's distantiation from it). One runs the risk of committing a *reductio ad Straussum/Scholemum* if one simply relies on Strauss or Gershom Scholem's characterizations of the *Wissenschaft* movement. This characterization, however, comes, in equal measure, from Leopold Zunz. In a crucial passage in his "On Rabbinic Literature" (1818), he writes that "[t]he entire literature of the Jews, in its widest scope, is presented here as the object of scholarly research; in this context it is not at all our concern whether the context of this entire literature should, or could, also be the norm for our own judgment."[8] In this statement, one detects the (unconcerned) neutrality characteristic of a Weber and thus constituting a variant of what Strauss (in his autobiographical preface to *Spinoza's Critique of Religion*) refers to as German Judaism's spiritual dependence on the modern (in this case, intellectual) practices of Germany as a whole. Strauss agrees with Zunz's estimation, but draws the opposite conclusion from it: insofar as it adopts a supersessionist attitude toward traditional Judaism, this form of Enlightenment, for Strauss, amounts simply to "Obfuscation."[9]

If the *Wissenschaft* movement exhibited its modernity in one direction, then the Jewish apologetics of the Maimonides anthologies did so no less in the opposite direction. Like the *Wissenschaft* movement, its beginnings were noble. As the Scientific Study of Judaism sought to resist superstition and prejudice through academic study, the Schocken Maimonides anthologies of the 1930s sought—in the words of Martina Urban—a "'spiritual resistance'" through a guarded (yet secretly impassioned) defense of Judaism.[10] This occurred through the publication of anthologies that "[p]resent[ed] a selection of representative writings from the Jewish past . . . accompanied with minimal scholarly commentary" in order to "be perceived as nonpolitical."[11] By making translational use of terminology that "had been central in conservative thought during and since the days of the Weimar Republic"[12] (e.g., *Sendung* [mission], *Schicksal* [destiny], *Geschick* [fate], *Ordnung* [order]—terms used by conservative thinkers such as Heidegger and Schmitt[13]), the Maimonides anthologies "aimed to counteract . . . the [National Socialist] state policy aimed at reghettoizing the Jews spiritually and culturally, by obliging them to stress their particularity and 'otherness.'"[14] While Urban holds that "these anthologies framed a defiant if muted response to the regnant political and existential nihilism of the Nazis and the theoretical descants of Schmitt and Heidegger," she also notes that they nonetheless "assumed an apologetic posture. And that posture betrayed the weakness that Leo Strauss diagnosed as the 'political-theological [*sic*] predicament' of German Jewry and ascribed to an unwillingness to let go of what he saw as the chimerical promises of liberalism."[15] In trying to assimilate to the strains of German conservatism, therefore, the Maimonides anthologies did exactly what the *Wissenschaft* movement had done (although precisely in the opposite direction)—that is, they attempted to make themselves acceptable to Germany at large. This, for Strauss, constitutes their "spiritual dependence." But this "spiritual dependence" has a philosophical counterpart or flipside equally as problematic for Strauss: in both cases, the *theoretical* aspects of the movements/projects were subordinated to *practical* outcome of societal acceptance (be it by an Enlightened or conservative polity). *It is the reduction of theory to practice that ultimately occludes both (1) recognition of the theological-political problem and the Jerusalem/Athens distinction and (2) an adequate perception of Maimonides.*

Not all of the modern Maimonides commentators listed above can be so easily fit into the aforementioned categories—for example, Wolfson was certainly no apologist, but he also (while conceptually closer) was not exactly a member of the *Wissenschaft des Judentums* either. It is nonetheless true that, according to Strauss, they all emerge in the same modern horizon that gave rise to the scientific and apologetic forms of modern Judaism. Put differently, they either assume the modern separation of theory and practice or assume the Enlightenment preference for practical over theoretical concerns (in some cases both assumptions are in play). In the present context, therefore, the modern Maimonides interpretations can be seen to exhibit the following features: (1) Aristotelianism, (2) an orientation toward practical issues, and (3) harmonization or synthesis of philosophy and religion.

Aristotelianism

For Wolfson, "Maimonides is a true convert to Aristotelian philosophy. To him, the thorough understanding of Aristotle is the highest achievement to which man can attain."[16] This shows, for Wolfson the profound affinity of Maimonides's thought with his age (unlike, e.g., the thought of Halevi).[17] For Wolfson, this derivative quality of Maimonides's Aristotelianism is coupled with a similarly derivative dualism between theoretical and practical matters: "In its speculative part the Law contains Aristotle's metaphysics couched in language suitable for the intelligence of the common people. In its practical part, it is a scheme of a social organization planned to produce 'actually intelligent beings' . . . Maimonides was not a rabbi employing Greek logic and categories of thought in order to interpret Jewish religion; he was rather a true medieval Aristotelian, using Jewish religion as an illustration of the Stagirite's metaphysical supremacy."[18] Stated otherwise, for Wolfson, Maimonides's Aristotelianism signifies not a religious application of philosophy to Judaism, but rather a philosophical application of religion to Aristotelian metaphysics. Most surprising is Wolfson's following claim: "That, naturally, he was unaware of the dualism must be clear. Indeed, he thought he had made a synthesis, and had given scientific demonstrations of poetic conceptions."[19] In this respect, Wolfson shows a predilection for the idealizing interpretation bequeathed from Kant to Cohen (as discussed in chapter 1).

Guttmann makes an attribution of Aristotelianism to Maimonides which is similar to Wolfson's except in two important respects: (1) he views the relation of philosophy to religion less as a "practical necessity" and more as a genuine theoretical synthesis and (2) the terminology he uses appears to emphasize the religious—rather than the philosophical—character of Maimonides's Aristotelianism: "[Maimonides's] spiritualization of Judaism interpreted the law in terms of the religious values of Aristotelianism, and thereby gave it a different religious meaning in some essential points. Maimonides' theistic Aristotelianism established the place of the biblical Creator-God within the framework of philosophical cosmology, and thus achieved a true metaphysical synthesis between biblical religion and Aristotelianism . . . But the religious ideals of this theistic Aristotelianism were still Aristotelian, though they were introduced into historical Judaism without any awareness of basic religious discrepancies."[20] Thus, although Guttmann's language replaces philosophy with religion as the center of Maimonides's Aristotelianism, and although he construes such religious Aristotelianism theoretically, he nonetheless preserves the idealizing interpretation one sees in Wolfson by holding that Maimonides was unaware of the basic religious discrepancies. In at least two of the three cases here, then, Maimonides's Aristotelianism is understood symptomatically as an inability (on Maimonides's part) to come to grips with the differences between Judaism and Greek philosophy. Although I will treat

Isaac Husik in a bit more detail below, it suffices to mention that his conception of the relation between Maimonides and Aristotle follows in the tradition just outlined.[21]

Orientation Toward Practical Issues

In breaking with Wolfson's and Guttmann's respective construals of Maimonides as an Aristotelian, Cohen specifically seeks to emphasize the practical character of Maimonides's thought—thus, the title of his essay *Ethics of Maimonides* (*Charakteristik der Ethik Mamunis*): "There is no greater testimony to Maimonides as the most vital and most inner representative of philosophy within Judaism than that his metaphysics has its interweaved center in his ethics."[22] In denying the unconditionality of the idea of the Good (i.e., insofar as the Good only has relative status),[23] Aristotle cannot, in Cohen's terms, form the philosophical impetus for Maimonides's thought: "Can Maimonides accept, without qualification, the formulations of Aristotle into his position? If this were the case, the whole of Maimonides' rationalism, which manifests itself in his pursuit of the grounds of the laws, would then be only of historical and anthropological interest. To be sure, Maimonides at times employs such an approach, but this does not represent his main emphasis. Rather, his basic tendency, that theology should culminate in ethics, attests to his rationalism; likewise every stage of Maimonides' dogmatics aims at ethics."[24] Maimonides's acceptance of the unity of God—and of God with the Good—forecloses the possibility of any serious dependence on Aristotelian ethics or metaphysics. The relative standing of the Good, and the absence of a related and personal divinity, in Aristotle have two consequences unacceptable to Cohen: (1) they relegate the practicality of ethics to a merely empirical status and (2) they fail to do justice to the divine-human relationship, which is the foundation of Judaism. This is the import of Cohen's oft-quoted statement to the effect that the God of Aristotle is "truly" not the God of Israel.[25] Cohen sums up his view in the following manner: "It is the ultimate meaning of Maimonides' theory of [divine] attributes [i.e., that they express God's actions in the world rather than God's essence] that God is not the God of metaphysics, or of cosmic substance, but the God of ethics, that is the God of humankind. God as the archetype (*Vorbild*) and ideal for the human race (*Menschengeschlecht*) and for the human self: solely as this human ethical ideal does God relate to the world and to the essence of humanity."[26] Philosophically speaking, for Cohen, Plato's conception of the unity of the Good provides a far better conception of ethics and divinity (with respect to Maimonides's thought) than does Aristotle.

Given the breadth and power of Cohen's interpretation, Baron and Altmann cannot help but appear as something akin to footnotes with respect to the present discussion. Nonetheless, their additions to this discussion further emphasize the role of the practical in the modern interpretations of Maimonides. Altmann's writings on Maimonides span much of the twentieth century and differ widely in their mode of presentation; it would, therefore, be unfair to claim that any one period suffices as a treatment of his interpretation. Nonetheless, because of its connection to the Schockensverlag Maimonides publications in the 1930s, I make use of Altmann's 1935 epilogue to the volume *Des Rabbi Mosche ben Maimon More Newuchim im Grundriss* (published by Schocken); as an expression of the apologietic character of the "practical wing" of the modern Maimonides interpretations, therefore, it is of special interest. In this text, Altmann critiques Maimonides for *failing to give adequate emphasis* to the practical character of Judaism: "Maimonides' interpretation of the law of the Torah does not do justice to the central position of *mitzvah* (commandment) in Jewish consciousness. He does not pay fundamental attention to the election of Israel, this basic theological fact of Judaism. The universal breadth of his thought made him overlook, in his philosophical position, the unique nature and intensity of what is specifically Jewish, which he expressed, in its entire particularity, in the *Mishneh Torah*."[27] For Altmann, Maimonides's treatment of law (in the *Guide)* does not pay sufficient attention to the election of Israel and (by implication) to the divine-human covenant set forth at Sinai. In this respect, Altmann's early critique of Maimonides is simply the flipside of Cohen's project of emphasizing the practical, if transcendent, Platonism that exhibits the divine-human couplet. In the same year (1935), Altmann writes that Maimonides's critics "see in his work halakhah cut off from its roots and leading a life of pure spirit. Here his opponents who are against systems have a stronger instinct for what constitutes the typically Jewish element. He sees halakhah as a logical system, the others see it as a living stream."[28] Altmann again notes the concern over Maimonides's intellectualism as a threat to the fundamentally practical character of Judaism. In this context, Baron's "The Historical Outlook of Maimonides" (1934–1935) provides a fascinating counterpoint.[29] If Altmann ultimately claims that Maimonides's construal of Jewish law takes too many intellectual liberties, Baron holds exactly the opposite concerning Maimonides's understanding of that most controversial root of Judaism—that is, the creation of the world: "Although he acknowledged, as is well known, that by strictly philosophical arguments the creation of the world can neither be proved nor disproved, he believed that creation *ex nihilo* at a certain date was an indubitable historical fact. He even followed the rabbinic chronology that about 2500 years elapsed from Adam to Moses."[30] While it may be the case that Maimonides has a complex and interesting relation to history,[31] Baron's claim locates such an interest as conditioning Maimonides's philosophical project, not the other way around. In sum, Cohen's emphasis on the primacy of the ethical in Maimonides dovetails with Altmann's concern over Maimonides's supposed neglect of Jewish election and Baron's construal of a strong historical sense in Maimonides. All three, in different ways, point to a concern with the practical over the theoretical when it comes to interpreting Maimonides.

Harmonization or Synthesis of Philosophy and Religion

I have already intimated that Guttmann's interpretation suggests a synthesis, in Maimonides, between philosophy and Judaism; he states this explicitly in the beginning of his discussion of Maimonides: "Maimonides endeavored to effect an inner reconciliation between the spiritual worlds whose opposition had been blurred and obscured . . . The wide sweep and penetrating power of his philosophical thinking were bent to this task of planting Aristotelianism in the soil of Judaism . . . Maimonides threw the opposition between Aristotelianism and biblical revelation into bold relief in order to overcome it by a genuine synthesis. This major achievement made Maimonides the leading philosophical figure of the late Jewish Middle Ages."[32] Guttmann holds that Maimonides attempted to rescue the oppositions inherent in Jewish philosophy from their prior obfuscation with the purpose of exhibiting a clearer and more profound synthesis. The "originality of [this] creative synthesis"[33] lies precisely (as stated above) in its construal of Jewish law in terms of Aristotle.[34]

Isaac Husik expresses a similar view when he claims that "From his youth we can trace the evident purpose, not finally completed until toward the end of his brilliant and useful career, the purpose to harmonize Judaism with philosophy, to reconcile the Bible and Talmud with Aristotle. He was ambitious to do this for the good of Judaism, and in the interest of a rational and enlightened faith."[35] For Guttmann philosophy and religion appear to operate "on the same level," as it were, in the Maimonidean synthesis; for Husik (*contra* Wolfson), however, Maimonides's *Guide* subsumes philosophy and science under a religious tent: "The work is not a treatise of science or philosophy. The latter are presupposed. He introduces philosophic principles, Aristotelian or Kalamistic, only with a view to their relation to Jewish theology."[36] Although I am unaware as to whether he makes this distinction, it is not unreasonable to assert, for Husik, that Maimonides's thought aims to contribute to a philosophically-tinged *theology* more than to a theologically-tinged *philosophy*. Appreciating the tensions between the Hebrew Bible and Talmud, on the one hand, and Aristotelian philosophy, on the other, Husik nevertheless repeats Wolfson's and Guttmann's idealizing contention (albeit in a more qualified manner): "Maimonides . . . endeavors to harmonize the intellectualism and theorism of the Stagirite with the diametrically opposed ethics and religion of the Hebrew Bible. And he is *apparently* unaware of the yawning gulf extending between them."[37]

From this standpoint, Rawidowicz's construal of Maimonides is of particular interest insofar as it stands as a possible critique of both Straus's Maimonides and the modern Maimonides commentators mentioned above. Rawidowicz understands Maimonides's thought within the broad context of the problem of *interpretatio*; taking his bearing from the relation between Biblical and post-Biblical Jewish literary activity, Rawidowicz construes the practice of commentary (and commentary on commentary, etc.) to constitute an attempt at "reshaping either the 'document' interpreted or the world it came from . . . It derives its strength both from a deep attachment to the 'text' and from an 'alienation' from it, a certain distance, a gap which has to be bridged."[38] Maimonides's thought is thus understood as "fighting for establishing in Israel the right, nay, the duty of *interpretatio.*"[39] Differently stated, in order for Judaism to remain a living religion, it must continue to be invested with a hermeneutic self-understanding sensitive both to tradition and the need for innovation. Insofar as such a self-understanding always operates between the familiar dichotomies of old/new, revelation/reason, (etc.), the decision for one term over another constitutes an obfuscation of both the problem and any possible solution: "Recent discussions as to whether Maimonides is to be considered a 'philosopher' or not do not make any contribution towards a deeper grasping of Maimonides' intellectual personality and achievement in Judaic thought."[40] For Rawidowicz, the very dichotomies, their critique, and (in fact) claims regarding Maimonides's self-awareness of his own project are side issues. What matters is the *historical* significance of his intellectual and literary contribution with respect to the issue of *intepretatio*. If Maimonides does not ultimately effect a harmonization or synthesis between philosophy and Judaism, he has certainly opened the space for further concrete attempts (which attempts constitute the very core of Jewish post-Biblical activity). Like Baron, Rawidowicz views history as a significant category in which to understand the import of Maimonides's thought; unlike Baron, history functions not as an *epistemic* category by which one makes claims about the past but, rather, as an *existential* one in which one navigates the future life of a people. Instead of attempting a conceptual harmonization or systemization of philosophy and Judaism, Rawidowicz's Maimonides effects a historical harmonization of opposing tendencies through the hermeneutic practice of *interpretatio.*

As stated above, the constellation of Maimonides commentaries all have this in common: they either (1) assert the separation of theory from practice, with Aristotle functioning as the name for "abstract theory," and either "Plato" or "Biblical thought" functioning as the name for "practice" (as do Wolfson, Guttmann, and Husik), or (2) manifest the Enlightenment orientation, which emphasizes (either by interpretation or critique) the practical over the theoretical with Plato or the Bible forming the locus into which Aristotelian cosmology or theology gets inserted (as do Cohen, Altmann, Baron, Rawidowicz). Even Rawidowicz's substitution of historical harmonization for conceptual harmonization remains within this modern horizon. Finally, in the cases of Wolfson's, Guttmann's, and

Husik's respective Maimonides interpretations, one clearly sees the "idealizing interpretation" characteristic of modern Jewish thought and philosophy. As was the case in chapter 1, this discussion has been necessary insofar as it helps one to understand and appreciate the originality of Strauss's Maimonides, especially in the light of Glatzer's warning to him. Indeed, Strauss's "Athenian Maimonides" constitutes a response to both the confluence of modern philosophy and modern Jewish thought (as discussed in the previous chapter) and the modern Maimonides interpretations discussed above. Before I can discuss the properly philosophical significance of Strauss's Maimonides (i.e., as a recovery of the theological-political problem and Jerusalem and Athens as the responses to this problem), it is necessary to sketch the contours of Strauss's arrival at—and development of—his reading of Maimonides. This can be accomplished largely (though not exclusively) through a consideration of Strauss's correspondence.

Strauss's Journey to Maimonides

While the periodization of Strauss's oeuvre is of secondary import from a philosophical perspective, it is crucial for purposes of tracing aspects of his intellectual biography. As noted in the first chapter, it is only when we have a sense of the development of Strauss's thinking that we can attempt to envision it as a "whole." For this reason, the conventional tripartite scheme (formulated by Bloom and applied to Strauss's Maimonides writings by Brague) is far from irrelevant.[41]

The first period of Strauss's development takes place during the years 1921 to 1938. The major writings dealing with Maimonides, in this period, include *Spinoza's Critique of Religion* (1930), "Cohen and Maimonides" (1931), *Philosophy and Law: Contributions to the Understanding of Maimonides and His Predecessors* [1935] (written with the intent on applying for professorship at the Hebrew University of Jerusalem[42]), "Some Remarks on the Political Science of Maimonides and Farabi" (1936), "The Place of the Doctrine of Providence According to Maimonides" (1937), and "On Abravanel's Philosophical Tendency and Political Teaching" (1937).[43] Strauss's encounter with Avicenna's *Divisions of the Rational Sciences*, in which (through a reference to Plato's *Laws* as treating the issues of prophecy and divine law) he discovers that divine law is the proper object of politics, occurs in 1929–30.[44] This begins his period of reorientation (according to Meier, 1929–1937), during which time he turns (in Socratic fashion) to political philosophy and undertakes his rediscovery of the esoteric/exoteric distinction characteristic of premodern philosophy.[45] Of significance during this reorientation are Strauss's contentions that he is not a believing Jew and the comparison between Maimonides's *Guide* and Nietzsche's *Zarathustra* (a comparison that ultimately goes in Maimonides's favor).[46] In sum, this early period is decisive insofar as it shows Strauss's emerging understanding of Maimonides as a genuinely free thinker who undertakes an authentic human search for wisdom—that is, as a citizen of Athens.

The second period of Strauss's development occurs between the years 1938 and 1954. The major writings dealing with Maimonides, in this period, are his review of Arthur Hyamson's translation of Book One of the *Mishneh Torah* (1939), "The Literary Character of *The Guide for the Perplexed* [1941] (contained in *Persecution and the Art of Writing*), the lecture "How to Study Medieval Philosophy (1944), and "Maimonides' Statement on Political Science" (1953). This period can be characterized by a deepening of the tendency occurring in Strauss's reorientation. Strauss's texts now exhibit the very esoteric character about which he wrote during his first period. One might put the point in the following way: if Strauss's first period signals a rediscovery of "political philosophy" as both a subject of inquiry and a manner of presentation, his second period amounts to an attempt to exemplify "political philosophy" in his own presentations (thus also the concern with "literary character" and "the art of writing" during times of persecution).

The third and final period of Strauss's development begins in 1954, and continues to the end of his life. This period sees the translation of Maimonides's *Guide* by Shlomo Pines (which Strauss organized and for which he provided his introduction). The major texts on Maimonides, in this period, are Strauss's Chicago Hillel lecture "Introduction to Maimonides' *Guide of the Perplexed*" (1960), his introduction to Pines's translation of the *Guide*—"How to Begin to Study *The Guide of the Perplexed*" (1963), and three short (posthumously published) texts from 1967 and 1968—"Notes on Maimonides' *Book Of Knowledge*," "Notes on Maimonides' *Treatise on the Art of Logic*," and "Notes on Maimonides' *Letter on Astrology*." This period is characterized by an extension and radicalization of the style Strauss had adopted during his second period.[47] Here, his texts become even less straightforward, and ever more removed from the conventional academic style of presentation. Alexander Altmann characterizes Strauss's Maimonides writings from this period as follows: "So much had [Strauss] immersed himself in the attempt to disentangle Maimonides' presumed esotericism that he discovered strange keys and often abstruse answers. The comparison with Beethoven's last quartets may not be completely out of place."[48]

Altmann's comparison of Strauss's late writings on Maimonides with Beethoven's last quartets may paradoxically remind careful readers of another twentieth-century German thinker who explicitly discussed Beethoven's late string quartets under the rubric "late style"—that is, Theodor Adorno. That Adorno and Strauss had little in common is easily enough understandable. However, insofar as Altmann picks up on a similar theme in Strauss's late Maimonides writings, Adorno's 1937 characterization is relevant in the present context: "in the very late Beethoven *the conventions find expression as naked representations of themselves*. This is the function of the often-remarked-on abbreviation of his style. It seeks not so much to free the musical language from mere phrases, as, rather, to free the mere phrase from the appearance of its subjective mastery. The mere phrase, unleashed and set free from the dynamics of the piece, *speaks for itself*."[49] While Strauss's thought exhibits none of the Romantic echoes still audible in Adorno's description, two things bear noting: (1) Strauss's late texts compel readers to wonder about his rejection of academic written conventions (in order, perhaps, to indicate what "freedom of thought" entails) and (2) Strauss's late texts oftentimes refer, in equal measure, to the writer in question and to Strauss's own thought. In other words, Strauss's late texts both make explicit the conventional character of said conventions and use the "commentary" form of writing as a means to speak directly about philosophical issues (in the style of Islamic commentaries on Plato and Aristotle). Paradoxically, this is one moment where Strauss's recollection of premodern (e.g., Farabian) forms of writing and Adorno's construal of aesthetic modernism, at least peripherally, touch. This is yet another way of making the point, familiar to readers of Strauss, that his later texts "speak in two voices"—one for the nonphilosophers, who hear the texts as simply communicating content and one for the potential philosophers, who may wonder whether Strauss is also performing what he speaks about.[50]

Even a brief consultation of Strauss's correspondence shows the movement toward understanding Maimonides as a citizen of Athens. This movement happens alongside a more forthright announcement of Strauss's own Athenian citizenship. Already in 1934, Strauss writes to Gershom Scholem that "I am not an orthodox and under no circumstances the right man for an orthodox institute since I cannot make any concessions, I hardly need tell you."[51] The following year he simplifies his message to Löwith: "Incidentally, I am not an orthodox Jew!"[52] If one recalls (from chapter 1) Strauss's 1932 draft letter to Krüger in which he declares his inability to believe, a picture emerges concerning Strauss's relation to Judaism (at least as *dogmatically* construed). This sentiment of Strauss's "*apiqorsiut* [radical unbelief]"[53] is one that accompanies Strauss to the end of his life. Whether such nonbelief would today be characterized as atheism is an interesting but somewhat irrelevant question; it certainly was thus characterized in 1935, when Scholem writes the following lines to Walter Benjamin: "[Strauss's *Philosophy and Law*] begins with an unfeigned and copiously argued (if completely ludicrous) affirmation of atheism as the most important Jewish watchword. Such admirable boldness for a book that will be read by everybody as having been written by a candidate for Jerusalem!"[54] Current readers do not have to simply grant Scholem's assessment to recognize the controversy that would ensue from Strauss's work; indeed, Strauss's own claims about Maimonides are equally as bold as Scholem suggests they are. In a June 1, 1938 letter to Ernst Simon, Strauss states his view in no uncertain terms: "Rambam was an actual philosopher—in the medieval sense of the word, which means radically unbelieving."[55] From the standpoint of his correspondence with Klein, 1938 was an especially revealing year regarding the development of Strauss's Athenian Maimonides; taking his cue from Avicenna's aforementioned reference to the treatment of religion in Plato's *Laws*, on January 20, he writes the following: "[Maimonides] was a truly free mind . . . The crucial question for him was not world creation or world eternity (for he was persuaded of world eternity), instead it was whether the ideal law-giver must be a prophet."[56] Continuing this connection with, and reliance on, Islamic political philosophy, on February 16, he tells Klein: "You can't imagine with what infinite refinement and irony Maimonides handles 'religion' . . . One misunderstands Maimonides simply because one does not reckon with the possibility that he was an 'Averroist': consider it and all the difficulties in principle just dissolve."[57] These statements throw an interesting light on Strauss's 1935 letter to Scholem, in which he mentions that he has completed an introduction to Maimonides's *Guide* titled "Hobbes' Political Science in Its Development."[58] While "Introduction" does not, in this context, connote a similarity of approach or understanding between Hobbes and Maimonides, it does suggest that Strauss clearly understands Maimonides to be concerned with the relation between religion (as divine law) and politics. It also suggests (contra Baron) that Strauss's Maimonides does not view the most important religious issues (like Creation) historically.

In subsequent periods, Strauss's understanding of Maimonides—as with his self-understanding—deepens but does not change its fundamental orientation. In a decisive letter on May 20, 1949 to Julius Guttmann, Strauss both (1) articulates the esoteric character of Maimonides's writing and (2) indicates that he views this style of communication as a current possibility or even necessity: "If my hunch is right, then Maimonides was a 'philosopher' in a far more radical sense than is usually assumed today and really was almost always assumed, or at least was said. Here the question arises immediately of the extent to which one may responsibly expound this possibility publicly—a question that certainly makes the problem of esotericism immediately a timely or, as one says these days, an 'existential' one. This was one of the reasons why I wanted to present the problem in principle of esotericism—or the problem of the relationship between thought and society—*in corpore vili*, thus with respect to some strategically favorable, non-Jewish object. I chose Xenophon, partly due to the connection with the problem of Socrates, partly because the assumption is that if *even* Xenophon, this seemingly harmless writer, then all the more . . ."[59] This is, perhaps, the clearest statement of Strauss's view that a premodern conception of philosophy (as a way of life operating with the esoteric/exoteric distinction) is currently practicable. Moreover, the replacement of Maimonides with Xenophon is an important precursor for his Hebrew University lectures of 1954–55.

Also characteristic of these subsequent periods is Strauss's attempt (both concerning his Maimonides interpretation and more generally) to work through issues normally construed as "metaphysical" or "theological." In a letter to Helmut Kuhn (written shortly after the German translation of *Natural Right and History*), Strauss counters the claim that he (perhaps along the same lines as Wolfson's construal of Maimonides) is ultimately and simply a disciple of Aristotle by stating that: "I am not an Aristotelian since I am not satisfied that the visible universe is eternal, to say nothing of other perhaps more important reasons."[60] One might surmise that these "more important reasons are connected with his construal of premodern political philosophy as inherently Platonic (to be discussed in the final section of this chapter). At any rate, one finds, alongside his reservations regarding Aristotelianism, statements that are fully compatible with Aristotle's thought (as one instance of premodern thought more generally)—for example, in a 1958 letter to Hans Jonas: "Our problem now is to recover physis [nature]."[61] Given that these two "metaphysical" issues are, for Strauss, also significantly raised in Maimonides's *Guide*, I believe that they cannot simply be understood as separate from Strauss's treatment of more "theological" matters—for example, of the kind raised in a 1963 letter to Scholem: "You imply that according to him [Maimonides] there is immortality of the individual soul; I am almost certain that this is not the case."[62] These "metaphysical" and "theological" issues come to find their place (for Strauss) within the context of political philosophy; Strauss makes this utterly clear in another late correspondence with Scholem (1960): "On the basis of *Guide* I.2 regarding Adam's pristine unawareness of the noble and base I would say that the messianic age is not necessarily higher but rather lower than Adam's original state. One must also consider the persistence of the Law in the messianic age and take this together with the depreciation of the Law (of all actions) in favor of pure contemplation."[63] That the law persists in the messianic age means that conventional moral categories—as well as political necessities—also persist; in this respect, the end is not equal to the beginning (where such categories did not yet exist). However, the depreciation of the law in favor of contemplation points to an interruption or denigration of moral stringency in the days of the messiah. Maimonides does, after all, hold (in the

Eight Chapters) that the acquisition of the moral virtues is propaedeutic to the acquisition of the rational virtues—and, ultimately, of intellect.[64] Sensitive readers might ask whether Strauss is suggesting that, for Maimonides, Athens ultimately "completes" Jerusalem. Strauss's remark does appear to indicate that he understands Maimonides to be advocating philosophical inquiry—albeit in a manner appropriate for its survival in one's given time and place. In this respect, Strauss's concerns over premodern philosophical issues (such as *physis* and the possibility of cosmological eternity)—as well as doctrinal issues (such as individual immortality)—always occur in proximity to questions about the law. In this way, these "metaphysical" and "theological" issues ultimately come to sight as concerns for political philosophy.

If my interpretation of Strauss's correspondence is correct, this suggests that politics is the initial horizon for both philosophy and religion. This is precisely what is at stake in the theological-political problem—that is, the concern over the best/most just way of life. That religion and philosophy—that is, Jerusalem and Athens—are two responses to this problem suggests that the proximity in which they find themselves related to one another needs to be navigated.[65] This, for Strauss, is the premodern configuration that becomes obfuscated in the modern attempts at synthesis or harmonization (or, for that matter, denial). Such navigation can never take place from a neutral, third place outside of either Jerusalem or Athens. The question then becomes: How can individuals navigate their relation to the other city without jeopardizing either (1) one's own city or (2) the relation between the two? The prudence that Strauss sees in Maimonides, and that he expresses in his published writings, is of apiece with his apparent reticence over making too visible the full extent of his Athenian Maimonides (in keeping with Glatzer's expressed concern) outside of specific moments in his correspondence—such as, for example, in his 1967 letter to Seth Benardete: "What you say about the bloodlessness of the gods [in Homer] reminds me of *The Guide of the Perplexed* I.1."[66] Having discussed Strauss's intellectual biography in reference to his Maimonides interpretation, however, I can now consider that interpretation in its philosophical significance. This discussion calls for a synchronic, rather than diachronic, approach.

Strauss's Maimonides

Strauss's rendition of Maimonides is sometimes seen as a way station: sandwiched in between (1) on the one hand, his early engagements with Nietzsche and Heidegger (both of whom provided the impetus for Strauss to return to premodern thought),[67] and on the other hand, his discovery of Farabi and Avicenna (from whom Strauss learned the political function of prophecy and—in the aforementioned case of Avicenna—its presence in Plato's *Laws*);[68] and (2) his subsequent return to the Greeks generally and Socrates and Plato particularly. Maimonides (in this reading) is therefore viewed as a transitional figure. Paradoxically, while these views are not incorrect, it remains the case that, as Brague holds, "Maimonides is the permanent object of [Strauss's] scholarly research."[69] Beginning with his early presentation in *Spinoza's Critique of Religion*, and continuing all the way to the final short above-mentioned essays (contained in *Studies in Platonic Political Philosophy*),[70] Maimonides is the one figure who accompanies Strauss in every period of his philosophical journey. That his study of Maimonides was "frequently interrupted but never abandoned" (LSM, 493) attests both to the abiding importance of Maimonides's thought, for Strauss, and to the necessity of integrating his interpretation of Maimonides's thought in terms of a philosophical "whole."

I have provided a brief discussion of the vicissitudes that Maimonides's thought takes throughout Strauss's career, indicating the changes between his pre- and post-1938 writings. Despite the differences, however, there are significant moments of affinity that show Strauss's relation to Maimonides to be in fact transdevelopmental: (1) Maimonides (as a medieval thinker) is intimately exposed to and involved in the Jerusalem/Athens distinction; (2) Maimonides understands what is at stake in both cities (i.e., forms of life); (3) Maimonides understands that both cities are responses to the question concerning the best/most just existence in and of the city—that is, they are responses to the theological-political problem; and (4) Maimonides understands the political and pedagogical importance of speaking in different ways to different audiences. I have also shown, however, that Strauss's understanding of Maimonides as a philosopher (akin to Averroes) who "described Athens through the specifics of Jerusalem"[71] is not *prima facie* at odds with the other Maimonides interpretations discussed in this chapter. Put differently, no one seems to disagree that Maimonides's thought, in some sense, brings together philosophy and religion. Where, then, does its unique character lie?

Jerusalem and Athens

The uniqueness of Strauss's interpretation turns on his understanding of Jerusalem and Athens (that "highest theme of [all]"[72]) as competing forms of life that nevertheless are both in proximity with one another and serve as the catalyst for the development of Western civilization. This theme (which, according to Velkley, is conceptually prefigured in the struggle between Plato's and Aristophanes's differing portrayals of Socrates[73]) first comes to sight in the Middle Ages: "the Middle Ages witnessed the first, and certainly the first adequate, discussion between these two most important forces of the Western world: the religion of the Bible and the science or philosophy of the Greeks. It was a discussion, not between ethical monotheism and paganism, that is., between two religions, but between religion as such and science or philosophy as such: between the way of life based on faith and obedience and a way of life based on free insight, on human wisdom alone" (LSM, 102).[74] To be a philosopher, in this highly charged context, means that one literally has to justify one's way of life in the court of revealed law; and this Maimonides does both by *zetetic* and esoteric means (i.e., he both "defends reason in the face of Orthodoxy" [SCR, 148] and writes between the lines for those "able to understand by themselves" [LSM, 398]). In being able to take up philosophy in general, and Platonic political philosophy in particular, within the central context of the "un-Platonic premise of revelation" (PL, 128), Maimonides's rationalism amounts to the "true natural model, the standard to be carefully protected against distortion" (PL, 21).

How is it that we are still able (i.e., in a modern horizon) to take Maimonides's thought as such a standard? It is at this point (as mentioned in chapter 1) that Strauss's thought shows its debt to modern German philosophy; for while the acceptance of Maimonides as such a standard is coeval with the conceptual move back behind modern philosophy, the very act of recovery is itself a crucial aspect of modern philosophy. It cannot, therefore, be a matter of construing Strauss simply as a premodern; such a construal, even if it were possible would not necessarily be desirable. However, Strauss does not rule out the possibility that we moderns can still approach Maimonides as Maimonides approached the Greeks: Readers are compelled, in other words,

> to make an entirely new beginning, which is in fact identical with Maimonides' own beginning. That beginning consists in not taking philosophy for granted, as all the historians of the nineteenth century have done; that beginning consists in not presupposing philosophy, i.e., the legitimacy of philosophy. Philosophy must be understood as in need of justifying itself before a higher or a pre-philosophical tribunal. That tribunal is the Torah, or [is] constituted by the Torah. In a word, the beginning of any understanding of Maimonides' work is to realize that the *Guide* is not a philosophic book; it is a Jewish book, written by a Jew for Jews. The *Guide* is based on the old Jewish premise that to be a Jew and to be a philosopher is mutually exclusive. (LSM, 434)

As Maimonides understood Socrates's tribunal in Athens as the horizon in which philosophy occurs, so (Strauss holds) should Jews understand the Torah as the horizon in which philosophy comes to sight. To say that the *Guide* is not a philosophic book—but, rather, a Jewish book written for Jews—is to say that its manner of presentation is aimed at Jews rather than philosophers. I will return to this issue during my discussion of Maimonides's understanding and appreciation of the esoteric/exoteric distinction. This much, however, can be stated up front: the need to speak differently to different audiences—that is, the need to conceal one's philosophical views (which means, in Strauss's terms, one's way of life) from nonphilosophers—is coextensive with "not presupposing the legitimacy of philosophy." As Strauss notes, "for the classics, the conflict between philosophy and the city is as little tragic as the death of Socrates" (WIPP, 127). In a certain respect, then, all that is needed to make the move behind modern philosophy is the awareness that philosophy is not (from the perspective of the city) transparently legitimate.[75]

The Stakes in the Two Cities

To say that Athens amounts to a way of life rooted in free insight and human wisdom is to, implicitly or explicitly, reject a way of life that takes its departure from the primacy of Creation and a personal deity. In this respect, Strauss holds (slightly paraphrasing Cohen) that "the God of Aristotle is not the God of Israel" (PL: 131). This might account for the "perplexing and upsetting character of Maimonides' teaching regarding Unity," which consists in "Maimonides's acceptance of the philosophic view according to which God is not only the efficient or moving and the final cause of the world, but also the form of the world" (LSM: 541).[76] One might, therefore, understand Strauss's pregnant, yet compressed, remark to Benardete (mentioned above) as indicating the fact that, in both Homer's *Iliad* 5.339 (the primary reference for the "bloodlessness [*ambroton*] of the gods") and in the *Guide* I.1, there is no similarity between humans and the divine—that is, that God is not personal.[77] This is not, to be sure, a pure denial of the existence of God. It is, however, a questioning—and, thus, an undermining—of the literal language of the Hebrew Bible. If Jerusalem is premised on obedience to divine law, this sort of inquiry would likely be construed as endangering belief in the literality (and, thus, actuality) of that law. Differently stated, Jerusalem is premised on a law that is not based in demonstration (LSM, 526). The two cities, therefore, cannot be simply reconciled through harmonization or systemization—they are, at root, opposed to one another. This does not mean, however, that they need be actually at war with one another; as stated in the chapter 1, Athens needs Jerusalem for its very self-understanding—that is, Athens needs and requires the permanence of Jerusalem. If Jerusalem does not need Athens in the same way, or to the same extent, it at least needs Athens as a subsidiary discourse for the purposes of rational explanation of the law on which it is based—that is, Jerusalem requires the permanence of Athens for purposes of Kalam (i.e., rational theology; argumentation that takes divine existence/authority as a given). Far from actual war, this situation indicates that the proximity of the two cities/capacities of the soul (either individually taken or "writ large") needs to be negotiated; for Strauss's Maimonides, this takes the form both of (1) a *zetetic* movement between rational argumentation and exegesis of the law, and (2) an esoteric discourse on the separation of Jerusalem from Athens provided, at times, by means of an exoteric discourse on their harmony.

Maimonides and the Theological-Political Problem

What allows for both the *zetetic* and esoteric modalities of communication to occur are the resemblances between Jerusalem and Athens; these resemblances are a result of analogous responses to the question concerning the best city and how one should live in it. Were such similarities merely insubstantial, there would be no catalyst for either the interaction or the resistance of the two cities. One might say that Strauss's construal of Jerusalem and Athens mirrors Heidegger's well-known quip about Schelling's relation to Hegel—that is, that it is precisely because they wanted the same thing that an agreement between them was impossible.[78] Both Jerusalem and Athens acknowledge the need for politics to be grounded in divine law—at issue are their competing conceptions of the relation of the polity to law. This is to acknowledge (as discussed in chapter 1) that the fundamental issue out of which the Jerusalem/Athens distinction grows (and to which it responds) is the theological-political problem—that is, the question of the right, best, or just life. This is not to say, with Carl Schmitt, that all politics is based in theological categories. The specific response to the theological-political problem known as "political theology" would hold true, if at all, only for Jerusalem insofar as "political theology" means "political teachings which are based on divine revelation" (WIPP, 13). In a Jewish context this view, according to Strauss, most clearly holds for a thinker such as Judah Halevi;[79] the question as to whether even Strauss's earliest readings of Maimonides (as a proponent of "enlightened Kalam") admit of "political theology" remains open.

For Strauss, both Jerusalem and Athens share the basic beliefs or tenets "on which an ideal law ought to be based" (LSM, 584). This similarity also shows itself in the reaction to dissent within the two cities (as stated in chapter 1)—that is, that both Socrates and the Biblical prophets had to wander far away from the center of their respective cities in order to search for justice (LSM, 584). But whereas Jerusalem construes the authority of divine law in a simply unphilosophical manner, Athens accepts it with qualification; divine authority is understood to be one of the "necessary beliefs, i.e., beliefs necessary for political reasons" (LSM, 584). In accepting the political necessity of divine authority for governance of the city, philosophy in the Islamic and Jewish medieval context "resembles, in this respect, its situation in classical Greece" (LSM, 112); in this way, it parts company with Jerusalem.

But (with an eye toward Cohen) *which* "Greece" does this context resemble—the Platonic or the Aristotelian? As stated above, Strauss disagrees neither with Cohen's claim that Maimonides is a Platonist, nor with his claim that the God of Aristotle is not the God of Israel. For Strauss, however, Maimonides's Platonism shows up not as morality but as political philosophy: "The Cohenian starting point, 'All honor to the God of Aristotle, but He is not the God of Israel,' leads no further if one interprets the God of Israel as the God of *morality*. Instead of morality, one must say: *Law*. The idea of law, of *nomos*, is what unifies Jews and Greeks; the idea of the concrete, binding order of life . . . this idea [is the one] under whose spell at least our philosophical thought moves" (LSM, 221). The problem with Cohen's interpretation, on Strauss's account, is that it takes the modern preoccupation with morality (as something like a normative idea) to be more foundational than the "concrete, binding order of life" expressed in (the idea) of law. Strauss's reversal of this priority is Platonic (rather than Aristotelian, and in contrast to Cohen's Platonism) insofar as it demands that the philosophical way of life account for itself in the court of nonphilosophy. Differently stated, Platonic political philosophy shows that the contemplative life does not have the luxury of construing itself as separate from the opinions of the nonphilosophical *polis*: [80] "What Plato *called for*—that philosophy stand under a higher court, under the state, under the *law*—is *fulfilled* in the age of revelation. With all their freedom in the pursuit of knowledge, the philosophers of this era are conscious at every moment of their answerability for the law and before the law: they justify their philosophizing before the bar of the law; they derive from the law their *authorization* to philosophize as a legal *duty* to philosophize. The Platonism of these philosophers is given with their *situation*, with their standing in fact under the law. Since they in fact stand under the law, they admittedly no longer need, like Plato, to *seek* the law, the state, to *inquire* into it: the binding and absolutely perfect regimen of human life is *given* to them by a prophet. Hence they are, as authorized by the law, free to philosophize in Aristotelian freedom: they can *therefore* aristotelize" (PL, 132–133). Whereas (for Strauss) Aristotle presupposes the freedom to philosophy, Plato does not; prior to its own activity, philosophy, in Strauss's construal of Plato, needs to view itself as subject to law. The original philosophical activity, Socratic questioning (as recorded by Plato)—insofar as it asks about the just regime—is therefore political rather than moral (LSM, 200). As a result of this, Socrates's "Platonic descendants" live under the law and, therefore, understand its necessity for society. Is this simply a politicized sentiment (of the kind for which Strauss has recently come under such scrutiny)? We might ask: is this not rather a subtle (if sobering) insight about the aforementioned potential dangers to the foundations of (nonphilosophical) society resulting from philosophy as a way of life (PAW, 140)?

The Question of Audience

If Maimonides is not merely unaware of the tensions between philosophy and revealed law (as Wolfson, Guttmann, and Husik maintain), if he is not simply attempting a straightforward harmonization or synthesis of the two (as Wolfson, Guttmann, Husik maintain and as Rawidowicz suggests in a more nuanced fashion), how does he attempt to navigate the tensions between the two? Strauss provides the beginnings of an answer to this question by noting both (1) Maimonides's awareness (as stated in the preface of the *Guide*) that the Bible is an esoteric text (LSM, 364), which prompts him to write in a similarly esoteric manner; and (2) that (in light of the problems of written discourse as discussed in Plato's *Phaedrus*) "what matters is always to say the One True [Thing] differently" (LSM, 201). The question of audience, for Strauss and Strauss's Maimonides is thus identical to the question of how to simulate oral discourse (which, unlike its written analogue, is flexible enough to communicate to different audiences simultaneously) in written form. Strauss's "response" to the aforementioned modern commentators is to refuse to take for granted the Enlightenment assumption that humankind is universally educable. Differently stated, if one attempts to "aristotelize" with people who are not able or willing to engage in philosophy, one runs the risk of both endangering their necessary societal beliefs as well as facing persecution as a result; hence, the necessity of Platonic political philosophy. The "noble lie," for Strauss, is aimed both at protecting the foundations of society (even if they are based on opinion rather than knowledge) as well as the freedom of those who are able to (and, by implication, desire to) engage in philosophy. What is the significant "mark" of the potential philosopher? In his review of Hyamson's translation of Book One of the *Mishneh Torah* (1939), Strauss states that "secret teaching, according to Maimonides' principles . . . means teaching the truth to those who are able to understand by themselves, while at the same time hiding it from the vulgar" (LSM, 338). In "The Literary Character of *The Guide for the Perplexed*" (1941), Strauss makes three additional references to this phrase: "[those] who are able to understand by themselves" (LSM, 375, 376, 398).[81] If we take this as our bearing, potential philosophers are those who are able to see the truth even when it is presented "between the lines." Moreover (to adopt Aristotelian terminology), they would also understand the necessity, or cause, of such a presentation.[81]

In Maimonides's context, the question of audience can, in fact, be approached from both sides of the Jerusalem/Athens distinction. Philosophers are at risk of persecution by the nonphilosophical Jewish majority (which adheres to an unproblematic construal of divine law), and Jews—philosophical or otherwise—are at risk of persecution by other religious polities. Maimonides is, therefore, concerned both about how to preserve the philosophical way of life and about how to preserve the Jewish polity. Thus, the relation of philosophy to law, for Strauss's Maimonides, takes on the appearance of a legal foundation of philosophy while maintaining the reality of a philosophical foundation of the law. To reiterate: philosophy continually needs to be justified in the court of law, even as the philosopher recognizes that—apart from its adoption of rational principles by means of belief—law is itself directed toward political exigency: "Law contains, apart from . . . rational beliefs, a number of other beliefs which, while being not properly true, but representing the truth in a disguised way, are necessary or useful in the interest of the political community" (LSM, 583).[82] Hence, for Strauss, Maimonides's *Guide* is open to both a "radical" and "moderate" interpretation depending on whether the reader excels in "consistency of . . . thought" or "fervor of . . . belief" (LSM, 584). Instead of either (1) exposing himself to the danger of heresy or (2) exposing the Jewish community to the dangers of the "spiritual hell" (PAW, 109) of unbelief (and the loss of the law's legitimacy), Maimonides "insisted on taking a middle course between impossible obedience and flagrant transgression" in the *Guide*—that is, "he had to become master of the art of revealing by not revealing and of not revealing by revealing" (LSM, 357). In attempting to present the secrets of Maimonides's Guide in the same manner that Maimonides presents the secrets of the Bible (i.e., during his middle and later periods), Strauss comes to drop any reference to Maimonides as a philosopher;[83] Maimonides, Strauss tells us, writes primarily Jewish books for a Jewish audience. However, given that he informs his readers of Maimonides's two assumptions—"that the Bible is an esoteric text, and that its esoteric teaching is closely akin to that of Aristotle" (LSM, 364)—he compels those readers to wonder which audience of Jews Maimonides has in mind for the composition of any given text. "Literary Character" closes with the following claim: "We conclude: The *Mishneh Torah* is primarily addressed to the general run of men, while the *Guide* is addressed to the small number of people who are able to understand by themselves" (LSM, 398). Insofar as Maimonides composes defenses of the law, he takes his point of departure from opinion and proceeds by means of rational exegesis of scripture (i.e., Kalam)—that is, he proceeds *zetetically*.[84] Insofar as Maimonides undertakes inquiries into the fundamental questions concerning both (1) the necessity of law and (2) the extent and limits of human knowledge and cognition—that is, concerning topics meant for those "who are able to understand by themselves"—he proceeds exoterically.

To summarize, I understand Strauss's Maimonides to be Socratic as well as Platonic. For Strauss, Maimonides does, in fact, defend Judaism. While it may be the case, for the later Strauss, that the *zetetic* movement of defending revealed law by reason and limiting reason by the possibility of revealed law is ultimately locatable on the exoteric level, it is not, for all that, dismissible; if Maimonides's writings do make use of the esoteric/exoteric distinction (at least in its premodern form), they are, by definition, concerned about the welfare of the many. Therefore, his "enlightened Kalam," while different in kind from philosophy, is not pure dissimulation. The view that the city needs both laws and legitimating authority—that is, the view that "[a] law, to be truly equal, must not be purely human" (LSM, 301)—is, after all, a philosophical view. Hence, while the harmonization of Jerusalem and Athens and the affirmation of Creation are exoteric, they are not simply unconnected to their philosophical counterparts; Strauss's Maimonides (in good Aristotelian fashion) lets his readers stop where they will. Put differently, it is possible to be compelled to wonder about the doctrine of Creation and about the harmony of philosophy and revealed law. The reader's intellectual apprehension of Maimonides's text functions like a trapdoor leading from the useful silver filigree to the true apples of gold.[85] Paradoxically, the same thinking that exhibits the access to philosophy also defends law: "If [Maimonides] had not brought the greatest sacrifice, he could not have defended the Torah against the philosophers as admirably as he did in his Jewish books" (LSM, 416). I do not understand this reference to sacrifice in the Augustinian sense of "sacrifice of intellect"—of the kind which Weber confronts in Strauss's *Natural Right and History*—but rather as a Platonic political-philosophical sacrifice both for the sake of the few and the many. Just as the city owes its real existence to the (albeit indemonstrable) belief in the exigency of law, "philosophy owes its authorization, its freedom, to the law; its freedom depends upon its bondage" (PL, 88). In following this thought to its conclusion, Strauss's Maimonides remains a citizen of Athens on the border of Jerusalem.

PART II

Jerusalem and Athens *in Deed*

CHAPTER THREE

Philosophy as a Platonic Dialogue, or Jerusalem and Athens *in Jerusalem*

In the light of my presentations both regarding (1) Strauss's critiques of modern Jewish thought and modern philosophy (chapter 1) and (2) his recovery of Maimonides as the exemplary figure illustrating the theological-political problem and the responses of Jerusalem and Athens (chapter 2), I can now begin to discuss his Hebrew University lectures of 1954 - 1955—lectures that formed the basis for the title essay of one of Strauss's most well-known books, that is, *What Is Political Philosophy?* My claim is that his Hebrew University lectures show (in a manner attuned both to the particular occasion as well as to posterity) Strauss's deep and abiding commitment to the recovery of the theological-political problem and Jerusalem and Athens over and against their occlusion by modern philosophy and modern Jewish thought. In a manner similar to the previous two chapters, I begin by setting the intellectual historical and biographical context for a consideration of Strauss's lectures. Unlike the previous chapters, however, the intellectual history and intellectual biography are somewhat more entwined and shall be treated as such. I then proceed to a discussion concerning why the lectures are best read in the manner of a Platonic dialogue (as Strauss understands it). This requires a discussion of the functions of (1) the prologue and (2) the argument, action, and argument of the action within the context of Strauss's presentation. Finally, I shall read the first paragraph of Strauss's text and show how it functions as such a prologue.

It may seem paradoxical to the reader that (1) the lectures are almost entirely silent about the question of Jerusalem and (2) the essay "What Is Political Philosophy?" is almost completely silent with respect to medieval thought. Given the amount of attention Strauss has dedicated to recovering the premodern over and against the modern (in order to recover Jerusalem and Athens), why does this seminal part of his work receive almost no attention in his lectures? Why, above all, when the lectures were delivered at the Hebrew University of Jerusalem during the 1954-1955 academic year (in three parts, each part corresponding to the sections of the written text, during December 1954 and January 1955[1]), and at the behest of Gershom Scholem?[2] Given the context, what accounts for his omission of Jerusalem in the lectures, and then medieval Jewish thought, in general, and Maimonides, in particular in the essay?[3]

As concerns the final published essay, one might be tempted to suggest that the answer to the above question lies in the secondary character of medieval thought. On the one hand, Strauss sometimes "designates philosophers such as al-Farabi or Maimonides as 'ancients,' because their quests for the single 'metaphysical' truth were undertaken within the framework of the Platonic striving for an external 'Divine' law that would guide humans towards their purpose."[4] If this were the case, the designation "medieval" would be simply derivative and historical, rather than philosophical. On the other hand, if "[g]enerally speaking, medieval philosophy has in common with modern philosophy the fact that both are influenced . . . by the teaching of the Bible," the designation "medieval" would amount to nothing other than the modern in its premodern stage.[5] While neither suggestion is simply false, they not only fail to account for Strauss's abiding interest in medieval thought (especially in its Jewish and Islamic forms), but, in the present context, they also fundamentally distort what the philosophical significance of that thought is. That the question regarding the absence of Jerusalem-the medieval/Maimonides in Strauss's text has been largely unasked is due, I surmise, to the fact that the text is primarily read simply as a conventionally construed essay (i.e., where the evident content is more important than the form). But given that Strauss's text was originally a series of public lectures at Hebrew University,[6] the question of context—as well as literary style—becomes significant. Differently stated, the occasional character of the communication matters in coming to a fuller understanding of Strauss's essay. Since (as mentioned in the Introduction), the essay amounts to a development out of the lectures that retains the same direction, I take care to distinguish which set of audiences (i.e., Hebrew University or posterity) had access to which statements.

Strauss and Israel

As mentioned above, Strauss's lectures were given during his stay at the Hebrew University of Jerusalem during the 1954 to 1955 academic year. What is the significance of Strauss's delivering a lecture in Jerusalem on political philosophy, which first "came to light in Athens" (WIPP, 10)? Laurence Lampert claims that Strauss was taking on the role of the Athenian Stranger from Plato's *Laws* who "travelled all the way to Crete to bring the original source of Greek law, and to its most powerful representative, Sparta, the blessings of Athens" (effectively reversing the situation in which Paul found himself when he delivered the Gospel of Christ to Corinth).[7] If this is correct, one would still have to ask why Strauss traveled so far to deliver this news: "[D]oes not philanthropy begin at home? Did [the Stranger] not have more pressing duties to perform at home?" (WIPP, 32) Given the apparent strangeness of this situation, one might emphatically ask the following question: why would Leo Strauss—after leaving Germany on the eve of the Nazi takeover—and after experiencing economic hardship in England[8]—depart for a year from the University of Chicago to go to the newly independent, and politically volatile, State of Israel? The Strauss-Scholem correspondence provides some background: in 1950, Scholem wanted Strauss to relocate to Jerusalem in the hopes of having him succeed Martin Buber at Hebrew University. Strauss declined for reasons having to do with exhaustion and "self-fragmentation" as a result of the traumatic exile from Germany.[9] This refusal, however, in no way addresses the question concerning the philosophical and perhaps political insight into the deed of the lectures themselves.

A beginning can be made if one recalls Strauss's well-known statement about his meeting with Jabotinsky (referred to in chapter 1) in which the latter inquired about whether the young Zionist Strauss had been engaging in rifle-practice (and Strauss's subsequent negative answer). Strauss's "no" is, as mentioned earlier, misunderstood if it is taken to be merely a retreat from the necessity of bearing arms. Its significance lies in the fact that Jabotinsky was advocating a practical and worldly solution to the so-called Jewish problem. Differently stated, the impulse of Zionism derives from the fact that the Jewish Enlightenment (Haskalah) in Europe did not work—Jews were still persecuted. Already in exile from Biblical Israel, the dispersal to Europe did nothing to secure Jews a "home." Zionism was an attempt to solve the Jewish problem by means of the creation of a modern, secular, nation-state. As discussed in chapter 1, Strauss views the State of Israel as a modern political answer to the Jewish problem but not a Jewish answer to the Jewish problem. It is, therefore, simply a continuation of the *diaspora/galut.* Qua modern state, therefore, Israel is no more a part of "Jerusalem" than Haskalah Jewish communities are. And this signals a third kind of exile for Jews—this time from Judaism itself. For Strauss, modernity—with its emphasis on historical and practical worldly "solutions"—has occluded the possibility of viewing Jerusalem (and therefore of viewing Athens) as it really is. Insofar as the state of Israel is a modern invention, it distorts the fundamental nontemporal Jerusalem/Athens distinction. The state of Israel, therefore, is indicative of a larger problem—that is, the distorting lens of modernity and modern political solutions: "To realize that the Jewish problem is insoluble means *never to forget* the truth proclaimed by Zionism regarding the limits of liberalism" (JPCM, 143; my emphasis). One does well to keep in mind (and, to that end, I will keep repeating it) the final clause of the opening paragraph of "What is Political Philosophy?": "I shall not for a moment forget what Jerusalem stands for" (WIPP, 10). If liberalism assumes that all problems have worldly solutions, Zionism testifies to its limits; and if Zionism, with its modern limitations, is understood by Jews to be an essential expression of Judaism, then Jews exist in exile from Judaism insofar as they have lost Jerusalem. For Strauss, the project of recollecting the limits of "modern solutions" (the title of the third lecture/part of "What is Political Philosophy?") is coeval with the project of recollecting "what Jerusalem stands for."

If this were Strauss's only word on the subject of Israel, it might mark a moment of despair rather than ambivalence; and despair would presumably have led neither to Strauss's year-long visit to

Israel nor to his delivering the series of lectures that would become, in 1959, the title of one of his most significant collections of essays. In fact, Strauss's views on Israel and Zionism are not so one-sided.[10] In 1957, reflecting back on his year-long visit at Hebrew University (in the context of an impassioned letter of January 5, to Willmoore Kendall of the *National Review* concerning its opposition to Israel), Strauss writes, "I taught at the Hebrew University in Jerusalem for the whole academic year of 1954–1955, and what I am going to say is based exclusively on what I have *seen with my own eyes*" (JPCM, 413; my emphasis). Given the extreme importance of sight, as a philosophical sense, for Strauss, the reference to it in the letter to Kendall cannot simply be discounted. This letter is an important document that recounts Strauss's encounter, *in Israel*, with the very material conditions that initially confront *all* polities: poverty, external and internal instability, and unstable founding conditions (JPCM, 413–414). It is instructive for two reasons.

First, it is a thoughtful defense of Israel, *while at the same time* indicating ambivalences: "political Zionism was the attempt to restore the inner freedom, that simple dignity, of which only people who remember their heritage and are loyal to their fate are capable. Political Zionism is problematic for obvious reasons. But *I can never forget* what it achieved as a moral force in an era of complete dissolution" (JPCM, 414; my emphasis). Again, this sentence must be read in the light of the prologue to Strauss's essay: "But while being compelled, or compelling myself, to wander far away from our sacred heritage, or to be silent about it, *I shall not for a moment forget* what Jerusalem stands for" (WIPP, 10: my emphasis). The imperative "not to forget," for Strauss, exerts a gravitational pull that cannot be ignored; recovery and/or reorigination of Jerusalem and Athens means, first and foremost, *recollection.*

Second, the letter discloses a political action undertaken by a political philosopher on behalf of Israel during a fragile period in Israel's development as a state. What, specifically, did Strauss see "with his own eyes"?[11] In the parlance of Strauss's reading of Genesis 1: 1, "We are not told; hence we do not know" (JPCM, 382). Nonetheless, Strauss makes some general claims in his letter that allows for reasonable speculation on the reader's part. He informs Kendall that "Israel is a country which is surrounded by mortal enemies of overwhelming numerical superiority, and in which a single book absolutely predominates in the instruction given in elementary schools: the Hebrew Bible . . . The country is poor, lacks oil and many other things which fetch much money . . . the university and government buildings are within easy range of Jordanian guns; the possibility of disastrous defeat or failure is always close" (JPCM, 413). While the immediate context of the letter is clearly a spirited defense in the face of evident opposition, Strauss's comments deserve further consideration; they do not merely refer to the "harsh necessity" characteristic of a new state, but to its *precariousness* as well: (1) Strauss's concern over Israel's "government and university buildings" being in easy range of Jordanian guns might easily have referred to the escalation of border conflicts between the two nations (leading to a rise in Israeli civilian deaths) in the autumn of 1953.[12] (2) Israel's being "surrounded by mortal enemies" might well have referred to the groups of *feyadeen* (armed Palestinians) crossing the Egyptian border into Israel in the winter of 1954–1955.[13] And Egyptian president Nasser's statements in August of 1955 (following a February Israeli raid on Gaza) that "no future Israeli army attack could go unanswered"[14] could have further substantiated Strauss's observations. (3) "Israel lacks important resources"—readers will of course recall the 1956 crisis when Nasser attempted to block off the Suez Canal from Israeli usage in an effort to exert commercial and monetary pressure on the new state. While the actual crisis occurred after the completion of Strauss's visit, it would certainly not be unreasonable to assume an awareness, on his part, of the likelihood of such an action occurring.

Perhaps the most interesting observation, however, is Strauss's reference to (4) the elementary educational system centering on the Hebrew Bible. The attempt to revive the Hebrew language and have it become "the base language of a new, Hebrew society"[15] had been going on since the late nineteenth century (the first manifestation of this revival being a Hebrew article written in Odessa by Joseph Klausner in 1893).[16] In 1954, a professional committee was instituted in Israel with the aim of launching a national educational program geared toward teaching the Hebrew Bible in primary schools. This program contained the following objectives: "to inculcate in the children love and respect for the book and the desire to read it always and an inner need to seek inspiration in it . . . [and that] starting in First Grade (the age of six) it is necessary to cultivate an emotional attachment towards the Book of Books of the People of Israel."[17] Even if Strauss were unaware of the specifics of this educational initiative, he might very well have been aware of the establishment, in 1955, of the Academy of the Hebrew Language as a culminating moment in this "effort to create a modern spoken Hebrew that, while making the fullest use of biblical forms, would also incorporate new words, chosen to replace foreign words that had not been in use at the time of the Bible."[18] The Hebrew Bible was, thus, the standard as well as the mode of transmission for the national language of Israel:[19] "Torah, Prophets, and Writings together became a primary source attesting to the ages-old continuity of a nation with historical and cultural roots. It provided evidence of the nation's constant possession of Eretz Israel, the land of its forefathers, and of Jewish attachment to it."[20]

Insofar as the willingness of this movement to "mix new words in with biblical forms" indicates a lack of concern over the blurring of the distinction between the sacred and the secular, it at least exemplifies the concerns discussed by Strauss in other contexts: if modernity is characterized by the forgetting of the theological-political problem and Jerusalem and Athens, the specific instance of using the Hebrew Bible as the basis for a largely secular national (i.e., political) culture would be, in the highest degree, modern. Further, such a project would unwittingly run the risk of giving rise to fanatically theocratic impulses. It is here that the connection between Strauss and Scholem becomes relevant; this was *exactly* the concern Scholem harbored and then expressed to Franz Rosenzweig in a 1926 letter: "if we pass on to our children the language that we have received, if we, the generation of the transition, revive the language of the old books that it may be revealed to them anew—will not the religious power latent therein one day break out against its speakers? And what will be the image of the generation toward whom its expressions are directed? We live with this language as on the edge of an abyss, yet nearly all of us walk there with confidence, like blind men. Does no one fear that, once our eyes are opened, we or those who follow us will roll down into it? Nor can we know whether the sacrifice of those lost in the abyss will suffice to cover it up again . . . One day the language will turn against its own speakers—and there are moments when it does so even now; moments which it is difficult to forget, leaving wounds in which all the presumptuousness of our goal is revealed. Will we then have a youth who will be able to hold fast against the rebellion of a holy tongue?"[21] While it is clear that Strauss did not share Scholem's mystical conception of language, both thinkers recognize the political problem *addressed by* such a conception. Simply put, this shared concern is: how can a people avoid the dangers of fanaticism in a polity with a religious foundation that remains unacknowledged? In this *particular* respect, Strauss and Scholem both recognize the dangers inherent in Jerusalem.

The problem of theocracy, as one modality of political fanaticism, is by no means particular to Israel—it is, in Strauss's terms, a problem coeval with political life. However, Israel, as a modern nation-state, faces a second difficulty: the *forgetting* of the *fundamentality* of the theological-political problem. This second difficulty is coeval with *modern* political life and, as such, affects Israel directly, if not exclusively. However, what does affect Israel exclusively is the degree to which the search for a modern political solution (Zionism) obscures the irresolvability of the Jewish problem. One might suggest that this is the Jewish equivalent, in Strauss's terms, to descending into the cave beneath the Cave. Strauss deals with this issue in his discussion of sectarianism in his debate with Kojève: sectarianism emerges when the desire for a solution to problems overcomes "the awareness of the problematic character of that solution" (WIPP, 116). Differently stated, if the Hebrew Bible is taken to direct people toward a way of life that provides a specific and determinate solution to problems, the possibility of sectarianism is intrinsic to it. Moreover, if the Hebrew Bible is taken as the basis of a people's national and civic education, then that sectarianism continually runs the risk of becoming a theocracy. Finally, if, on top of these two conditions, an awareness of the theological-political problem is lacking, guarding against theocracy becomes that much more difficult.

Posing, to an originally Jewish audience, a thoughtful challenge to the modern forgetting of the theological-political problem through a recovery and reorigination of Jerusalem and Athens[22]—this, nothing less, is Strauss's philosophical project as it comes to light in his Hebrew University lectures. His willingness to travel to Jerusalem, and then—after seeing the "political things" (WIPP, 12) with his own eyes—to deliver this message indicates at least that the significance of this forgetting is not limited to any particular place or time. And to the extent that the lectures deal with a fundamental philosophical problem, I agree with the observation that Strauss's lectures have "one foot in the 1950s and one foot in eternity."[23] In this respect, visiting Israel would afford a unique opportunity to "see with one's own eyes" a concrete instance of both the theological-political problem and the Jerusalem/Athens distinction. If Strauss adopts the role of the Athenian Stranger at the Hebrew University of Jerusalem, one answer to his question over whether philanthropy begins at home is that the problem is endemic to all modern regimes; while this problem attains a particular intensity in Israel, it cannot be exclusive to Israel.[24] Hence, wherever "home" may be (and, *qua modern life*, the answer might actually be: *nowhere*), it is not simply limited to one's "fatherland" (be it Germany, the United States, or Israel). Strauss's lecture is, thus, not only a unique statement of his views; it is also a unique *formulation* of views he expressed throughout his philosophical career. This formulation is what makes his specific recollective recovery of the theological-political problem and Jerusalem and Athens, in "What Is Political Philosophy?" a reorigination.

One other point bears mentioning: In a 1953 letter to Peter H. Odegard, Strauss mentions that he has "a kind of moral obligation to the Hebrew University in Jerusalem (Israel) to teach there during the academic year 1954–55."[25] The remainder of the letter deals with administrative issues and thus is not relevant here. Readers might wonder what the status of this "moral obligation" is for Strauss. If Strauss is a citizen of Athens, he presumably views the contemplative life as higher than the moral life. Is this remark, then, simply a denigration of his perceived obligation to Hebrew University? I do not believe so. Strauss's concerns are not so much over morality *per se* as they are with the modern construal of morality as located on a cultural plane. For Plato and Aristotle, morality—or better, ethics—is located in the sphere of politics—hence, it is concerned with the question of justice. If my interpretation is correct, Strauss's concern over his "moral obligation" toward Hebrew University is not condescending (even if such a "moral obligation" does not ultimately rise to the level of a "contemplative" one). Rather, in his going to Israel, "seeing with [his] own eyes" what life is like and attempting to recover Jerusalem and Athens, Strauss enacts *in Jerusalem* the classical political philosophical stance par excellence.

With this intellectual historical and biographical context for Strauss's lectures at the Hebrew University in mind, let me now turn to the character of his lectures: What makes these lectures a reorigination of Jerusalem and Athens?

The Literary Character of "What Is Political Philosophy?"

If, for a moment, one considers a visual image of the internal character of "What is Political Philosophy?"—that is, the trajectory of its arguments—it becomes clear that it is a grid formed by two axes: one vertical and one horizontal.[26] The vertical axis charts the fundamental, philosophical distinction of Jerusalem and Athens. The horizontal axis charts the historical, worldly opposition of the Ancients and the Moderns. In order to even begin to recover, let alone reoriginate, Jerusalem and Athens, one would first have to become aware of the distorting tendencies in modern appropriations of classical political philosophy (of the kind indicated in chapter 2 during my discussion of the modern interpretations of Maimonides). This awareness comes about through an encounter with the Ancients/Moderns distinction. In this respect, the "slashes" (/) in the Jerusalem/Athens distinction and the Ancients/Moderns distinction are not equivalent. To say that the Ancients/Moderns distinction is worldly and historical is to say that, for Strauss, it is not an essential (i.e., philosophical) distinction. Differently stated, the Ancients/Moderns distinction is practically difficult—but not, in principle, impossible—to overcome. The Jerusalem/Athens distinction is a fundamental problem admitting of no worldly solution. In order to become receptive to the "primary" education provided by classical political philosophy, that is, we are first "in need of a second education in order to accustom our eyes to the noble reserve and the quiet grandeur of the classics" (WIPP, 104). Or, in more familiar imagery, we are in need of historical awareness insofar as it "makes possible the ascent from the second, 'unnatural' cave, into which we have fallen less because of the tradition itself than because of the tradition of polemics against the tradition, into that first 'natural' cave which Plato's image depicts" (PL, 136).[27] Once one has started the process of this second education and begun the ascent out of the second cave, the ability to see

Jerusalem and Athens becomes possible. In this respect, historical inquiry, for Strauss, is today an absolutely necessary precondition for the possibility of *philosophy*.[28] Strauss's concern is not over history as such, but rather over the grounding of philosophy in history.

From the standpoint of modern thought, therefore, Strauss's challenge (in his essay) is double: the Ancient/Modern distinction must first be addressed in order to approach the Jerusalem/Athens distinction. That historical challenge, however, is coupled with the challenge that constitutes the Jerusalem/Athens distinction: Insofar as "[p]hilosophy as such is nothing but genuine awareness of the problems, i.e., of the fundamental and comprehensive problems" (116), it necessarily comes into conflict with nonphilosophical individuals/members of a polity that solely seek solutions (modern States being the most characteristic of this tendency).[29] Such solutions have traditionally (in both their Greek and monotheistic iterations[30]) emerged from political-legal[31] institutions that are taken to embody divine authority. In other words, the primary way in which Jerusalem and Athens comes to light is as the opposition between philosophy and straightforward obedience to divine law (PAW, 20; LSM, 276–281). The problem, according to Strauss, is that philosophically addressing nonphilosophers leads to potential persecution of the philosopher and the interruption (however momentary) of the status quo (thereby endangering the order inherent in nonphilosophical society). One can, therefore, discern a twofold double challenge in Strauss's lectures and essay: (1) how to move his potential-philosophical listeners in Jerusalem (both at the time and *sub specie posteritatis*) from an appreciation of the Ancients/Moderns distinction to an appreciation of Jerusalem and Athens; and (2) how to appropriately and simultaneously address both potential "citizens of Athens" (i.e., philosophers) in Jerusalem and "citizens of Jerusalem" (i.e., nonphilosophers) in Jerusalem. Given that Strauss's lectures are the basis for, but not identical to, his final published essay, he has essentially four different audiences—the non- and potential philosophers at Hebrew University, and the non- and potential philosophers reading his text.

Strauss characteristically addresses just this problem of communication (in the context of his critique of Buber's "I-Thou" relation) in "What Is Political Philosophy?":

> [P]hilosophic . . . *analysis* is not speaking to a friend, i.e., to this individual here and now, but speaking to anyone concerned with such *analysis*. Such an *analysis* cannot be meant to be a substitute for living together as friends; it can at best only point to such living together or arouse a desire for it. . . . [In forgetting this distinction] I am trying to preserve in *objective* speech that which cannot be preserved in *objective* speech; I am trying to *objectify* something that is incapable of being *objectified*. I am trying to preserve in "speaking about" what can be actual only in "speaking to" . . . While attempting to lay a foundation for genuine human communication, I preserve an incapacity for genuine communication. (WIPP, 29; my emphasis)

If one takes modern philosophy to be the attempt to express analyses of universal and objective truths that simultaneously apply adequately to all concrete phenomena, then Strauss's comment amounts to a critique of all modern modes of philosophical communication as incomplete, and so inadequate. Put differently, philosophical communication cannot occur directly without loss to the phenomenon being discussed; one cannot adequately "speak about" Jerusalem and Athens, one can at best point to them in the hopes of awakening a desire in potential philosophers to engage them.[32] If Strauss's lectures are an attempt to "point to" an object rather than simply speak about it, they follow in the tradition of Plato's *Republic*, Maimonides' *Guide*, and Spinoza's *Ethics*—that is, texts which lead the reader to the properly noetic/intellective moment but, strictly speaking, never contain such a moment. Or, as Strauss puts it, "there exists no Platonic utterance about the meaning of Platonic dialogues" (RCPR, 151). We should also note that, in speaking about communication in this context, Strauss is also speaking to a particular community of students and professors (which professors are, in a certain respect, authority figures). One cannot help but notice the resemblance to Socrates speaking to a mixed audience of students with authorities present.

What, then, is the character of a text/speech that seeks intentionally to "talk to some readers and be silent to others" (CM, 53)? I believe that we are justified in viewing Strauss's account of the Platonic dialogue as the model he adopted in "What Is Political

Philosophy?" For Strauss, "the undogmatic character of the Platonic dialogues" is characterized as follows: "For presenting his teaching Plato uses not merely the 'content' of his works (the speeches of his various characters) but also their 'form' (the dialogic form in general, the particular form of each dialogue and of each section of it, the action, the characters, names, places, times, situations and the like); an adequate understanding of the dialogues understands the 'content' in light of the 'form.'"[33] Strauss makes use of additional terminological distinctions to express his claim about the relation of content to form—for example, "how/what" and "form/substance" (CM, 52) as well as "speech/deed." While these distinctions are not strictly identical to the form/content distinction, they do refer to the same point. His overall claim is that the speeches contained in the dialogues can only adequately be understood against the indirect, background horizon of the unfolding action in and of the dialogue (NIPPP, 352).

Moreover, this indirect, background horizon itself silently indicates aspects of the dialogue's teaching that are not visible to the dialogue's content. Seth Benardete puts the point as follows: "the key to each [dialogue is] something absent from the dialogue, which [is] necessary for understanding the issue at hand."[34] Strauss refers to this strategy of intentional omission as "abstraction" (RPCR, 150–151, 164; CM, 62). This is, to be sure, exotericism. However, on Benardete's extension of Strauss, the political usage of exotericism (based on the view that "it is in the nature of the city as now constituted" that things are hidden) leads to the (Heraclitean) metaphysical esoteric insight: it is in the nature of things that they are hidden.[35] That some people will pay insufficient attention to the horizon of the dialogue—thereby missing the unstated, "absent" aspect of the dialogue—indicates that the dialogic character intends to communicate to different audiences simultaneously (RCPR, 151). Potential philosophers will sense that something unstated is at play in the dialogue when their attention is drawn to the indirect horizon. Finally, philosophers presumably appreciate the *inter-action* between the argument in the dialogue and the "literary" (CM, 52) or "mimetic"[36] horizon that indicates the unstated "argument of the action." This phrase—"the argument of the action" is Benardete's and not Strauss's own. Nonetheless, as Benardete holds, it was Strauss's "discovery . . . that once argument and action are properly put together an entirely new argument emerges that could never have been expected from the argument on the written page."[37] This "new argument," however, is not simply unrelated to the "argument on the written page." In a different context, Benardete explains it thus: "One might say, in general, that the action of a Platonic dialogue both explains the inadequacies of the argument and deepens the argument. Strauss was the first, as far as we know, to give a coherent account of this double function. He showed that, how, and why the linking up of *logos* and *psyche*, which is dialectics, was of the essence of the Socratic revolution" (as exemplified in, among other places, the Platonic dialogue).[38]

This complex and subtle *inter-action* between the argument (content) and mimesis (form)—allowing for the absent teaching to silently come to light—constitutes the *deed* of the dialogue's words (CPM, 18; RCPR, 152). In "What Is Political Philosophy?" Strauss refers to this complex and subtle inter-action as revealing "the mysterious character of the whole" (WIPP, 39).[39] In order to understand the dialogic character of Strauss's lectures, therefore, one must view the inapparent *inter-action* of the apparent content and form as it comes to indicate a (mysterious) whole. Again, one does well, in this context, to return to the final sentence of the opening of Strauss's lectures (this time giving emphasis to different parts than before): "while being compelled, or compelling myself, *to wander far away from our sacred heritage, or to be silent about it,* I shall not for a moment forget what Jerusalem stands for" (WIPP, 10; my emphasis). This sentence indicates the inseparability of speech and deed. This maintanence is, I believe, only deepened when one considers the differences between the lectures and the final published essay.

While "What Is Political Philosophy?" is not (in the strictest sense) a dialogue, I claim that it makes use of the aforementioned dialogic strategies in order to approach the twofold double challenge of communicating to both potential philosophers and nonphilosophers with the hope of recovering the theological-political problem and reoriginating the Jerusalem/Athens distinction in those of his listeners (and readers) who are open to it. I can now turn my reflections specifically to reading the prologue of Strauss's Hebrew University lectures in order to begin to show how Strauss's aim in his *speech* is accomplished through the *deed* of his lectures.

Strauss's Prologue

"What Is Political Philosophy?" has three sections—corresponding to the three lectures promised to be delivered at the Hebrew University—the last two of which overlap: (1) "The Problem of Political Philosophy," (2) "The Classical Solution," and (3) "The Modern Solutions." Sections/lectures 1 and 2 discuss political philosophy, its origination in Athens, and its distinction from Jerusalem. Sections/lectures 2 and 3 provide Strauss's philosophical history of the development of political philosophy in the West (and, by implication, the concomitant forgetting of Jerusalem and Athens). Although the first paragraph of Strauss's lectures occurs under the first section/lecture heading, I believe it stands apart for the following reason: if the section/lecture did not provide the context for the whole, the account of history (especially in section/lecture 3) would be scarcely different from another, seemingly more conventional, lecture Strauss gave titled "The Three Waves of Modernity."[40] Because it contains this crucial prologue, a narrative frame, a "setting," occurs which indicates that the parts are to be understood within the context of a whole (CM, 59–60; RCPR, 150–152)[41]—in this case, Jerusalem (both the actual city and the city as the "soul writ large"). This narrative frame holds *both* for the actual lectures as well as for the final version of the essay. The prologue, therefore, points to the whole without "attempting to speak about" it.[42]

Since the prologue both provides the overall setting for Strauss's lectures and introduces the themes to be contained therein, I believe it should be quoted in full. I number the six sentences of the prologue for ease of reference. In the case of differences between the lectures and the essay, I place the lecture formulations in italic brackets.

> [1] It is a great honor, and at the same time a challenge to accept a task of particular difficulty, to be asked to speak about political philosophy in Jerusalem. [2] In this city, and in this land, the theme of political philosophy—"the city of righteousness, the faithful city" *[justice and the just city]*—has been taken more seriously than anywhere else on earth. [3] Nowhere else has the longing for justice and the just city filled the purest hearts and the loftiest souls with such zeal

> as on this sacred soil. [4] I know all too well that I am utterly unable *[incompetent]* to convey to you what in the best possible case, in the case of any man, would be no more than a faint reproduction or a weak imitation of our prophets' vision. [5] I shall even be compelled to lead you into a region where the dimmest recollection of that vision is on the point of vanishing altogether—where the Kingdom of God is derisively called an imagined principality—to say here nothing of the region which was never illumined by it. [6] But while being compelled, or compelling myself, to wander far away from our sacred heritage, or to be silent about it, I shall not for a moment forget what Jerusalem stands for : *[I shall not for a moment cease to think of it]*. (WIPP, 9–10)

1. It is a great honor, and at the same time a challenge to accept a task of particular difficulty, to be asked to speak about political philosophy in Jerusalem. One might hold that the first sentence, in Platonic fashion, stands in the same relation to the rest of the prologue as the prologue stands to the rest of "What Is Political Philosophy?" First, readers should recall Strauss's earlier intended (but disregarded) application for professorship at Hebrew University (which intent saw the composition and eventual publication of *Philosophy and Law*). His actual visiting of Hebrew University was (in a certain sense) a revisiting of Hebrew University—this quite apart from his continuous revisiting of the theological-political problem and Jerusalem and Athens. If it was, in fact, an honor and challenge to speak there, this consideration is not irrelevant. Moreover, while I have not been able to locate actual lists of attendees, a number of faculty members at Hebrew University would have quite likely attended his lectures. Among those whom one presumes to have attended are Martin Buber, Shlomo Pines, Yehoshua Bar-Hillel, Gershom Scholem, and both Nechama and Yeshayahu Leibowitz.[43] We might similarly wonder whether Nathan Rotenstreich (who joined the faculty in 1949), the Biblical scholar Yehezkel Kaufmann (who also joined in 1949), and the Talmudic scholar Ephraim Urbach (who joined in 1953) were in attendance. Even if Strauss did consider all of the above-mentioned figures to be potential philosophers or philosophers, one might wonder just who the nonphilosophers actually in attendance might have been. One possible candidate might have been the political scientist, admirer of Jabotinsky, and Dean of the Faculty in 1954, Benjamin Aksin. While these specifics can amount to no more than informed guesses, the open and public character of these lectures[44] allows us to reasonably assume the presence of both nonphilosophers and (at least) potential philosophers in the audience. Conceptually speaking, the first sentence explains the difficulty that Strauss faces and shows that it is precisely the difficulty that Lampert indicates;[45] Strauss acts the role of the Athenian "Stranger"—that is, he delivers a message to a foreign and potentially opposed audience. Strauss could not be clearer about the specific message and occasion: he is bringing Athens to Jerusalem. One might still wonder, however, about the destination to which Strauss is delivering Athens—is it *really* Jerusalem? If he is, in fact, speaking to the newly formed nation-state of Israel, is he not actually bringing Athens to modernity? If my reading is correct, this would have to be the case—that is, Strauss cannot *simply* proceed to the Jerusalem/Athens distinction because the conditions for its reception are still obscured by one of the "modern solutions." One would have to say, then, that Strauss both is and is not delivering Athens to Jerusalem—and this double aspect corresponds to the two distinctions that serve as the axes for these lectures: Ancients/Moderns and Jerusalem/Athens. Perhaps it would be more accurate to state that, in delivering Athens to Jerusalem, Strauss is first delivering Jerusalem and Athens to modern Jewry and modern philosophy.

2. In this city, and in this land, the theme of political philosophy—"the city of righteousness, the faithful city" [justice and the just city]—*has been taken more seriously than anywhere else on earth.* With the second sentence, the reader is confronted with what appears to be a paradox: how can Jerusalem take—or have taken—political philosophy more seriously than anywhere on earth if political philosophy is the province of Athens? But Strauss does not say that political philosophy *itself* has been taken seriously in Jerusalem; rather, the *theme* of political philosophy has been taken seriously. If the theme of political philosophy concerns the question of justice—that is, the search for the "just city"—then Strauss's statement makes immediate sense. This is true, first and foremost, because the Hebrew Bible (focused, for Strauss, as it is on deeds) is continually concerned with justice. And this is simply to restate Strauss's claim that Greek philosophy and the Hebrew Bible are concerned with a great deal of overlapping themes. One sees this also by recalling Strauss's statement (discussed in chapter 1) that "the Middle Ages witnessed the first, and certainly the first adequate discussion between these two most important forces of the Western world: the religion of the Bible and the science or philosophy of the Greeks" (LSM, 102).[46] The import of this passage for Strauss's lectures is both philosophical and historical-political: philosophically construed, the Middle Ages witnessed the first sustained exposure (after Philo and Hellenic Judaism about which, for Strauss, knowledge is still wanting [LSM, 102]) of the Hebrew Bible to Platonic and Aristotelian philosophy. That this took the form of a justification of philosophy before the tribunal of law indicates that it was not fully (or even partially) a friendly encounter.

The historical and political import of this statement (i.e., for the nonphilosopher) must be thought within the modern context of political Zionism. Despite Strauss's discussion of *teshuvah* (return) for traditional Judaism (in his lectures "Progress or Return?" [JPCM, 227–270]), in opposition to the modern attempt to found a nation-state in Israel, this was in fact how the original political Zionists understood their project; it was also how they portrayed the history of Judaism until the nineteenth century—that is, as the desire to *return* to Israel. For nonphilosophers (to the extent that they are interested in, or knowledgeable about, medieval thought) the Middle Ages was the time in which Greek philosophy was placed in the context of Jewish law—that is, Greek philosophy facilitated observance to the Torah, which, among other things, calls for the return to Israel. Strauss's sentence, therefore, communicates different thoughts to different audiences.

While Strauss's Jerusalem audience heard "justice and the just city", it is reasonable to suppose that they would have understood the connection between "justice" and "righteousness" in the analogous Hebrew terms *tzedek* (justice) and *tzedakah* (righteousness). For the final version of his essay, Strauss sharpens the point (presumably for readers who might not have had the analogous education or background as his Hebrew University audience) in his hyphenated reference. How does the hyphenated Biblical reference (which Strauss does not name) interact with the rest of sentence 2? The concept of the righteous and faithful city occurs in Isaiah 1:21 and 1:26, respectively, and refers, in both cases, to Jerusalem. Isaiah

1:21 states that Jerusalem "has become a harlot / The faithful city / That was [once] filled with *justice*, / Where righteousness dwelt."[47] Isaiah 1:26 speaks of restoration: "I will restore your magistrates as of old, / And your counselors as of yore. / After that you shall be called 'City of Righteousness, Faithful City." Strauss comments on these passages, in "Progress or Return?": "A perfect beginning—the faithful city is followed by defection, decline, sin; and this is followed by a perfect end. But the perfect end is the restoration of the perfect beginning: the faithful city at the beginning and at the end" (JPCM, 227)[48] The nonphilosopher might think in this the pattern of initial paradise, transgression, and the World-to-Come in otherworldly terms. But Strauss's reference in the prologue includes the phrase "righteous"—a political designation. Further, the scriptural reference as a whole seems to be related to "political philosophy" (Athens). The nonphilosopher might realize that, insofar as Judaism is based in divine law, the substance of the best political order is always close by; what else do the 613 commandments and prohibitions (contained in the Torah) refer to if not an attempt to set up a divinely ordered, and just, polity? The nonphilosopher might understand an unbroken continuity between prophetic attestation, exile from a homeland, and subsequent return to traverse all the phases of the history of the Jewish people. If righteousness and faith deal with political philosophy, then the historically existing Jerusalem and Israel would be a manifestation of the concern with political philosophy to the highest degree. Hence, Jerusalem and Athens do not *appear* so very far apart, after all.

The potential philosopher, in contrast, might notice that the apparent symbiosis of the second sentence conflicts with the "difficulty" mentioned in the first sentence. The potential philosopher might raise the question as to what a Torah-based polity would look like. Given that it is precisely such a polity that forced philosophy to justify itself in the Middle Ages, the potential philosopher might wonder whether or not political *philosophy* can ever exist within the context of the Torah in a mutually receptive and nontoxic manner. Seeing the similarity with Socrates' relation to the city of Athens, the potential philosopher might realize that optimism over the possibility of philosophy ever being at ease in the city is, at best, unjustified. This might be all the more difficult for nonphilosophers to see, insofar as *concern over the theme* of political philosophy (which

Jerusalem shares)—*appears* to be the same as the *activity* of political philosophy.

3. *Nowhere else has the longing for justice and the just city filled the purest hearts and the loftiest souls with such zeal as on this sacred soil.* The third sentence of Strauss's prologue can be understood as an announcement of Jerusalem as one response to the theological-political problem: the question of the just city fills the citizens of the "sacred soil" of Jerusalem with zealous longing. Here again, bringing Athens to Jerusalem by no means amounts to an *unrecognizable* activity; the two are alternative responses and recognize each other as alternatives—this is what causes the tension. The nonphilosopher might hear in this the association of goodness and justice with purity and loftiness. Hearing it thus, it would not strike one as strange that the concatenation of purity with loftiness and goodness with justice (whether it be understood in terms of the lineage of Abraham, Isaac, and Jacob, or the questions motivating the *Euthyphro*, *Philebus*, and *Republic*) finds its profoundest expression in the Holy Land. Both the nonphilosopher and the potential philosopher might wonder about the connection between zeal and justice; the nonphilosopher might wonder whether such a connection could lead to dangerous fanaticism; the potential philosopher might wonder if a religiously oriented politics (or any political order that denies nature, limits, or both) can *ever* avoid it. This question characterizes the nonphilosophical character of Athens every bit as much as Jerusalem. Was not Euthyphro zealously pursuing justice? This, again, indicates that, philosophically understood, Jerusalem/Athens refers in the first instance to aspects of the human soul (irrespective of geographical location).

4. *I know all too well that I am utterly unable* [incompetent] *to convey to you what in the best possible case, in the case of any man, would be no more than a faint reproduction or a weak imitation of our prophets' vision.* Sentence four can also be understood as an announcement. Strauss, in his own account, will (at the very least) not be able to shine a faithful light on righteous longing. His Jerusalem audience was given the more forceful statement of his own incompetence. About what is Strauss unable or incompetent to convey to his audiences? Strauss lacks zeal. He thus lacks the ability to make ultimate sense of the affect that most characterizes Jerusalem. Nonphilosophers might hear this as an expression of the religious (perhaps

moral) virtue of humility/modesty. The potential philosopher may wonder whether political philosophy is being set up as an alternative to such righteous longing and zealotry. In fact, if this reading of Strauss is correct, he will be unable to shine a light on righteous longing precisely because he lacks zeal; he thus lacks the affect most characteristic of Jerusalem. This in no way means that he is not a Jew. It does corroborate his own statement (discussed in chapter 1) that he is not a *believing* Jew.

5. I shall even be compelled to lead you into a region where the dimmest recollection of that vision is on the point of vanishing altogether—where the Kingdom of God is derisively called an imagined principality—to say here nothing of the region which was never illumined by it. What is interesting (and, paradoxically, straightforward) about the fifth sentence is that it refers both to the historical category of modernity as well as to the philosophical category of Athens (depending on the audience addressed). Strauss will lead the audience into a region where the prophetic vision threatens to disappear completely—without even a dim recollection. Certainly modern political philosophy—as concomitant with the declining influence of the Church and the rise of the secular nation-state in Europe—takes religion far less seriously than its premodern analogue does. The potential philosopher may again wonder whether a fundamental distinction between philosophy and revelation is in the process of being substantiated. Might the ultimate consequences of political philosophy be that God's kingdom becomes construed as an "imagined principality" or worse, is from the very beginning "never illuminated" by such a kingdom? This question is not abated by the realization that Strauss has silently juxtaposed a phrase from the fifteenth chapter of Machiavelli's *The Prince* (i.e., "many have imagined republics and principalities that have never been seen or known to exist in truth"[49]) with the title of one of Martin Buber's most controversial books (i.e., *Kingdom* [Königtum] *of God*, translated in English as *Kingship of God*[50]) in a manner that seems to favor Machiavelli. At this point, readers should note that Machiavelli returns later on in Strauss's lectures in an important way.

Given the presence of Martin Buber at Hebrew University, this last juxtaposed double reference is indeed bold. Yet it does not, for all that, simply indicate a rejection of Jerusalem. As discussed in chapter 1, Buber's thought, like Cohen's, is problematic for Strauss not because it is *Jewish*, but because it is *modern*. While Strauss rejects Jewish belief, he does not reject Judaism *tout court*. He does, however, understand himself to be a critic of modern Judaism (based as it is in modern philosophy). Therefore, while one would be correct in seeing the Jerusalem/Athens distinction emerge, this distinction is not the one being critiqued/rejected. Rather, Strauss is attempting to first lead his potentially philosophical audience away from modern thought in order to subsequently confront them with the Jerusalem/Athens distinction. We might state this point differently: Strauss's "leading away" from Jerusalem has a fundamentally different character than his "leading away" from modernity—in the latter case, "leading away" means simply "leaving behind"; in the former case, it means choosing one side in the (premodern) dialectic of the West.

6. *But while being compelled, or compelling myself, to wander far away from our sacred heritage, or to be silent about it, I shall not for a moment forget what Jerusalem stands for* [I shall not for a moment cease to think of it]. This final sentence (with which readers are, by now, familiar) highlights the nondogmatic character of Strauss's prologue (as well as, in my view, his overall project). While he is, to be sure, continuing to substantiate the Jerusalem/Athens distinction, he makes problematic the notion that this distinction is prescriptively uncomplicated. From both a nonphilosophical and a potentially philosophical perspective, Strauss's imperative to "not for a moment forget what Jerusalem stands for" makes sense; the nonphilosopher ought not to forget in order that political atrocities toward the Jewish people never happen again; the potential philosopher ought not forget in order that Jerusalem/Athens (as a fundamental distinction) be recovered. As stated above, Strauss intimately recognizes—that is, he sees with his own eyes—*both* the practical achievements of political Zionism for the Jewish people *and* the inessentiality of political Zionism for Judaism. While this final sentence does speak differently to both audiences, it expresses neither simple admiration nor simple criticism. We might say that it expresses a respectful and appreciative ambivalence. Given that the horrors of the Shoah were only one decade past, the sentiment expressed herein—be it as Jerusalemite remembrance or Athenian recollection—could not have been (as it is not now) foreign to Strauss's audience.

Four particulars of Strauss's final sentence are worthy of remark. The first is Strauss's reference to "being compelled, or compelling myself." If the choice between Jerusalem and Athens is based in a need/desire of the soul (rather than an arbitrary act of a capricious will), then the efficient cause of such a choice can only be a compulsion. Insofar as this compulsion occurs intrinsically to the soul of the one choosing, it can justifiably be called "self-compulsion"; it would thus resemble Spinozan *conatus* at least as much as Kantian will. Second, aside from the clear reference to the Israelites' journey through the desert (Numbers 14; Deuteronomy 1:3), Strauss's "wander[ing] far away from our sacred heritage" should (again) not, I believe, be understood as a rejection of Jerusalem. Rather, it indicates that Strauss is located on the border of Jerusalem and Athens. This is precisely the place where one experiences the *limits* of one's own city in order (through an encounter with the alternative city) to better *understand* one's own city. This would hold equally for citizens of any city—almost. Strauss's wandering is an Athenian wandering, and one has the right to ask whether such wandering would/could ever occur in Jerusalem. Interestingly (as discussed in Chapter 1), Strauss's answer is "yes," at least insofar as the prophets occupy the same "location" in Jerusalem as Socrates does in Athens—that is, on the border. In this respect, wandering both is and is not an exclusively philosophical activity (unless one wishes to grant that Jeremiah was a philosopher). Third, Strauss's "silence" regarding his sacred heritage is paradoxical. On the one hand, he has just announced this silence and, in so doing, negated it. On the other hand, his relative silence about Jerusalem (other than through the hints I shall discuss in the next chapter) brings renewed emphasis to Jerusalem precisely as a fundamental alternative to Athens. This deed constitutes a significant aspect of *the argument of the action* in Strauss's lectures. These three particular moments of Strauss's final sentence come together as a whole in the following way: Strauss's compelled wandering toward Athens takes the form of a pregnant silence about Jerusalem that continually brings focus to this distinction for potential philosophers.

The fourth particular of Strauss's final sentence concerns the term *forget*. Strictly speaking, his Jerusalem Hebrew University audience heard Strauss's proclamation that he "will not for a moment cease to think of it." Given that "it" refers to the "sacred heritage" from which Strauss will "wander far away," there doesn't seem to be a great distinction between "ceasing to think" and "forgetting." It is reasonable to suppose that his Hebrew University audience would have the Biblical education to make the association between such "cessation of thinking" and "forgetting." Again, in terms of posterity, Strauss sharpens the formulation for his essay."[51] In keeping with the rest of the prologue, Strauss speaks here in his own voice—"I shall not for a moment forget what Jerusalem stands for." In addition to the aforementioned meanings of "forgetting," it should be recognized that this term has tremendous resonances for an audience familiar with the Hebrew Bible. These references do not so much constitute a unified and systematic standpoint as they indicate the significance of memory for Jerusalem. In this context, it would not at all be surprising if Strauss's imperative was additionally aimed at having his audience recall Deuteronomy 25:17–19 and Psalm 137:1–6. Insofar as both texts refer to memory in the light of disaster, they would both (1) set the context for the movement away from the historical to the philosophical, and (2) indicate that the Bible, too (with characteristic zeal, longing, and, yes, immoderation), speaks with one foot in the present and one foot in eternity:

> Remember what Amalek did to you on your journey, after you left Egypt—how, undeterred by fear of God, he surprised you on the march, when you were famished and weary, and cut down all the stragglers in your rear. Therefore, when the LORD your God grants you safety from all your enemies around you, in the land that the LORD your God is giving you as a hereditary portion, you shall blot out the memory of Amalek from under heaven. Do not forget! (Deuteronomy 25:17–19)

> By the rivers of Babylon,
> there we sat,
> sat and wept,
> as we thought of Zion.
> There on the poplars
> we hung up our lyres,
> for our captors asked us there for songs,
> our tormentors, for amusement,
> "Sing us one of the songs of Zion."
> How can we sing a song of the LORD

> on alien soil?
> If I forget you, O Jerusalem,
> let my right hand wither;
> let my tongue stick to my palate
> if I cease to think of you,
> if I do not keep Jerusalem in memory
> even at my happiest hour. (Psalm 137:1–6)

As with every other substantial aspect of Strauss's prologue, these lines (if Strauss does indeed intend to reference them) carry a dual meaning. Nonphilosophers might resonate with the *thymos* expressed therein. In the context of Strauss's prologue, this might suggest Strauss's appreciation (not to say "love") of one's own (fatherland). Potential philosophers might wonder whether such a zealous longing for one's own can form a secure basis for a polity—that is, whether such *thymos* is politically good.

Regardless of how one answers this final question, there can, I think, be little doubt that the prologue of Strauss's lectures—juxtaposing as they do philosophical and Biblical references—provides the context within which a sustained engagement between Jerusalem and Athens can take place. In juxtaposing these two sets of references, Strauss begins to restage (if not yet reoriginate) the Jerusalem/Athens encounter. Moreover, irrespective of his own relation to religious belief, Strauss situates his writing nondogmatically on the border between the two cities. This "location," I claim, stays the same throughout the entirety of "What Is Political Philosophy?" and allows for Strauss to communicate a practical Athenian message (the argument) to the nonphilosophers as well as a contemplative one (the deed), to those who are on the path toward understanding by themselves.

CHAPTER FOUR

The Theological-Political Significance of "What Is Political Philosophy?"

A number of reasons present themselves for turning to Strauss's "What is Political Philosophy?" as a vantage point from which to look at Strauss's work as a whole. In one respect, it provides a comprehensive overview of Strauss's characteristic themes: the Ancients and the Moderns, the relation of law and justice, the critique of modern social science, and the relation of political philosophy to prephilosophic political life are all treated seriously and provocatively therein. One can similarly appreciate the unique conception of history developed in the final two sections. That uniqueness (at least with respect to other contemporary conceptions of history) stems, in large measure, from its point of origin: the history of political philosophy emerges as a way of responding to the fundamental tension between Jerusalem and Athens—an opposition that, for Strauss, is not itself historical. This conception of history is significant for at least two reasons. First, without simply denying the current necessity of approaching philosophy through its history, it steadfastly refuses to "ground" philosophy in that history. To the contrary, history itself is indexed, for Strauss, to the more primordial horizon of philosophy. Second, the origin of that history does not amount to anything like a closed, conceptual answer. Instead, it lies in a fundamental duality that exceeds humans' cognitive grasp (let alone any worldly resolution).[1] Finally, this philosophical origin is not a simple unity. Rather, it is something like an eidetic constellation of opposites/questions, a series of "permanent characteristics of humanity" (WIPP, 26) that, taken as a whole, make up a "noetic heterogeneity" (RCPR, 132, 142).[2] This last point might be put differently: unlike Heidegger's *Seinsfrage*, for example, which both remains the one thought of a great thinker and occurs as a potentiality that resists ontic determination, Strauss's realm of fundamental questions/problems/oppositions admits of both plurality and actuality. Far from being a historicizing "philosophy of history" Strauss's conception of history stands out as a genuinely philosophical conception of history. This is, perhaps, a main reason why the essay (and the book that it inaugurates) has such enduring significance.

It is my contention that Strauss's lectures and subsequent essay illustrate (and serve as a model for) what it means to be a citizen of Athens on the border of Jerusalem. Strauss accomplishes this in two ways: First, in the lectures, he articulates classical political philosophy and reticently (i.e., through hints) indicates its relation to Jerusalem. Second, in the essay, he extends his deed by silently indicating a predecessor to his own "thinking on the borders" in the context of his interpretation of the history of political philosophy in the West. And this is, for me, the most striking aspect of Strauss's essay—that is, his near total silence with respect to medieval Jewish thought. I therefore ask again the question raised in the last chapter: how is one to understand Strauss's apparent omission of medieval Jewish thought in general and Maimonides in particular?

The situation is initially not made clearer by the fact that there is as yet no consensus as to whether Strauss is, at bottom, a modern or not. This obviously determines the lens through which one views "What Is Political Philosophy?" Some commentators view Strauss's performance in Jerusalem as that of a radical modern operating under the guise of a premodern.[3] In a certain respect, my reading of the lectures is a response to this view. It is not a denial of the fundamental point (made by Velkley and others) that the project of return, which Strauss undertakes, is a fundamentally modern one. Instead, Strauss's modern project of return/recovery/reorigination, insofar as it develops in the form of *recollection*, brings one to an alternative construal of modernity—that is, one in which a genuine contemplative relation to premodern thought is possible. *I hold that, in the lectures, Strauss silently brings Athens into contact with Jerusalem such that potentially philosophical listeners can recollect the distinction for themselves. Similarly, I hold that, in the essay, it is Maimonides who functions as the unnamed presence. Strauss's apparent silence with respect to medieval thought in general, and Maimonides in particular, amounts to a strategy of sharpening the work originally undertaken in the lectures—that is, of both recovering the theological-political problem and reoriginating the Jerusalem/Athens distinction in the souls of his potentially philosophical readers of "What Is Political Philosophy?" Far from being an inessential historical index to what comes before or after, medieval thought amounts to an important mode of access for this recovery and reorigination.* In order to substantiate my claim, I will dedicate this chapter to a close reading of "What Is Political Philosophy?," augmented by other related material.[4] I believe that I can best illustrate the relation between the content, form and *inter-action between* content and form (what I have been calling the argument, action, and argument of the action), in Strauss's essay by focusing on (1) Strauss's reticent hints, which are intended to draw the distinction between Jerusalem and Athens as well as between Jerusalem/Athens and modernity, and (2) the historical account of the development of political philosophy in the West, in which account is contained Strauss's nearly invisible treatment of Maimonides.

As discussed in the previous chapter, much depends on how one understands the relation of the prologue to the rest of the lectures and essay. If one views the prologue in terms of its *speech*, one would conclude that the Jerusalem/Athens distinction is not an important part—that is, Strauss tells the reader that he will be silent about Jerusalem (and, of course, we ought to "take him at his *word*"). If, however, one views the prologue, in Platonic fashion, in terms of its *deed*, one would view it as exerting a gravitational pull on both the lectures and essay—that is, Jerusalem (and its "other," Athens) would be the beginning and the end of "What Is Political Philosophy?" At the level of speech, then, "What is Political Philosophy?" quickly dispenses with Jerusalem and Athens in favor of Ancients/Moderns. Is it then fair to say that, at the level of deed, "What is Political Philosophy?" adopts the Ancients/Moderns distinction as a presentational "veil" with which to hide the Jerusalem/Athens distinction? Not exactly. Insofar as the reorigination of the (vertically determined) Jerusalem/Athens distinction requires the horizontal movement back to premodern thought, the Ancients/Moderns distinction never simply becomes a salutary doctrine—that is, it never amounts to pure dissimulation. Rather, from the standpoint of the Jerusalem/Athens distinction, the distinction between premodern (i.e., Ancient and Medieval) and modern philosophy would come to lose its *historical* character in favor of a philosophical one. At this point, one would simply speak of philosophy. Due to the prejudices of modern philosophy (qua *historical* designation), however, this end point is still wanting. For this reason, one remains at the level of the second cave.

Finally, readers should note the following as a major feature of both the Hebrew University lectures and essay: they are presented largely in the form of a critique of both Buber and Cohen analogous to the critique discussed in chapter 1 of the present study. Coupled together with his silent indication of Maimonides in his historical account of political philosophy, Strauss's final essay can be understood as a bringing-together of the themes discussed in the first two chapters, but now recast in the form of a Platonic dialogue (as discussed in chapter 3).

Jerusalem/Athens and Ancients/Moderns

The first sentence of the "The Problem of Political Philosophy" announces the fundamentally nonhistoricist quality of political philosophy, as the premoderns understood it: "The meaning of political philosophy and its meaningful character is as evident today as it always has been since the time when political philosophy came to light in Athens" (WIPP, 10). Once we are able to view political philosophy from a standpoint exceeding the modern conceptual horizon, we see that political philosophy strives after a clear view of evident political activity: desiring preservation or change, political activity is proximally motivated by notions of better and worse and ultimately motivated by some "awareness of the good." Having initially the "character of opinion," this awareness is unquestioningly presupposed by political actors who are oblivious to the fact that such an awareness remains questionable. Having become aware of the questionableness of this awareness of the good, the philosopher becomes aware of the possibility (the "thought") of a good "which is no longer questionable." Strauss does not assert that there is actually such a good; he leaves even this possibility as a question. One can infer, however, that the political philosopher's activity is (at least in a sense) coeval with the awareness of this possibility. The political philosopher, then, is the one who searches for knowledge of the good—"If this directedness [toward knowledge of the good] becomes explicit, if men make it their explicit goal to acquire knowledge of the good life and of the good society, political philosophy emerges" (WIPP, 10).

Strauss then begins to explicate the adjective "political" in the present context. For Strauss, it refers both to "the subject matter and the function" of the philosophical inquiry. This distinction between "subject matter" and "function" seems to replicate the aforementioned distinction between "speech" and "deed"; political philosophy both deals with the political things and does so in a "politic" manner, "in a manner that is meant to be relevant to the political life" (WIPP, 10).[5] Insofar as political philosophy encompasses both the subject matter (speech) and function (deed), it is that part of philosophy that is the most relevant to nonphilosophical life. Strauss then ends with a reference to Aristotle's *Politics*: "Only in his *Politics* does Aristotle make use of oaths—the almost inevitable accompaniment of passionate speech." The reader/listener is supposed to understand, by this reference, Aristotle's "politic" attunement to the passionate character of the nonphilosophical citizen. If a human being is "an intellect marked by a certain longing, or longing marked by thinking" (as Aristotle states in the *Nicomachean Ethics*),[6] and if only some humans have philosophical sensibilities, then the deed of political philosophy amounts to the communication of (some) philosophical ideas in the mode of passionate speech. This may strike intellectual or academic nonphilosophers as an obvious aspect of political philosophy. Understood in the light of the prologue, however, the reference to Aristotle's "politic" presentation of politics also begins to silently substantiate the movement away from the un-ironic zeal that characterizes "the sacred soil" of Jerusalem.

Given that philosophy, for Strauss, is "essentially not possession of truth, but quest for the truth" (WIPP, 11), it is by definition limited. Strauss holds that Socratic ignorance, and its inducement to strive after knowledge, is the distinctive trait of the philosopher. At this point, Strauss raises the issue of philosophy's limitation that, I believe, directly contradicts the particular late modern readings of Strauss given by commentators such as Stanley Rosen and William Altman. "It may be," Strauss holds, "that as regards the possible answers to these questions, the pros and cons will always be in a more or less even balance, and therefore that philosophy will never go beyond the stage of discussion or disputation and will never reach the stage of decision. This would not make philosophy futile. For the clear grasp of a fundamental question requires understanding of the nature of the subject matter with which the question is concerned" (WIPP, 11). The usage of the term *decision* here is not innocent; Strauss is well aware of Carl Schmitt's conception of politics as resting on sovereign decision. That conception of decision is, in fact, one half of Kant's conception of moral choice as being the product of will. For Kant, however, the will that wills morally does so by submitting itself to the universality of the moral law. For Schmitt, in contrast, the will that decides politically is the arbitrary and capricious will that takes the leap of faith. Far from advocating "decisionism," Strauss holds that philosophical activity is valuable even if the moment of decision in favor of one view over another remains forever deferred. This view is reiterated in his "Restatement on Xenophon's *Hiero*": "philosophy . . . as such is neither dogmatic, nor sceptic, and still less 'decisionist,' but zetetic (or skeptic in the original sense of the term). Philosophy as such is nothing but the genuine awareness of the problems, i.e., of the fundamental and comprehensive problems . . . [T]he philosopher ceases to be a philosopher at the moment at which the 'subjective certainty' of a solution becomes stronger than his awareness of the problematic character of that solution. At that moment, the sectarian is born" (WIPP, 116). If philosophy forsakes its properly Socratic character, it transforms into sectarianism. Moreover, as discussed in chapter 1, the very turn to the path of philosophy is motivated by the compulsion or desire to search after knowledge. Rosen's claim that Strauss's conception of philosophy is based on a modernist notion of willful and decisive subjectivity can be sustained only if one forgets or ignores its connection to desire (or compulsion) and awareness of the whole (of which it is a part and knowledge of which would constitute its *telos*). Differently stated, the philosophical life does not call for *decisive* action.

Strauss ends this discussion with a juxtaposition of a statement by Thomas (one of the two explicitly cited references to medieval thought in the lectures) in Latin prefaced by his own interpretation of that statement. In the lectures, he supplies the English: "The least which can be obtained of the knowledge of the highest things is more desirable than the most certain knowledge which can be obtained of the smallest things." Prior to this, Strauss offers a context-setting preface: "Genuine knowledge of a fundamental question, thorough understanding of it, is better than blindness to it, or indifference to it, be that indifference or blindness accompanied by knowledge of the answers to a vast number of peripheral or ephemeral questions or not" (WIPP, 11). The nonphilosophers might take Strauss's statement to be simply his own "creative rendering" of Thomas's point without bothering to wonder whether the two statements really say the same thing. Potential philosophers reading the essay might wonder about the *deed* of leaving Thomas's statement in Latin; might it say something different from Strauss's rendition? If so, why bother to even cite it?

A careful inspection shows that the two statements are similar only in the most general sense—that is, they both *can* be taken to refer to the idea that the search for knowledge is better or nobler than the possession of opinion. But notice the structure of each statement: whereas Thomas opposes "the least which can be obtained of the knowledge of the highest things" to "the most certain knowledge which can be obtained of the smallest things," Strauss opposes "genuine knowledge of a fundamental question, [a] thorough understanding of it" to "blindness or indifference to it [the fundamental question]" regardless of whether or not it is "accompanied by knowledge of the answers to a vast number of peripheral or ephemeral questions." Is the slenderest knowledge of the highest things" the same as "genuine knowledge [or thorough understanding] of a fundamental question"? Is "the most certain knowledge obtained of lesser things" thc same as "blindness to genuine knowledge of a fundamental question accompanied by knowledge of the answers to a vast number of peripheral or ephemeral questions"? It seems as if Strauss is using the authority of Thomas to legitimate his own Socratic understanding of philosophy. If, as Strauss believes, nonphilosophers have little patience for philosophy, the deed of Strauss's citation conflicts with the argument put forward by his own rendering. Could Thomas have really held a *zetetic* view of philosophy? Potential philosophers might wonder what it is about philosophy (in any case, the philosophy presented in Strauss's essay and lectures) that would call for such a legitimation or "veiling."

In any case, since political philosophy is a branch of philosophy in general, it stands or falls within the realm of a specific inquiry—that is, an inquiry about the nature of political things: "One does not understand them as what they are, as political things, if one does not take seriously their explicit or implicit claim to be judged in terms of goodness or badness, of justice or injustice, i.e., if one does not measure them by some standard of goodness or justice. . . . If political philosophy wishes to do justice to its subject matter, it must strive for genuine knowledge of these standards. Political philosophy is the attempt truly to know both the nature of political things and the right, or the good, political order" (WIPP, 12). The inquiry proper to political philosophy deals both with understanding political things as they are—that is, their nature—and understanding them in the light of the best political order. Were Strauss to have stopped with the first criterion (the nature of political things), his view would resemble early moderns like Machiavelli, Hobbes, and Locke. By emphasizing the second criterion (the best political order), he comes into conflict with the early moderns (at least as Strauss presents them) insofar as they reject any semblance of natural political teleology (i.e., questions concerning the good and the just). It is the refusal to capitulate to such rejection that, in Strauss's terms, characterizes both Jerusalem and Athens over and against modern political philosophy.

Strauss then gives some definitions with the aim of providing clarification as to the nature and character of political philosophy. While a complete explication of these definitions would exceed the purpose of this chapter, there are a few that merit close consideration. Strauss distinguishes political philosophy first from "political thought in general," which is simply "the reflection on, or the exposition of political ideas" whose form is expressed in "laws and codes, in poems and stories, in tracts and public speeches *inter alia*" (WIPP, 12). A political idea is, in turn, are "any significant 'phantasm, notion, species, or whatever it is about which the mind can be employed in thinking' concerning the political fundamentals" (WIPP, 12).[7] Strauss leaves his quotation unnamed and, to nonphilosophers, the definition might seem basic enough. Potential philosophers (especially readers of early modern thought) might recognize the passage from Locke's *Essay Concerning Human Understanding.*[8] Why would Strauss characterize "political ideas" with reference to a definition of "idea" taken from Locke? Further, why would he take it from Locke's epistemological treatise rather than attempt to derive it from one of his political works? Certainly Locke's straightforward definition occurs in the *Essay*. Is Strauss's citation due simply to convenience? If one grants Strauss's overall claim that our thoughts inhabit a modern philosophical horizon, then starting with a modern definition of ideas allows Strauss to work backward to a conceptual horizon that precedes modernity. Finally, after one encounters the third section of his final essay (on modern political philosophy), careful readers might recall Strauss's citation of Locke with the following statement: "There is a hidden kinship between Machiavelli's political science and the new natural science" (WIPP, 47). Insofar as Machiavelli's thought constitutes the basis for early modern political philosophy (taken up by thinkers such as Locke), the kinship between new natural science (with its emphasis on epistemology) and modern political philosophy would equally apply to Locke; and the secrecy of this kinship would, *by and large*, be preserved by Strauss's presentation. Despite the modern presentation of his definition, Strauss notes that "Political thought is as old as the human race; the first man who uttered a word like 'father' or an expression like 'thou shalt not . . .' was the first political thinker; but political philosophy appeared at a knowable time in the recorded past" (WIPP, 12–13). We should (at least) note that these examples make appearances in both Biblical and Greek thought. Familial narratives such as Jacob and Esau and the commandments and prohibitions given throughout the Torah serve as instances in the Hebrew Bible. Sophocles's *Antigone* and Plato's *Euthyphro* can serve as instances in Greek thought.

Strauss's next definition concerns "political theory." In the first definition, Strauss employs the phrase "we understand"; in this definition he employs the phrase "people frequently understand today." Is Strauss simply using common parlance in order to orient his definitions? Careful readers and listeners might wonder whether his usages of the first-person plural and the third person are meant to proceed in a Socratic dialectical fashion. Given that his concern is not with beginning from abstract and technical definitions (characteristic of modern philosophy), but from commonly accepted ones, I believe that Strauss tacitly substantiates his intent to move away from common notions toward (1) political philosophy in general and (2) classical political philosophy in particular. In this case, the *deed* of Strauss's definition accords with the *speech* contained in his definition: "By political theory, people frequently understand today comprehensive reflections on the political situation which lead up to the suggestion of a broad policy. Such reflections appeal in the last resort to principles *accepted by public opinion or a considerable part of it*; that is, they dogmatically assume principles that can well be questioned" (WIPP, 13; my emphasis). One can also, indeed, question whether the principles underlying the definitions presented by Strauss are adequate. While nonphilosophers might not question his definitions, careful readers might find them inadequate in two respects: first, in depending on modern philosophy, they presuppose much (Strauss would acknowledge this); second, insofar as Strauss uses them strategically—that is, in order to move beyond them—his concern is less with establishing their veracity than with establishing them as common notions (which is precisely the opposite of establishing veracity). Potential philosophers might wonder whether they are being actively moved away from modern philosophy toward something very different.

The examples of political theory given by Strauss are Pinsker's *Autoemancipation* and Herzl's *Judenstaat*. It is not too much of a stretch to suggest that the entirety of Strauss's audience at Hebrew University would have recognized the significance of these two examples: Pinsker and Herzl were among the two earliest and most important of the nineteenth-century political Zionist figures. The example of Pinsker affords Strauss the opportunity to illustrate the political usage of abstraction: "Pinsker's *Autoemancipation* carries as its motto the words: "'If I am not for myself, who will be for me? And if not now, when?' It omits the words 'And if I am only for myself what am I?' Pinsker's silent rejection of the thought expressed in the omitted words is a crucial premise of the argument developed in his tract. Pinsker does not justify this rejection. For a justification, one would have to turn to the 3rd and 16th chapters of Spinoza's *Tractatus theologico-politicus*, to a work of a political philosopher" (WIPP, 13).[9] Pinsker's selective usage of Hillel's statement from the Talmudic tractate *Pirke Avot* both makes an argument and silently indicates the alternative. Recounting Pinsker's omission in his 1962 lecture "Why We Remain Jews," Strauss adds: "[Pinsker's] omission of these words constitutes the definition of pureblooded political Zionism" (JPCM, 318). Or in Pinsker's own words, "Help yourselves and God will help you!"[10] Strauss's immediate audience at Hebrew University would have recognized what many today will have to recall—that is, that the alternatives to the political Zionism of Pinsker's and Herzl's day were cultural and religious Zionism. Insofar as Pinsker's text is put in the service of a practical political aim (i.e., garnering support for political Zionism), his omission can be understood, in Strauss's terms, as propaganda. In this respect, Strauss silently indicates the kinship between political Zionism and its modern foundation in the thought of Machiavelli (the figure who, for Strauss, first makes use of propaganda in a secularized context [WIPP, 45–46]). His reference to chapters 3 and 16 of Spinoza's *Theological-Political Treatise* (which deal respectively with the prophetic gift of the Hebrews and with questions concerning the foundations of the state and sovereign authority) is a somewhat less reticent indication that the modern political philosophy—on which Herzlian and Pinskerian political Zionism was based—views the Jewish problem ultimately as a practical (rather than a fundamental) problem.

Is Strauss also using propaganda on his audience/readership? The answer to this question depends on how one construes Strauss's intention: if Strauss intends to influence policy, then the answer is yes; if not, then the answer is no. I believe that Strauss intends (1) to convince the nonphilosophers to undertake moderate political action, and (2) to show potential philosophers the fundamental problems and questions (involved in the theological-political problem) that become manifest in the Jerusalem/Athens distinction. To the extent that Strauss's lectures contain a practical teaching, they run the inevitable risk of making use of propaganda. This is to say only that, insofar as it is a practical endeavor, politics cannot demand the kind of thoroughness that other endeavors demand—a point about which, paradoxically, both Aristotle and Kant would agree. This raises another question: would practical endeavors be served well or ill by attempting the thoroughness of theoretical inquiry? Readers will ultimately make up their own minds on this issue. Insofar as Strauss believes that, in politics (as *opposed to* philosophy), one needs to adopt some of the tactics being used by the other side, propaganda is inevitable. This raises the final question (which exceeds the purview of the present study): is propaganda in the service of moderate political action (concerning the founding of a State) necessarily inappropriate? Asked differently: is the cautioning away from theocratic fanaticism a bad thing?

Returning to the discussion of "political theory," one might wonder how Strauss's Spinoza reference would be understood by his different audiences. Nonphilosophers might simply take this reference as Strauss's attempt to explain a technical distinction—that is, between "political philosophy" and the more derivative "political theory." Strauss would then be suggesting that Pinsker and Herzl (who wrote as "men of action") derived their legitimacy from philosophers such as Spinoza. This reference would then be traditional and restorative insofar as it seeks to legitimate political Zionism by virtue of "returning" it to a properly Jewish lineage (albeit a recent one).[11] Furthermore, that Spinoza's philosophy is taken to signal the birth of the Enlightenment might suggest that the secular project of political Zionism is simply a further extension of the Enlightenment project—that is, one which confronts and rejects religious superstition and theocratic fanaticism. Even aside from the question concerning its propagandistic character, potential philosophers might wonder why Pinsker chose to leave out the middle statement from *Avot* ("and if I am only for myself, what am I?"). Might this omission signal a radical change in conception with respect to the self-understanding of Judaism as a religious community? Perhaps it indicates a peculiarly modern emphasis on individuality instead of one concerning how such individuality occurs within community (let alone "the whole"). Might it also suggest that the simple securing of land for the *Jewish people* is here being accorded a greater importance than that of adhering to the principles of *Judaism*? This suspicion is born out when one considers that, in "Why We Remain Jews," Strauss invokes the following passage from chapter 3 of Spinoza's *Theological-Political Treatise* as an "explanation" for Pinsker's omission: "If the principles of their religion did not effeminate the Jews, I would regard it as perfectly possible that one day, if the political constitution is favorable, they might succeed in restoring their state" (JPCM, 318).[12] Seen in this light, Pinsker's omission would signal that his writings had an ideological rather than a philosophical purpose (i.e., Pinsker is not concerned with presenting both sides of the argument, but rather with tendentiously advancing one side of the argument while suppressing the other side[13]). Hence, potential philosophers might begin to wonder if the conflict between (1) a *modern* solution to the Jewish (and, philosophically speaking, human) problem, and (2) a *Jewish* solution to that problem is not simply an occasional, but rather a fundamental one.[14]

Strauss then—almost in the manner of an afterthought—raises the issue of "political theology." It is the first of the definitions presented thus far that contains no quotation, citation, or reference (explicit or implicit) to any thinker current or otherwise. His statement runs as follows: "We are compelled to distinguish political philosophy from political theology. By political theology we understand political teachings which are based on divine revelation. Political philosophy is limited to what is accessible to the unassisted human mind" (WIPP, 13). Strauss immediately follows this definition up with a definition of "social philosophy" that deals with the same material as political philosophy but looked at from a different standpoint; whereas political philosophy looks at political phenomena from the standpoint of country or nation, social philosophy looks at it "as part of a larger whole which it designates by the term 'society'" (WIPP, 13). This apparently minimal statement contains a number of significant issues which (without claiming to know what was going through Strauss's mind as he composed the statement) allow one to make important and extremely interesting conjectures.

On the most basic level, one might ask about why there are no named sources or quotations concerning the term *political theology*. Surely the academics (potential philosophers and otherwise) in the audience—coming, as they mostly did, from central Europe—would have been aware of Carl Schmitt, the legal theorist (first associated with the Weimar Republic, then with National Socialism) who popularized the term in the 1920s (his book *Political Theology* was published in 1922). Perhaps Schmitt's name recognition was so great that there was no need to invoke his name. Might Strauss have been attempting to hide the fact that he read and commented on Schmitt (his "Notes on Carl Schmitt's *Concept of the Political*" was written in 1932) and that the two had corresponded for a short period (1932–33)?[15] But if this were the case, why even mention political theology at all? Was the term so familiar—so familiar in Israel—that dealing with it became unavoidable? Is this, perhaps, what Strauss means when (at least in the context of his immediate audience) he speaks of "being compelled" to speak about political theology? According to Nitzan Lebovic, Schmitt's conception of political theology had a substantial presence at the Hebrew University of Jerusalem—particularly in the 1940s—largely (but by no means exclusively) as a result of Martin Buber's presence there.[16] Along with Jacob Taubes and Samuel Hugo Bergmann, Buber created an intellectual environment that allowed religious and political activists (like the "mother of the Jewish settlers movement in the West Bank," Geulah Cohen[17]) to emerge and flourish. Given Strauss's familiarity with Buber (as discussed in chapter 1), I believe that it is not unreasonable to wonder whether his invocation of "political theology" (in the immediate context of Hebrew University) was an attempt to both (1) distinguish his conception of political philosophy from Buber as much as Schmitt and (2) to hint at the kinship between the thought of Buber and that of Schmitt. It is therefore relevant, I believe, to discuss the similarities between Schmittian "political theology" and Buberian "theopolitics" in order to substantiate this conjecture.

Schmitt's two most famous lines from *Political Theology* (1922) are the opening sentences of chapters 1 and 3, respectively: "Sovereign is he who decides on the exception" and "All significant concepts of the modern theory of the state are secularized theological concepts not only because of their historical development—in which they were transferred from theology to the theory of the state, whereby, for example, the omnipotent God became the omnipotent lawgiver—but also because of their systematic structure."[18] For Schmitt, the concept of the sovereign who wills the decisive legitimacy of the exception (in the state of siege or state of emergency) is a secularized form of the Biblical God who performs miracles.[19] On this basis, it is impossible not to hear in the friend/enemy distinction (as articulated by Schmitt in *The Concept of the Political* [1932][20]) echoes of Matthew 12:30 where Jesus says to his disciples, "Whoever is not with me is against me, and whoever does not gather with me scatters."[21] Similarly, the conception of a concrete decision (which exceeds the purview of normative rationality) carries with it echoes of the Lutheran-Kierkegaardian leap of faith. Finally, Schmitt articulates a political-theological conception of the Pauline "restrainer" in his description of the continuity of the Christian empire in the Middle Ages (in *Nomos of the Earth* [1950]): "The decisive historical concept of this continuity [characteristic of the Christian empire] was that of the restrainer: *katechon.* 'Empire' in this sense meant the historical power to *restrain* the appearance of the Antichrist and the end of the present eon; it was a power that withholds . . . as the Apostle Paul said in his Second Letter to the Thessalonians . . . I do not believe that any historical concept other than *katechon* would have been possible for the original Christian faith. The belief that a restrainer holds back the end of the world provides the only bridge between the notion of an eschatological paralysis of all human events and a tremendous historical monolith like that of the Christian empire of the Germanic kings."[22] In short (much like the notion of the sovereign, exception, decision, and friend/enemy), the "restrainer" becomes transformed from an eschatological-religious conception to a historical-political one.[23] And yet, the religious connection remains significant insofar as (for Schmitt) religious imagery is the only imagery powerful enough to *catalyze* and *motivate* the historical and political movement of peoples. This is another way of articulating the claim that Strauss understands to be at the root of the theological-political problem: only divine legislation can bring about an identity of justice and law. In the light of this, Strauss seeks to preserve the theological-political problem *as a question* by highlighting the responses to it given in the Jerusalem/Athens distinction. Schmitt, in sharp contrast, decides in favor of the friend/enemy distinction as it comes to light within the secularized religious context of political theology.

It is arguably a conception of faith in revelation that lies at the bottom of Schmittian political theology.[24] In his 1950 review of Karl Löwith's *Meaning in History*, "Three Possibilities for a Christian Conception of History," Schmitt (speaking in his own voice) clearly articulates this as follows: "Christianity is in its essence no morality and no doctrine. It is no penitential sermon, and no religion in the sense of comparative religious studies, but a historical event of infinite, non-appropriable, non-occupiable singularity. It is the incarnation in the Virgin Mary. The Christian Credo speaks of historical events. Pontius Pilate belongs there essentially. He is not just a pitiful creature who oddly ended up there. Christians look back on completed events and find a basic reason and an archetype. Through the active contemplation of them, the dark meaning of our history continues to grow."[25] For Schmitt, enmity is not only a constitutive and grounding feature of the political, but an ineradicable aspect of political theology as well.

The relation between Schmitt and Buber is anything but straightforward and (if my conjecture is correct) it is this fact that makes Strauss's reference to political theology at Hebrew University so interesting and controversial. Buber was certainly not a right-wing political or religious fanatic; he did not, in the main, advocate enmity as a constituent feature of politics or of religion; and he criticized Schmitt in print in 1936 precisely both for (1) basing his conception of politics on the extreme and "labile," rather than on the lasting and continuous (thus committing a methodological error), and (2) basing his view of the wickedness of human beings in the theological doctrine of sin (thus attempting to explain a universal human condition by means [again] of an extreme conception of humanity).[26] Finally, Buber's "theopolitics" is, in one respect, not so much a political *secularization* of religion, but rather a full-blown *theologization* of politics: unlike Schmitt (for whom the figure of God becomes secularized in the sovereign ruler), Buber describes "theopolitics" as "the realization of the all-embracing rulership of God [as] the Proton and Eschaton of Israel."[27] For Schmitt, God's sovereignty is the religious archetype of secular political sovereignty; for Buber, in contrast, God's sovereignty is *actual political sovereignty*.

The kinship with Schmitt is nonetheless evident in Buber's "Messianic Trilogy"—that is, *Kingdom of God* (1932), *The Prophetic Faith* (1944), and *Moses* (1946). As with my discussion of Schmitt, I can do no more than present a brief summary of Buber's kinship with him here. Such a discussion inevitably gives less emphasis to the historical development of Buber's thought than to a systematic presentation of it (but insofar as Buber composed his Trilogy out of chronological order, this approach perhaps has some precedent). In the end, such summary is (I believe) helpful for showing what may have been involved in Strauss's enigmatic statement. There are three basic features to this kinship: (1) Buber's practical intention, (2) the development of religious-historical concepts into political-historical actualities, and (3) God as sovereign. Even taking into account the vast differences summarized above, Buber's conception of theopolitics shares the above three characteristics with Schmittian political theology.

First, Buber's intention is irreducible to simply theoretical concerns; Buber writes as a man of action. This is as true of his scholarly texts as it is of his Zionist texts and his early lectures on Judaism. Buber is, above all, interested in a *renewal of Judaism* (this is the title of one of his most famous early addresses on Judaism, delivered in 1911). As with Rosenzweig, this renewal consists to a great extent in being oriented toward the future in the mode of "preparedness." Buber's description of this preparedness, in his early address, is stunning in its rhetorical power and fascinating insofar as it exhibits precisely the practical and historically teleological elements which Strauss finds problematic with Enlightenment philosophy and modern Jewish thought: "To be prepared means . . . to realize Judaism's great tendencies in our personal lives: the tendency toward unity, by molding our soul into a single entity, in order to enable it to conceive unity; the tendency toward the deed, by filling our soul with unconditionality, in order to enable it to realize the deed; the tendency toward the future, by unbinding it toward the goal, in order to enable it to serve the future."[28] It is no mistake, therefore, to hold that Buber's writings are aimed at producing such a renewal in his readers.[29] That this is the case in his Trilogy can be seen from the final remark in Buber's preface to *Moses*: "That Moses experiences [God] in this fashion [i.e., as revelatory in and through human deeds] and serves him accordingly is what has set that man apart as a living and effective force at all times; *and that is what places him thus afresh in our own day, which possibly requires him more than any earlier day has ever done.*"[30] For Schmitt, the practical character of his own endeavor comes to sight when one considers again the fundamental role of enmity in the political: "War is neither the aim nor the purpose nor even the very content of politics. But as an ever present possibility it is the leading presupposition which determines in a characteristic way human action *and thinking* and thereby creates a specifically political behavior."[31] Given Schmitt's aversion to the ideology of the "nonpolitical," it seems that Schmitt would have to understand his very discourse on the political (and, by implication, political theology) as a manifestation of the same antagonistic polemics about which he writes. This is precisely what follows from Schmitt's well-known remark that "all political concepts, images, and terms have a polemical meaning. They are focused on a specific conflict and are bound to a concrete situation."[32] Schmitt's texts are, therefore, tactics and arms in a battle. While Buber's particular practical concerns in the 1940s were the diametrical opposite of Schmitt's, their kinship lies in their modern preoccupation with theory in the service of practice. Differently stated, insofar as both Schmitt and Buber are primarily interested in advancing their own causes, they are not concerned with presenting all sides equally.[33] Their projects, in this respect, have (at least in part) an ideological component.

Second, the relation between the categories of "eschatology" and "politics" are complex in Buber's thought. On the one hand, he holds (contrary to Schmitt) that eschatology occurs subsequent to history: "the 'eschatological' hope [concerning Israel] . . . is first always historical hope; it becomes eschatologized only through growing historical disillusionment. In this process faith seizes upon the future as the unconditioned turning point of history, then as the unconditioned overcoming of history."[34] In much the same way as Jacob Taubes would (decades later) respond to Scholem's construal of the messianism/history relation,[35] Buber holds that history always precedes eschatology. On the other hand, Buber's conception of "direct theocracy" (characteristic of the early period of Israel's history) amounts to "a religio-historical concept which tends to actualize itself as a constitutional history: as that which attains expression in the beginnings of a people, in its subsequent history actualizes itself as effective striving for a real-earthly divine authority."[36] While the category of the "religio-historical" is surely more concrete than that of "eschatology" it comes to serve the same function in Buber's discourse as the latter term does in Schmitt's—that is, as the originary impulse which gives rise to the properly political situation. Hence, when Buber says of Moses that he "is not to be comprehended at all within exclusively 'religious' categories. What constitutes his idea and his task: the realization of the unity of religious and social life in the community of Israel, the substantiation of a ruling by God that shall not be culturally restricted but shall comprehend the entire existence of the nation, the theo-political principle,"[37] it means that the significance of Moses has migrated from the realm of the "exclusively religious" to that of the "(theo)political." In substituting "religion" or "religio-history" for "eschatology," Buber has maintained the secularization of politics even within the context of his illustrations of "direct theocracy."

Finally, in Buber's *The Prophetic Faith* (particularly in the section titled "The Theopolitical Hour"),[38] one sees both (1) the movement from the religious or religio-historical to the political-historical and (2) the absolute sovereignty of the divine (both in terms of His wrath and his ability to decide): "In order that the divine regime may be truly real, it is necessary that all the actual life of the community be subject to it. This regime cannot be compressed in the 'religious domain,' that is to say, in the 'upper spheres' of being, it is not to be reduced to special holy times and special holy places only. At the center is the holy *God*, Who demands all and gives all. His regime cannot but be political in the highest and most comprehensive sense."[39] Characteristic of God, as "judge or king"[40] (at least in the context of Isaiah) is his zeal: "The memoir of Isaiah closes with the song of the child, with the saying about the 'zeal of YHVH of hosts,' the zealous God, Who zealously demands decision and brings decision."[41] The language of decision is not *per se* Schmittian—it is present in much existentialist philosophy and religious thought (e.g., Kierkegaard, Heidegger, Barth, Sartre). Coupled with a conception of divinity, divine wrath, and an articulation of sovereignty, however, the parallel with Schmitt becomes more specific: "Those who know YHVH dare dread no earthly power. He who so gives himself to YHVH's will and 'sanctifies Him,' to him 'He will be for a sanctuary,' in which he will find a refuge. Whereas to all the rest, 'to the two houses of Israel,' *when He arises to act terribly in History* He will be for a stumbling-block, upon which they will stumble and fall."[42] While Buber construes God and sovereignty in a far more "directly theocratic" sense than Schmitt does, the way in which Buber treats divine sovereignty exhibits clear parallels with Schmitt's understanding of sovereignty as a secularization of divine power.

I reiterate: We cannot know for certain what occupied Strauss's thought as he composed the aforcmentioned statement. At issue here is not a Cartesian-type certainty over the mental contents of Strauss's mind, but rather the description and elucidation of the context in which Strauss delivered his remarks. Insofar as his remarks (both initially and in print) are characterized by "orality," they are suited both to a particular occasion as well as to posterity.

Given Strauss's familiarity with the thought of both Schmitt and Buber, and given the fact that his lectures were presented at the Hebrew University (where people were aware of Schmitt's thought and where Buber's presence was unmistakable), I believe this digression helps to draw together a likely connection in an otherwise enigmatic statement. One final question, however, needs to be raised. Strauss immediately (i.e., in the same paragraph) follows his definition of political theology with a definition of social philosophy. Might he be suggesting to careful listeners/readers that the two are somehow linked? Asked differently, does political theology—in both its Schmittian and Buberian iterations—have anything to do with modern conceptions of society?

Like Schmitt, Strauss is sharply critical of such conceptions insofar as they pretend to a value-neutrality that relegates religion and politics to the derivative spheres of culture and morals. It is in this context that Strauss can be understood as integrating a tacit critique of social philosophy into his tacit critique of political theology. In his "Notes on *The Concept of the Political*," Strauss holds that Schmitt's political critique of liberalism is actually a moral critique insofar as it involves a moral (i.e., universal and normative) judgment on pacifism[43]—that is, in taking for granted an "unpolemical concept of the state of nature,"[44] Schmitt makes use of the very normative and universal type of claim about human nature characteristic of liberalism's advocacy of societal neutrality. Paradoxically, while Schmitt desires to break with liberalism, "his critique of liberalism remains in the horizon of liberalism."[45] With respect to Buber, Strauss's caustic remark in his autobiographical preface to *Spinoza's Critique of Religion* about cultural and religious Zionism is relevant here (insofar as Buber was a major proponent of religious Zionism): "Cultural Zionism [e.g., as propounded by figures such as Ahad Ha'am] believed itself to have found a safe middle-ground between politics (power politics) and divine revelation, between the subcultural and the supracultural, but it lacked the sternness of the two extremes. When cultural Zionism understands itself, it turns into religious Zionism. But when religious Zionism understands itself, it is in the first place Jewish faith and only secondarily Zionism" (JPCM, 143). Viewed in the present context, Buber's "theopolitics" suffers from being a political conception that avoids "power politics," and thus reduces Zionism to a cultural manifestation and ultimately to a religious faith of the kind that can only exist in the private or public sphere of an otherwise neutral societal matrix. For different reasons, both Buber's and Schmitt's thought cannot escape a modern conceptual horizon. Insofar as they do not question this horizon (the horizon in which society remains neutral), their conceptions of political theology presuppose "the larger whole . . . designat[ed] by the term 'society'" (WIPP, 13).

The discussion of political theology is not the only place in the lectures where Strauss engages Buber's thought. In addition to the mention of the "kingdom of God" in the prologue (discussed above in chapter 3), Strauss directly confronts Buber's conception of the "concrete human relation . . . the I-Thou-We relation" (WIPP, 28). Strauss mentions Buber's conception as an instance of a fundamental change in orientation between premodern political philosophy and modern political philosophy (the dependence on which, according to Strauss, still plagues recent philosophers such as Buber [WIPP, 28]). Classical political philosophers "look at political things in the perspective of the enlightened citizens or statesmen [but] look further afield in the same direction . . . They do not look at political things from the outside, as spectators of political life" (WIPP, 27–28). In this way, classical political philosophy begins from "simple and primary issues." In sharp contrast, by assuming an artificially neutral (and thus external) stance toward the political things, modern and contemporary political philosophy begins from an abstraction. This problem is less an issue for the initial phase of modern philosophy—what Strauss refers to as the "first wave"— insofar as it understood the prior philosophical presuppositions that it was in the process of rejecting. The offspring of this initial phase—the "second" and "third" waves—simply took the veracity of this rejection for granted without actually inquiring into it. The move toward "concreteness" (characteristic of Buber, but also of Heidegger and Rosenzweig as well), albeit an attempt to remedy the abstract quality of modern philosophy, is a symptom of this lack of inquiry: "It was thought that by virtue of this movement toward the concrete, recent philosophy has overcome the limitations . . . of modern philosophy . . . It was overlooked, however, that this change of orientation perpetuated the original defect of modern philosophy because it accepted abstractions as its starting point, and that the concrete at which one eventually arrived was not at all the truly concrete, but still an abstraction" (WIPP, 28). Differently stated, the language of "concreteness" concealed its own abstract character.

Buber's "I-Thou-We" relation is Strauss's only example, in the Hebrew University lectures, of the abstract character of modern and contemporary philosophy. This does not mean, according to Strauss, that it refers to a phenomenon wholly unrecognizable by premodern philosophy; rather, it means that modern/contemporary philosophy deals with the same things in a derivative, abstract, and ultimately deficient manner. I can now give full play to the passage (partially quoted in chapter 3) dealing with the problematic character of Buber's thought:

> The phenomenon which is now called the I-Thou-We relation was known to the classics by the name of friendship. When speaking to a friend I address him in the second person. But philosophic or scientific analysis is not speaking to a friend, i.e., to this individual here and now, but speaking to anyone concerned with such analysis. Such analysis cannot be a substitute for living together as friends; it can at best only point to such living together or arouse a desire for it . . . By speaking of "the Thou" instead of "the friend," I am trying to preserve in objective speech what cannot be preserved in objective speech; I am trying to objectify something that is incapable of being objectified. I am trying to preserve in "speaking about" what can be actual only in "speaking to." Hence I do injustice to the phenomena; I am untrue to the phenomena; I miss the concrete. While attempting to lay a foundation for genuine human communication, I preserve an incapacity for genuine human communication. (WIPP, 29)[46]

If correct, this is a quite devastating critique of Buber, insofar as the I-Thou-We relation permeates the entirety of his philosophical, psychological and theological work. At the very least, one can say that, on Strauss's account, Buber's appeal to concreteness manifests the same obscuring tendencies as do modern philosophy and modern Jewish thought more generally.

Insofar as Strauss is communicating to different audiences—both immediately and with respect to posterity—however, his statement also indicates the limitations of his own lectures. While nonphilosophers might simply take his statement as a description of modern and contemporary attempts at concreteness, potential philosophers might wonder whether they are also being directly addressed. Speaking in the first person, Strauss acknowledges (as discussed in chapter 3) that the public and general nature of his lectures necessarily have a similarly abstract character. But this, in no way, precludes the possibility of "pointing to" or "arousing the desire for" the philosophical life (which life is characterized by friendship). Put differently, for the nonphilosophers, Strauss is (objectively) speaking about the Ancients/Moderns distinction; for the potential philosophers, Strauss is attempting to arouse their philosophical desire (i.e., the "Athenian" capacity of their souls) by speaking to them. This point would have been clear enough to his Hebrew University listeners, even without Strauss's final statement to the effect that he preserves (by means of the I-Thou-We relation) the incapacity for communication in the attempt to lay a foundation for it. The addition of this final statement, in his final essay, is yet another instance of Strauss's sharpening the point in the same direction.

The modern tendency toward neutrality, objectivity, and abstraction amounts to a subsumption of political thought by science such that "[t]oday, political philosophy is in a state of decay and perhaps of putrefaction, if it has not vanished altogether" (WIPP, 17). Political philosophy is now either a directly scientific endeavor—to be undertaken by political *scientists*—or it exists as the academic ("human scientific") study of the history of political philosophy. As stated earlier, Strauss believes the historical study of political philosophy to be necessary in order to clear away the modern occlusion of the theological-political problem and the Jerusalem/Athens distinction, but it cannot serve as an adequate replacement for the genuine article. In this context, Strauss makes a somewhat enigmatic statement concerning the status of political philosophy among philosophers: "As regards the philosophers, it is sufficient to contrast the work of the four greatest philosophers of the last forty years—Bergson, Whitehead, Husserl, and Heidegger—with the work of Hermann Cohen in order to see how rapidly and thoroughly political philosophy has become discredited" (WIPP, 17).[47] Strauss here references Cohen as a political philosopher—but in what sense? Is it not the case (as discussed in chapters 1 and 2) that Cohen substitutes a concern over politics by a concern over morality (both in terms of his philosophy and in terms of his Jewish thought)? If Cohen's substitution simply amounted to an abstract move in an argument, this would be of little consequence for Strauss. He fills out the point in the third (undelivered) section of his essay in his discussion of German idealism (as part of the "second wave" of modernity). Here, Strauss notes the following: "one may very well wonder whether the separation of law and morality of which German legal philosophy was so proud, is in itself a sound suggestion" (WIPP, 52). If (1) German legal philosophy effected the separation of law and morality (with the exception of the "moral law" as construed by Kant), and (2) no less a thinker than Kant (the explicit philosophical inspiration for Cohen) bases political law on morality (thus deemphasizing the political), then (3) Cohen, as a philosopher who concerned himself with political things, becomes the beneficiary of the modern reduction of politics to a subsidiary and derivative status. Political philosophy thus construed is rightly criticized (by Heidegger) for amounting to a derivative ("ontic") mode of inquiry that fails to address the fundamental way humans exist in the world. As such, "[w]e hardly exaggerate when we say that today political philosophy does not exist any more, except as matter for burial, i.e., for historical research, or else as a theme of weak and unconvincing protestations" (WIPP, 17). I believe that the reference to political philosophy "as matter for burial, i.e., for historical research" would have been recognized by his audience at Hebrew University, because (according to Gershom Scholem in 1944) this was precisely Moritz Steinschneider's final verdict on the role of the *Wissenschaft des Judentums* movement with respect to Judaism: "'we [the *Wissenschaft* movement] have no other task but to conduct a 'proper funeral' for all that.'"[48] In referencing Scholem's usage of Steinschneider, Strauss is again tacitly drawing the comparison between modern political philosophy and modern Jewish thought (as they are illustrated together in the personage of Cohen) for potential philosophers—that is, these movements of thought are in their death throes. A less dramatic way of making this point would be to say that neither is able to adequately address the fundamental problem concerning the right way of life—that is, the theological-political problem. Insofar as this problem can be framed in terms of humanity in general, it concerns philosophy; insofar as it can be framed in terms of Judaism in particular, it concerns Jewish thought. This question returns Strauss's potentially philosophical audience to the question as to whether or not the "human/Jewish" problem is a fundamental one.

But perhaps the philosophical equation of the "Jewish problem" with the "human problem" is inappropriate. Is this not, in some sense, precisely what Enlightenment Judaism attempted to do when—confronted with the charge of particularity—it responded by touting the universal ethical content of the Jewish religion? During his discussion of the relation between "political knowledge" and "political opinion," Strauss supplies a hint: "[T]he scholarly and non-scholarly quest for political knowledge are identical in this decisive respect: their center of reference is the given political situation, and even in most cases the given political situation in the individual's own country. It is true that a botanist of Canada pays special attention to the flora of Canada. But this difference . . . has an entirely different character than the only apparently similar difference between the preoccupation of the Israeli political scientist and the Canadian political scientist. It is only when the Here and Now ceases to be the center of reference that a philosophic . . . approach to politics can emerge" (WIPP, 16). Strauss's point is that philosophical knowledge both *emerges from* the here and now and *ascends beyond* it. Philosophy, as a quest for knowledge of the whole, is never simply satisfied with the given particular situation; rather, it strives to understand what all apparently similar particulars have in common. The nonphilosopher might hear this as a further validation of the Enlightenment project of grounding the political realm in a universal ethics (thus reconciling modern philosophy and modern Jewish thought). For the nonphilosopher, the construal of this situation as a "human problem" is not itself problematic because it views the universality of the State of Israel in three decisive respects: (1) it is a continuation of the legitimate, modern desire to pursue political autonomy via the formation of a nation-state, (2) it maintains the most noble aspect of the European Jewish Enlightenment—that of grounding the particularity of the Jewish people in a universal ethics, and (3) it amounts to the only acceptable and available response to the experience of the Shoah. Put differently, if it is right for the Canadians (or Americans, or British, etc.) to concern themselves with their own country, it is right for (Israeli) Jews as well—the very particularity of national concerns would itself be a universal value.

In the light of Strauss's statement, the construal of the Jewish problem as the human problem might appear, to the potential philosopher as appropriate for an entirely different reason: the human problem, philosophically understood, is constituted precisely by the fact that particular occasional circumstances are *not* inevitably aligned with the whole in which they occur. Stated in political terms, "[t]he actualization of the best regime depends upon the coming together, on the coincidence of, things which have *a natural tendency to move away from each other* (e.g., on the coincidence of philosophy and political power); its actualization depends therefore on chance" (WIPP, 34, my emphasis; WIPP, 132). The potential philosopher might, therefore, wonder whether political knowledge consists in just this insight: given that political power and the search for wisdom follow naturally opposite trajectories,[49] nation-states succeed largely by chance circumstances. In this way (as Strauss states in his essay), modern thought's continuous "attempt[s] to be absolutely sovereign, to become the master and owner of nature, to conquer chance" (WIPP, 55), amounts to an obliviousness with respect to real political knowledge. Further, the potential philosopher might begin to doubt whether people too immersed in the political Here and Now are ever able to attain knowledge of their own times—that is, absent a knowledge of the future, and being driven by strong political passions, they cannot see how their situation relates to the whole of which it is a part. In other words, "philosophy requires a radical detachment from human concerns: man must not be absolutely at home on earth, he must be a citizen of the whole."[50]

For Strauss, genuine political philosophy—which would constitute the appropriate basis of social science—cannot adopt the neutral, value-free attitude characteristic of modern social science: "A social science that cannot speak of tyranny with the same confidence with which medicine speaks, for example, of cancer, cannot understand social phenomena as what they are" (WIPP, 95). This same impulse undergirds the far more moderate statement, in Strauss's lectures, that "if we cannot decide which of two mountains whose peaks are hidden by clouds is higher than the other, cannot we decide that a mountain is higher than a mole-hill? If we cannot decide, regarding a war between two neighboring nations, which have been fighting each other for centuries, which nation's cause is more just, cannot we decide that Jezebel's action against Naboth was inexcusable?" (WIPP, 23) The scriptural reference here is to I Kings 21:8–16, which describes Jezebel's deceitful precipitation (for her husband) of Naboth's death in order to regain ancestral land that was originally part of Jezreel, thus committing a legal transgression.[51] The nonphilosopher might recognize this passage as a statement affirming the value judgments that inevitably accompany the founding of any polity. Put differently, founders are never value-free; they must affirm decisions as at least provisionally right or wrong. Whether or not Strauss's statement is construed *simply* as a blanket affirmation of the particular policies involved in the founding of the State of Israel depends on the reflective capacity of the nonphilosophically inclined audience members. The potential philosopher might recognize that this scriptural passage deals specifically with the use of an ancestral claim for justifying the taking of Naboth's land by illegal means. Does this suggest that Strauss intends for his potentially philosophically inclined audience to perceive him as taking critical aim specifically at the formation of the State of Israel? This cannot be the case, given what we have already seen regarding Strauss's views both about Israel and about the nonparticularizing character of philosophy. Rather, potential philosophers might wonder whether the problem of political founding *as such* consists in just this type of extra- or illegal activity (given that political, or positive, laws always presuppose a founding moment as their basis [WIPP, 34]). This problem would by no means be exclusive to Israel, but it would apply to Israel as an instance of a fundamental (philosophical) problem. Finally, potential philosophers might wonder about which value judgment would be philosophically called for in deciding whether a political founding occurs in a noble or base manner.

The distinction between "noble" and "base" is, for Strauss, one of the "permanent characteristics of humanity" (WIPP, 26). It is this (and other such fundamental distinctions) that contemporary political and social science denies. The most extreme form of this "value-free" social science Strauss refers to as "historicism"—that is, the view that all value is based solely on historical context and circumstance: "The historicist . . . looks down on the permanencies in question because of their objective, common, superficial and rudimentary character: to become relevant, they would have to be completed and their completion is no longer common but historical. It was the contempt for these permanencies which permitted the most radical historicist in 1933 to submit to, or rather to welcome, as a dispensation of fate, the verdict of the least *wise* and least *moderate* part of his nation while it was in its least *wise* and least *moderate* mood, and at the same time to speak of *wisdom* and *moderation*. The biggest event of 1933 would rather seem to have proved, if such proof were necessary, that man cannot abandon the question of the good society, and that he cannot free himself from the responsibility for answering it by deferring to History or to any other power different from his own reason" (WIPP, 26–27; my emphasis). Whether or not the audience would recognize the specific references to fate (*Shicksal*), mood (*Stimmung*), and History (*Geschichte*) as categories present in Heidegger's thought would depend largely on the audience's familiarity with his writings. If one assumes that the likely candidates for attendance at Strauss's lectures were, in fact, present—for example, Martin Buber, Gershom Scholem, Yeshayahu Leibowitz, and Shlomo Pines (all of whom came from German educational backgrounds[52])—then Heidegger's terminology would likely have been recognized as such.

I believe that the terms *wisdom* and *moderation*, in this passage, exert a gravitational pull with respect to the specific audiences in question. Nonphilosophers might construe the passage to contain two significant political insights: (1) moderation in governance leads away from fanaticism and tyranny, and (2) reason, not brute passion, serves to provide such moderation. If the State of Israel was created as a solution, and alternative, to European dictatorships, it ought to adopt the opposite political characteristics of such governments. Neither excessive aggression nor impotent pacifism, but rather moderation, should be the attribute characterizing Israeli policies. In construing this passage thus, Strauss would be communicating a moral virtue to his audience. With an eye towards "What is Political Philosophy?" one ought to recall that, for Maimonides (as for Aristotle before him), moral virtue *is* seeking the mean in action. To keep one's actions in accordance with reason (instead of with the passions) might be what (in this context) nonphilosophers understand by "wisdom." This would be in keeping with Strauss's contention that Machiavelli—the pallbearer of classical political philosophy—"separates wisdom from moderation" (WIPP, 103).

Potential philosophers might wonder about Strauss's conjunction of "wisdom" and "moderation"—are these two categories fundamentally related, as nonphilosophers might assume? If not, is the attribute of "moderation" a virtue with respect to thought, action or both? Strauss certainly holds that moderation is a virtue with respect to that action which most closely appears to touch thought—that is, speech (WIPP, 32). Is moderation in speech the same as moderation in thought? For Strauss, the answer is no: "moderation is not a virtue of thought: Plato likens philosophy to divine madness . . . thought must not be moderate, but fearless" (WIPP, 32).[53] Potential philosophers might wonder about the possibility of thought and action having diametrically opposed virtues; what might this suggest about philosophy's role with respect to politics? Further, what if the most profound thought of the greatest current philosophers appears to be accompanied by dangerous political judgment? "Only a great thinker could help us in our plight," Strauss notes in a different lecture, "But here is the great trouble: the only great thinker in our time is Heidegger."[54]

If this is true—if historicism accompanies radical thought with disastrously immoderate political judgment and action—then "one is forced to *think* of the restoration of classical social science" (WIPP, 95; my emphasis) based, as it is, in classical political philosophy. What, for Strauss, is the guiding theme of classical political philosophy? It is, simply, the question concerning the best "political order, the *politeia*, the regime" (WIPP, 34).[55] "Regime," according to Strauss, "becomes the guiding theme of political thought when the derivative character or questionable character of laws has been realized. There are a number of Biblical terms which can properly be translated by 'law'; there is no Biblical equivalent to 'regime'" (WIPP, 34). The nonphilosopher might hear this as an attempt by Strauss to describe the uniqueness and originality of Athens and the theoretical contribution that it has made to Western civilization. In this way, the nonphilosopher might find the question to be applicable to concrete discussions concerning how the political order of a new state should be brought into being. The potential philosopher might wonder whether Jerusalem—as a response to the theological-political problem—forecloses the possibility of even *asking* the question concerning the best regime. If the Bible is the embodiment of divine law, the question of the best regime is already answered—or rather, it is not even raised. Differently stated, Jerusalem would always already have provided a *solution* to the fundamental problem of the best regime. Finally, if Jerusalem has already solved this problem in thought, how might *actual* cities (adopting the "Jerusalemite" standpoint) attempt to solve it?

I have noted that, on Strauss's account, the "actualization of the best regime" is, according to classical political philosophy, a product of chance (WIPP, 34). This leads Strauss into a discussion concerning the dichotomy between a "good citizen" and a "good man"; the designation "good citizen" is always relative to the standards of the given regime; the designation "good man" is not (WIPP, 35). Strauss here works into his lectures the distinction between patriotism (love of one's fatherland, the actual place of one's birth, insofar as it is one's own) and philosophy (love of the best regime insofar as it is good) (WIPP, 35): "The relation between one's own and the good finds its expression in the relation between the fatherland and the regime. In the language of classical metaphysics, the fatherland or the nation is the matter whereas the regime is the form. The classics held the view that the form is higher in dignity than the matter . . . The practical meaning of this idealism is that the good is of higher dignity than one's own, or that the best regime is a higher consideration than the fatherland. The Jewish equivalent of this relation might be said to be the relation between the Torah and Israel" (WIPP, 35–36).[56] That the final sentence of this passage does not occur in the lectures may suggest that Strauss was leaving the dual association between Torah/form and Israel/matter at the level of a hint. Although he only makes it explicit in the final essay, the point remained for careful listeners to discern. Would the nonphilosopher see the setting apart of terminology, which Strauss enacts, under the heading of the distinction between fatherland and regime? Would the nonphilosopher see that Israel is being located in the realm of "one's own"(or, in the essay, matter) rather than in the realm of "the good" (or, form)? Would the nonphilosopher (especially the political Zionist) agree that the Torah is higher in dignity than Israel? To do so would be to raise the fundamental question over the *progressivist* project of political Zionism. It would also be, in Strauss's terms, to *return* to a presupposition inherent in medieval Jewish thought. Perhaps, instead, the nonphilosopher would see Strauss as setting up a dichotomy that is intended to work together in the founding of a just State of Israel. The potential philosopher might wonder again whether the distinction between the idea of justice and the actuality of statehood is of a fundamental (rather than simply practical) sort.

My claim here is not that Strauss's message to nonphilosophers is simply insubstantial or dissimulative. Strauss, in fact, argues that the fundamental problem between the philosopher and the city lies precisely in the fact that the philosopher—insofar as he or she is human—*needs* the security and structure of the very city in which he or she lives (WIPP, 119–120). For this reason, the moral virtue of moderate action (as advocated by Strauss) does, in fact, amount to a genuine *political* insight—but not a fundamental *philosophical* insight. Strauss's message to potential philosophers is intended to point to that aspect of human being that exceeds the actual, historical, and political circumstances in which particular human beings live. Differently stated, Strauss's philosophical insight concerns both (1) the insoluble character of the theological-political problem and (2) the dynamic tension between the responses to this problem—in the forms of Jerusalem and Athens—which have given rise to Western civilization. I believe that both aspects of his insight are summed up (if only implicitly) in the final statement of the second lecture (the statement of which deals with the *zetetic* and partial nature of philosophy): "Philosophy strives for knowledge of the whole. The whole is the totality of the parts. The whole eludes us, but we know the parts: we possess partial knowledge of the parts. The knowledge which we possess is characterized by a fundamental dualism which has never been overcome. At one pole we find knowledge of homogeneity . . . At the opposite pole we find knowledge of heterogeneity, and in particular of heterogeneous ends [i.e., political knowledge] . . . As knowledge of the ends of human life, it is knowledge of what makes human life complete or whole; it is therefore knowledge of a whole. Knowledge of the ends of man implies knowledge of the human soul; and the human soul is the only part of the whole which is open to the whole and therefore more akin to the whole than anything else is. But this knowledge—the political art in the highest sense—is not knowledge of *the* whole. It seems that knowledge of the whole would have to combine somehow political knowledge in the highest sense with knowledge of homogeneity. And this combination is not at our disposal" (WIPP, 39).[57] As humans—and as searchers after wisdom—we are unable to unify the different parts (or capacities, or needs) of our soul as well as the different parts of the soul "writ large" in the form of cities. This elevated, yet still partial, relation to the whole is what constitutes the fundamental position of the citizen of Athens (i.e., the classical political philosopher) in relation to both the theological-political problem as well as to the fundamental alternative of Jerusalem. To recollect, recover, and reoriginate this distinction is the task that Strauss has set for himself in these lectures.

Having discussed Strauss's presentation of the Ancient/Moderns and the Jerusalem/Athens distinctions, I can now turn to his historical account and the place left open in it for Jewish medieval thought—in particular, the thought of Maimonides. Although not delivered at Hebrew University, it again sharpens and accentuates Strauss's point and follows in the direction set by the lectures.

Strauss's Historical Account of Political Philosophy

As a general account of both the demise of premodern thought and the rise of modern thought, Strauss's historical narrative is quite familiar (WIPP, 27–55; IPP: 81–98). One version of it might run as follows: classical political philosophy and its medieval appropriation are decisively and radically rejected by the turn toward modernity as it occurs in Machiavelli, Bacon, and Hobbes. This rejection—specifically of the questions concerning the best regime and whether happiness (understood in terms of the contemplative life) is possible for most people—opens a space for the modern scientific presumption of a universal method for delivering happiness to most people in the practical form of labor, wealth, and property. The emerging doctrine of natural rights, still justified via appeals to nature and God in the first wave of modernity (Machiavelli, Hobbes, Locke), eventually transforms into a philosophy of history in the second wave (Rousseau, Kant, Hegel) where history forms the basis for the metaphysical necessity and the epistemological access for the development of the just society. By the third wave (Nietzsche, Heidegger), history overtakes its philosophical grounding and simply becomes the movement of life itself—that is, philosophy of history transforms into historicism; what becomes evident in this transformation is that the ordering principle of human life—construed formerly under the aegis of God, nature, and chance—now shows itself to be man. The human being, in other words, becomes the one who orders the world by setting it as his or her mission to "conquer chance" (WIPP, 54–55). Nietzsche's inability to reconcile history with rationality is thus symptomatic of the breakdown of modern political philosophy (WIPP, 54–55). In recounting this narrative here, I will focus on its *transitional* moments in order to locate where and why medieval thought in general, and Maimonides in particular, is silently expressed in Strauss's essay. This allows me to better elucidate the import of this particular abstraction.

If we return to the classical question of the best regime, as explicated above, we see that it is first and foremost a philosophical question. This means that it is not the same as the question concerning one's fatherland. It can be said, however, that the former question emerges out of the experience of the latter. As Strauss notes in "On Classical Political Philosophy" (in many ways the companion piece to "What Is Political Philosophy?"), "[c]lassical political philosophy was related to political life directly, because its guiding subject was a subject of actual political controversy carried on in pre-philosophical life . . . [Classical political philosophy] is concerned primarily with the inner structure of the political community, because that inner structure is essentially the subject of such political controversy as essentially involves the danger of civil war" (WIPP, 84–85). In refusing to simply be a partisan for one or another political opinion, the classical political philosopher "is ultimately compelled to transcend not merely the dimension of common opinion, of political opinion, but the dimension of political life as such; for he is led to realize that the ultimate aim of political life cannot be reached by political life, but only by a life devoted to contemplation, to philosophy" (WIPP, 91; my emphases). However, this transcendence, characteristic of political philosophy, in no way distorts the initial frame of reference as it first develops in prephilosophical political life. As Strauss states in "What Is Political Philosophy": "the classical philosophers . . . look at political things in the perspective of the enlightened citizen or statesman. They see things clearly which the enlightened citizen or statesman do not see clearly, or do not see at all. But this has no other reason but the fact that they look further afield in the same direction as the enlightened citizen or statesman . . . Hence their political philosophy is comprehensive; it is both political theory and political skill" (WIPP, 27–28). The political philosopher, then, is the one who is removed from the immediacy of political life, but not taken away from the fundamental orientation of such a life.

In one decisive respect, therefore, the argument against Strauss's dealing with medieval thought as a separate period clearly has validity: qua history, such a periodization would be at best meaningless and at worst distorting, given that no premodern philosophy takes history as an essential basis for philosophy. Strauss clearly makes this point in "Political Philosophy and History": "Classical philosophy originally acquired the fundamental concepts of political philosophy by starting from political phenomena as they present themselves to 'the natural consciousness,' which is a pre-philosophical consciousness. These concepts can therefore be understood, and their validity can be checked, by direct reference to the phenomena as they are accessible to 'the natural consciousness.'[58] The fundamental concepts which were the final result of the philosophic efforts of classical antiquity . . . remained the basis of the philosophic efforts of the Middle Ages . . . For medieval philosophy too was 'dependent' on classical philosophy, and yet, it was not in need of the history of philosophy as an integral part of its philosophical efforts. When a medieval philosopher studied Aristotle's *Politics, e.g.*,[59] he did not engage in a historical study. The *Politics* was for him an authoritative text . . . His philosophical study was *identical* with the adequate understanding of the Aristotelian teaching . . . It is precisely that *contemporaneity of philosophic thought with its basis* which no longer exists in modern philosophy, and whose absence explains the eventual transformation of modern philosophy into an intrinsically historical philosophy" (WIPP, 75–76; my emphases). Insofar as the historical separation of medieval thought from its basis in classical philosophy implies no philosophical distortion, it *can* be treated as another expression of classical thought. Further, insofar as Strauss aims to bring his potentially philosophical audience to this awareness of premodern philosophy, he aims to make that audience *philosophically contemporaneous* with it.

Strauss provides two *related* insights that should make one cautious about holding the aforementioned view as Strauss's final word on the topic of medieval thought. The first is a seemingly programmatic statement about the transformation from foundations to successors. While it occurs in a discussion concerning the particular transition from illiterate (ancestral) societies to literate ones (with respect to divine beliefs), it exhibits an isomorphism with the relation of medieval thought to its classical founding: "[the original society] cannot know whether the fathers or grandfathers have not deviated from what the original founders meant, or have not defaced the divine message by merely human additions or subtractions . . . Only letters which have come down from the founders can make it possible for the founders to speak directly to the latest heirs."[60] Even if the medieval understanding of classical thought is adequately identical with the founders of that thought, therefore, it is still the case that medieval thought is related to its founders in the mode of *transmission*. This alone would not constitute an essential, but merely a historical, point. Is there is anything about the Middle Ages, in Strauss's view, which *would* constitute a significant difference from its classical founding?

Taken together with Strauss's second point, however, it becomes clear that medieval thought is not *in every important sense* identical with classical thought. In "Maimonides' Statement On Political Science," Strauss focuses on Maimonides's interest in the different senses of "governance." In his *Treatise on the Art of Logic*, Maimonides provides a decisive reference to classical political philosophy: "On all these things, the philosophers have many books that have been translated into Arabic, and the ones that have not been translated are perhaps even more numerous. *In these times, all this—I mean the regimes and the nomoi—have been dispensed with, and men are being governed by divine commands.*"[61] Strauss interprets this statement as an indication that the Middle Ages faced a *new* problem concerning "the effects produced upon the character of laws by the change from paganism to *revealed* religion" (WIPP, 165; my emphasis). Differently stated, the classical problematic of the best regime is not *simply* applicable to medieval thought in the way it was to antiquity; medieval thought thus must deal with a problem not present to antiquity—that is, the problem of monotheistic theocracy. The philosopher in the Middle Ages, therefore, must deal with *a form of the theological-political problem hitherto unseen*—that is, reason versus revelation (which form illuminates the Jerusalem/Athens distinction).[62] As discussed in chapter 2, Strauss sees in Maimonides a clear awareness of this new situation.

Jerusalem and Athens become radically obscured to modern thought not only because of their surface similarities (as explained in chapter 1) but, additionally, because of the character of modern thought; Jerusalem and Athens, as fundamental alternative ways of life, were both closer to each other than either is to modernity. This occlusion by modernity, has to do with a conceptual orientation and basis nowise philosophically emphasized by the premoderns—history: "Classical philosophy is 'ahistorical' insofar as it is a search for . . . the fundamental questions . . . 'History' in the strict sense belongs in the practical dimension, in the dimension that is subordinated to the theoretical. Historicizing means the forgetting of eternity. This forgetting must be understood in terms of the rejection of the classical concept of philosophy."[63]

Modern political philosophy, for Strauss, can be summarized as a continuous progression from Machiavelli to Nietzsche with the aim of replacing chance (as an ordering principle of the world) with scientific necessity and predictability. The phrase "conquering chance" occurs twice in the final lecture—that is, at the very end of the lecture and in the discussion of Machiavelli. By working back through Strauss's account, we can better understand (1) how Machiavelli functions as the transition point from classical political philosophy to modern political philosophy, and (2) how this transition point silently announces the absent figure of Maimonides (as the best representative of medieval thought). I will now trace back Strauss's account of modern political philosophy—with an eye to the transitional moments—in order to substantiate the claim that Maimonides as the central figure of Strauss's reorigination of Jerusalem and Athens in "What Is Political Philosophy?"

As the inauguration of the third wave of modernity, Nietzsche's historicism asserts that the historical movement characteristic of all life is not fundamentally rational (WIPP, 54). In this sense, he is no longer a "philosopher of history" (as were thinkers in the second wave). His thought, therefore, comes to light as the irresolvable dichotomy that modernity ultimately faces: if all life is based in historical consciousness, but history is not rational, then the modern project to conquer chance falls into the morass of romanticism—that is, the attempt to conceive life aesthetically and control life through the "horizon-forming" (WIPP, 54) productions of the "solitary creator" (WIPP, 54). This breakdown was itself the end product of the attempt at grounding the just societal order through the philosophy of history. German idealism (e.g., Kant and Hegel) sought to reconcile the juridical concept of Rousseau's "general will" with morality by showing how the "actualization of the right order" (WIPP, 53) of society (and, ultimately, the world) is the result of an "essential necessity" (WIPP, 53) detailed, if not completely predicted, by history. The philosophy of history, therefore, sought to illuminate the thoroughgoing rationality implicit in the dialectical relations between law and morality, and the individual and society. As such, the philosophy of history was *itself* a response to the bifurcation of law and morality that was implicit in Rousseau's "general will": "On the basis of Rousseau, the limitation of license is effected horizontally by the license of other men. I am just if I grant to every other man the same rights which I claim for myself, regardless of what these rights may be. The horizontal limitation is preferred to the vertical limitation because it seems to be more realistic . . . Rousseau's doctrine of the general will . . . gives way to 'formal' ethics with the result that it becomes impossible ever to establish clear substantive principles" (WIPP, 51–52).

To what was Rousseau responding with this formalistic doctrine? As the inaugural figure of the second wave, Rousseau attempted to "return from the world of modernity to pre-modern ways of thinking" (WIPP, 50). No more were the concerns over property (characteristic of Locke and Montesquieu) good enough to sustain society; Rousseau believed that there needed to be a recovery of the classical "world of virtue and the city" (WIPP, 50). This was problematic insofar as it occurred within the context of an "interpret[ation] of the classical city in the light of Hobbes' scheme" (WIPP, 50). In other words, the "right of self-preservation," as seen in Hobbes and Locke, still functioned as the basis of the Rousseauian world of virtue (WIPP, 50). Rousseau was unable to break with the liberal individual self as the fundamental *datum* of political thought. Hence, the problem of the state of nature (as prior to society) continued in much the way it had for Hobbes and Locke. Even if Locke had given the Hobbesian view a more "acceptable" look by replacing the desire for immediate self-defense with that of a stable lifestyle (i.e., property), the problem they faced remained the same: alienated, disordered individuals just desiring to stay alive constituted the primary object of reflection for the first wave of modern political philosophy.

To what was Hobbes's conception of alienated individuals driven by blind self-interest and fear of violent death in the state of nature (thus necessitating the social contract) responding? Hobbes's political philosophy was essentially a "mitigation" of Machiavelli's thought (WIPP, 47). It was a response to the "revolting character" of Machiavelli's thought when it stated that the realistic way to obtain a just society was to create "institutions with teeth in them" (WIPP, 43). If Machiavelli held that sometimes governments needed to act in a criminal fashion, Hobbes refocused the discussion onto the question of the "duties of subjects" (WIPP, 48). The "state of nature," therefore, comes to light as a doctrine concerned with taming Machiavelli's assertion that blind self-interest can only be dealt with by institutionalized violence. Put differently, if individuals can consent to being governed because they realize that it is in their best interest to do so, there will be less need for—or at least less attention focused on—institutional violence. As for Machiavelli, his doctrine occurs within the context of attempting to do away with the classical focus on ideal regimes (and other such utopias); better to concern oneself with the fatherland—which can actually be changed—than with the perfect city (which Plato's *Republic* Book 9 makes clear exists nowhere on earth): "Machiavelli consciously lowers the standards of social action. His lowering of the standards is meant to lead to a higher probability of actualization of that scheme which is constructed in accordance with the lower standards. Thus the dependence on chance is reduced: *chance will be conquered*" (WIPP, 41; my emphasis).[64]

If Machiavelli was the first thinker to break with the classical emphasis on the best regime as well as the predominance of chance (with respect to the actualization of such a regime in the world), he nonetheless (in Strauss's account) accomplished something positively noteworthy: he recognized the inherent dangers of theocratic tendencies. During Machiavelli's time, religion showed itself to be fully at home with violence and injustice: "Concern with the salvation of men's immortal souls seemed to permit, nay, to require courses of action which would have appeared to the classics, and which did appear to Machiavelli, to be inhuman and cruel: Machiavelli speaks of the pious cruelty of Ferdinand of Aragon, and by implication of the inquisition, in expelling the Marranos from Spain. *Machiavelli was the only non-Jew of his age who expressed this view. He seems to have diagnosed the great evils of religious persecution as a necessary consequence of the Christian principle, and ultimately of the Biblical principle*" (WIPP, 44; my emphasis). That Strauss does not find this to redeem Machiavelli's rejection of classical thought in no way mitigates its importance in the structure of "What Is Political Philosophy?"; for it is during this discussion that Strauss mentions, for the only time in the lecture, a non-Christian medieval thinker (by referencing his 'school'): "[Machiavelli's] critique of religion, chiefly of Biblical religion . . . is not original. It amounts to a restatement of the teaching of pagan philosophers as well as of that medieval school which goes by the name of Averroism" (WIPP, 41).[65] Machiavelli's critique of religion, Strauss suggests, is blasphemy the "charm and gracefulness" (WIPP, 41) of which would be lost to modern listeners behind "their shocking character" (WIPP, 41). "Let us keep them under the veil which he has hidden them" (WIPP, 41).[66] It is not Machiavelli's usage of propaganda that will strike modern readers as shocking; modern philosophy (as discussed earlier), in attempting to tendentiously argue for its own agenda, is quite familiar with propaganda. What is the significance of Strauss's mentioning of Machiavelli's veil? Might Machiavelli himself be a veil for someone or something in Strauss's lectures?

One can put this point differently in the following manner: Strauss mentions a non-Christian medieval thinker (as befitting the only non-Jew of his age to raise the problem concerning religious persecution) and then diverts the reader's attention away from its possible, blasphemous significance in order to speak about the two important things (radical, in themselves, in different ways): the rejection of chance in favor of attainability, and the problem of theocratic impulses. A space has thus been opened up. What might it indicate? At this point, one does well to recall two potent statements from Strauss's *Thoughts on Machiavelli*: "Machiavelli does not go to the end of the road [of his enterprise]; the last part of the road must be travelled by the reader who understands what is omitted by the writer" (TM: 34–35); "By concealing his blasphemy, Machiavelli compels the reader to think the blasphemy by himself and thus to become Machiavelli's accomplice" (TM, 50). Is Strauss taking his attentive readers up to the last part of a road on which they are expected to travel? Is he compelling his attentive readers to think Strauss's own blasphemy for themselves?

Perhaps the nonphilosopher is satisfied with the suggestion that Machiavelli, for all his immoderate ideas, did at least recognize the problem of theocratic impulses leading to immoderate practice. Perhaps he or she will take away the following message: we ought to both (1) resist and reject the extremity characteristic of theocracy (and its concomitant religious fanaticism) and (2) extend such moderation to other aspects of policy making. What will the potential philosopher understand from this all-to-brief passing over of medieval thought? Such silence might inaugurate the following inquiry: Machiavelli is the philosopher who *affirmatively* rejects theocracy but *problematically* wants to do away with the classical conception of nature, displacing chance as a constitutive and eternal feature of that order, and thus allowing for the possibility that such chance can be humanly conquered (OT, 106).[67] Is Machiavelli effectively a trapdoor for Strauss that is set to open under those who stray far enough away from nonphilosophical perception? Without mentioning the names of any specific figures, Strauss compels his listeners and readers to ask the following question: *Is there a philosopher who both rejects theocratic impulses* and *preserves the classical ordering principle of nature which includes an acknowledgement of nature's limits (i.e., of chance)?*[68]

My answer to this last question is: Maimonides. The mention of "Averroism," which at first might appear to reference specifically *Islamic* Aristotelians, in no way excludes Maimonides insofar as the character of his thought is (with respect to political philosophy) very similar to his Islamic counterparts.[69] The case for Maimonides, however, can be made in a more direct way: First, Maimonides's aforementioned statement about the insufficiency of the classical *nomoi* in the time of divine legislation suggests that he is indeed aware of the problem of theocracy/fanaticism/religious persecution. Second, he was the exemplary Jewish figure during the time when Jerusalem and Athens were most intimately exposed to each other; hence, all his writings (save, perhaps, the medical treatises) are, in one respect, a response to the Jerusalemite alternative. Finally, he did not reject the classical construal of chance. We see all these aspect of Maimonides's thought at play in the following passage from his *Guide of the Perplexed* (book 3, chapter 27):

> The Law as a whole aims at two things: the welfare of the soul and the welfare of the body. As for the welfare of the soul, it consists in the multitude's acquiring correct opinions corresponding to their respective capacity . . . As for the welfare of the body, it comes about by the improvement of their ways of living with one another. This is achieved through two things. One of them is the abolition of their wronging each other . . . The second thing consists in the acquisition by every human individual of moral qualities that are useful for life in society so that the affairs of the city may be ordered. Know that as between these two aims, one is indubitably greater in nobility, namely, the welfare of the soul—I mean the procuring of correct opinions—while the second aim—I mean the welfare of the body—is prior in nature and time . . . This [can only be attained] through a political association, it being already known that man is political by nature. His ultimate perfection is to become rational in actu, I mean to have an intellect in actu; this would consist in his knowing everything concerning all the beings that it is within the capacity of man to know in accordance with his ultimate perfection . . . [T]his noble and ultimate perfection can only be achieved after the first perfection has been achieved. For a man cannot represent to himself an intelligible even when taught to understand it and all the more cannot become aware of it of his own accord, if he is in pain, or is very hungry or is thirsty or is hot or is very cold.[70]

Viewed in the context of the above discussions of Maimonides, this passage can be understood as follows: in order to acquire the theoretical virtues constitutive of correct opinion (or, depending on the capacity of the inquirer, perhaps even knowledge or wisdom), one must first acquire the moral virtues that bring about a stable political community consisting of peace, and lack of hunger, thirst, inclement weather, and persecution. While the theoretical virtues are nobler, they need, for their very acquisition, the prior acquisition of the moral virtues. Hence, one must live in a moderate society so that one can think fundamentally. And political philosophy, as a mode of fundamental thinking, is the attempt to understand what the best political association would be given the replacement of classical *nomoi* by monotheistic law. Put differently, Maimonides preserves classical political thought and transmits it to the altered context of the Middle Ages, where he discovers that the theological-political problem has taken a specifically monotheistic form. It is thus through a partially concealed recollection of the thought of Maimonides that Strauss wants to recover the theological-political problem and reoriginate Jerusalem and Athens in the souls of his readers. And although Strauss appears not to have delivered this material to his Hebrew University audience, the dramatic, setting of the text, *as determined by the prologue*, invites the reader to still wonder about the deed of Strauss's silence over Maimonides as it occurs in the *narrative frame of Jerusalem*.

Why must Strauss present Maimonides in the mode of being hidden? Surely in Jerusalem, of all places, Maimonides would get a fair hearing. Why the need to remain at the level of gesture? One issue perhaps has to do with protecting the nonphilosophers from the truth. Paradoxically, in this situation, Machiavelli is a less controversial figure than Maimonides (especially when Strauss takes care to pass over the "shocking" character of Machiavelli's thought). After all, he was the first non-Jew to appreciate the gross injustice and inhumanity of the inquisition. A modified Machiavelli is certainly more palatable to nonphilosophers than (recalling Glatzer's letter to Strauss) a deeply "disturbing" Maimonides. And if a nonphilosopher were to associate Machiavelli with Maimonides, he or she might (in an analogous way to my aforementioned discussion) appreciate Maimonides as the preserver of tradition and critic of theocracy—both eminently decent virtues from the standpoint of the founding of Israel's identity.

The potential philosopher, who has carefully understood Strauss's remarks thus far, might wonder about just what Maimonides illuminates with respect to Jerusalem and Athens. First, no actual synthesis occurred between them; philosophy did not become more accepted in medieval Islamic and Jewish communities. Second, Maimonides did not succeed in camouflaging his thought—he continually had to justify himself to the tribunal of religious and legal authorities (most of whom understood enough of what he thought to pronounce many of his views dangerous). Finally, the reason why no actual synthesis occurred (and why Maimonides's exotericism met with only qualified success) is because when Athens confronts Jerusalem, only one of them prevails; one simply cannot "inhabit" both cities in equal measure. From the perspective of the religious and political authorities (according to Strauss's account), Maimonides's problem was simple: he was a citizen of Athens donning the outfit of Jerusalem.[71] Aimed at the understanding of potential philosophers, this point expresses the argument of the action of Strauss's lectures and essay: *the Jerusalem/Athens distinction is a fundamental, essential, perennial, philosophical problem coeval with humanity that admits of no worldly solution.* Would the nonphilosopher be able to tolerate this insight? Would the realization that the new State of Israel is a practical, but not Jewish, solution to the Jewish (and, by example, human) problem really help Israeli statesmen govern? Not being a moral virtue, such insight (according to Strauss) could only harm nonphilosophical individuals and societies; hence, it would be the height of imprudence to act as if it could be of practical utility; theoretical virtues are not immediately applicable to particular worldly events. For the nonphilosophers' sake, therefore, *even* Machiavelli is preferable to a heterodox Maimonides.

However, the philosophical recognition that Jerusalem and Athens, while irreconcilable, exert a "mutual influence" on one another gives rise to two possible responses. One might choose to affirm Jerusalem or Athens and simply ignore the other. For Strauss, this would constitute a retreat into dogmatism (be it conceptual or doctrinal). To affirm an awareness of both Jerusalem and Athens as necessary for an understanding of each requires that one be able to make the case for either side when the occasion calls for it. This willingness to argue in support of that which one opposes has the character of a sacrifice. It certainly can be argued that both Farabi and Averroes made such sacrifices at certain moments. Strauss, however, discusses this characteristic (and its concomitant mutuality), specifically with respect to Maimonides: "If he had not brought the greatest sacrifice, he could not have defended the Torah against the philosophers as admirably as he did in his Jewish books" (WIPP, 169). Consequently, to reread "What Is Political Philosophy?" in the light of the "argument of the action," would mean to see Strauss's sacrifice in bringing the fundamental distinction between Jerusalem and Athens to Jerusalem without *simply* resting in an affirmation of either side; it would mean to see Strauss in his Maimonidean capacity.

Insofar as this experience of reorigination exceeds the limits of both "speaking about" and "pointing to," is one justified in suggesting that Strauss's role both at the Hebrew University and in "What is Political Philosophy?" reflects that of the friend? Before one can begin to answer this, one needs to address a prior question: What is the ultimate accomplishment of "What Is Political Philosophy?" In my view it is something quite notable: in bringing a philosophical Maimonides—in Platonic fashion—to the *narratival* Hebrew University, Strauss has provided an illustration of what it means to be a citizen of Athens on the border of Jerusalem.

PART III

Conclusion

CHAPTER FIVE

The Transmission of Philosophy as a Way of Life

Maimonides Viewed Through a Spinozan Lens

> The first part of this art [i.e., political science] is in Aristotle's book known as the *Nicomachea*, and the second in his book known as the *Governance* [*Politics*] and also in this book of Plato's that we intend to explain since Aristotle's book on governance has not yet fallen into our hands.
>
> —Averroes, *On Plato's Republic*[1]

> Spinoza—who stood on the foundation of modern philosophy laid by Descartes and Hobbes—had carried along into the modern world, which he already found in existence, the ideal of life of the premodern (ancient-medieval) tradition[.]
>
> —Leo Strauss, "The Testament of Spinoza"[2]

Having shown both (1) how Strauss critiques modern philosophy and Jewish thought in order to recover the theological-political problem and the Jerusalem/Athens distinction (as illuminated in the thought of Maimonides) and (2) how Strauss enacts this recovery in "What Is Political Philosophy?" in the manner of a Platonic dialogue, I now owe the reader a discussion of one question still lurking in the background: How is it possible for Strauss to recover premodern thought if modern philosophy amounts to a decisive rejection of such thought? How is the thought of Maimonides at all available to Strauss? And what makes me think that Spinoza (in Strauss's terms) is a viable candidate for the transmission of Maimonides?[3]

The above epigrams serve as the contours, in the ensuing discussion, for my answer to this question. They are, to be sure, problematic statements. Regarding the first epigram, is Averroes speaking plainly about Aristotle's *Politics*? According to Strauss, Farabi may have had access to it "through the intermediary of those of his friends who knew Greek" (LSM, 278n5). If so, Averroes's decision not to comment on this text might have been "because [its] reception would have made impossible the philosophical explication of the shari'a [Law]" (LSM, 279).[4] For present purposes, this interesting debate need not be decided. What matters is this: even if Averroes is telling the truth, his statement shows that he is aware of the existence of Aristotle's text. Such awareness, even when the content of the text is lacking, supplies the possibility of entering a horizon not simply limited by the circumstances of one's own time. If Averroes is aware of Aristotle's text, he might be compelled to wonder whether there is a difference between that text and Plato's *Republic*. And insofar as this question leads to the distinction between Platonic and Aristotelian political philosophy (between one that, in Strauss's terms, actively speaks to different audiences and one that does not), it allows for the possibility of genuinely recovering Platonic political philosophy.

The second epigram is problematic for a different reason. Strauss wrote "The Testament of Spinoza" in 1932—i.e., at a time during which his relation to both the Ancients/Moderns and Jerusalem/Athens distinctions were anything but clear. Doesn't Strauss come to realize that Spinoza's thought is the precise rejection of Maimonides's thought? At the very least, this question is as yet undecided. Strauss modifies his formulation, without ultimately rejecting the substance, of his above-stated view of Spinoza in the preface to *Persecution and the Art of Writing*: "The three last essays deal with the problem [of the relation between philosophy and politics] as it appears from the writings of the two most famous Jewish medieval thinkers (Halevi and Maimonides) and of Spinoza who has been called, *not altogether wrongly*, 'the last of the medievals'" (PAW, unnumbered preface; my emphasis). Finally, Strauss's 1965 preface to *Spinoza's Critique of Religion* shows that his view remained largely the same throughout his life: "far from being a revolutionary thinker, Spinoza is only the heir of the modern revolt and the medieval tradition as well . . . [He] attempts to restore the traditional conception of contemplation: one cannot think of conquering nature if nature is the same as God. Yet Spinoza restored the dignity of speculation on the basis of modern philosophy or science, of a new understanding of 'nature'" (JPCM, 154–155).[5] That Spinoza was a modern and not an ancient is clear for Strauss; yet, Spinoza also bears a quite particular relation to premodern thought that cannot simply be denied. The very fact that Strauss ends *Persecution* with an essay on Spinoza and *not*, for example, Machiavelli or Hobbes (both extremely likely candidates for Strauss's discussion of philosophy and politics) suggests that Spinoza bears a privileged relation to premodern Jewish and Islamic thought. I claim that Spinoza's thought preserves and transmits not only the premodern construal of "the relation between philosophy and politics"—that is, the theological-political problem and the Jerusalem/Athens distinction as it occurs in Maimonides's writings—but in fact the very structure of "argument/action/argument of the action" that characterizes Platonic political philosophy.

What does this all mean for my interpretation of Strauss? This question can be posed both with respect to the Ancients/Moderns distinction and with respect to Jerusalem and Athens: If Strauss is neither (1) *simply* a pre-modern political philosopher nor (2) a modern political philosopher (or propagandist, in Rosen's terminology) if he is neither (3) a traditional Jew nor (4) a modern atheist proclaiming (however quietly) the death of God, *what is he?* In answering this question, I shall briefly consider the important work on Strauss done by Heinrich Meier and Miguel Vatter. For Meier, Strauss is a political philosopher who never wavers from his attempts to disprove revelation; he thus holds that philosophy needs the existence of revelation only insofar as that existence allows philosophers to better see the alternative to the philosophical way of life; in seeing this alternative, philosophers better understands their own way of life. For Vatter, Strauss is a political theologian insofar as he understands the Platonic return to the Cave (and, therefore, Platonic political philosophy) as a transhistorical response to revelation; for Vatter, therefore, Platonic political philosophy is validated (one might say, legitimated) by the "historical happening of divine revelation."[6] I believe that both interpretations of Strauss have great merit, but that, in their respective advocacy for political philosophy and political theology, they risk missing the forest for the trees. I thus attempt to show what a mean between Meier and Vatter's provocative readings—that is, between a modern atheist political philosopher and a political theologian—looks like. In the previous chapter, I briefly referred to this mean as Strauss's alternative construal of modernity.[7] I will return to this in my discussion of Meier and Vatter.

If Maimonides's thought stands on the border of Jerusalem and Athens, and if Spinoza's thought stands on the border of premodernity and modernity, then Strauss's thought stands (as it were) on the borders of Judaism, philosophy, and history. In making this case, the present chapter assumes the following structure: (1) a discussion of Strauss's "How to Study Spinoza's *Theologico-Political Treatise*" (within in the greater context of the whole of *Persecution and the Art of Writing*) in order to show how Spinoza's thought (for Strauss) transmits Maimonides's Platonic political philosophy into a modern context, (2) a discussion of Meier's and Vatter's interpretations, and therefore my own interpretation, of Strauss's thought, and (3) some concluding remarks as to the more general significance of Strauss's Maimonidean-Spinozan rendition of Platonic political philosophy.

The Significance of Spinoza in Strauss's *Persecution and the Art of Writing*

The familiar story about Strauss's engagement with Spinoza goes something like this: in the aforementioned 1962 autobiographical preface to his Spinoza-book, Strauss locates his initial interest in Spinoza as resulting partly from the Weimar debates between atheism, liberal theology, and neo-Orthodoxy; amid the intellectual crossfire of Cohen, Nietzsche, Rosenzweig, Barth, and Gogarten, Strauss becomes interested in "the greatest man of Jewish origin who had openly denied the truth of Judaism and had ceased to belong to the Jewish people without becoming a Christian" (JPCM, 154). In this context, (neo-)Orthodoxy would stand or fall based on whether or not Spinoza's critique of religion is correct: "Orthodoxy could only be returned to if Spinoza was wrong in every respect" (JPCM, 154). Insofar as Spinoza does not (indeed, cannot) disprove religion, however, his thought discloses a sobering truth about modern atheism—that is, that its failure to demonstrate the untruth of revelation signifies nothing so much as its own arbitrariness and capriciousness: "the last word and the ultimate justification of Spinoza's critique is the atheism from intellectual probity which overcomes orthodoxy radically by understanding it radically . . . Yet this claim . . . cannot deceive one about the fact that its basis is an act of will, of belief, and, being based on belief, is fatal to any philosophy" (JPCM, 172). Spinoza's thought, in "the self-destruction of rational philosophy" (JPCM, 172), shows the great difference between premodern rationalism (which acknowledges its own limits) and modern rationalism (which does not). This, in turn, obscures the theological-political problem and the Jerusalem/Athens distinction; it is the difference between these two conceptions of rationalism that ultimately leads Strauss back to Maimonides in *Philosophy and Law*.[8] I do not dispute the broad outlines of this narrative. Given the above statements regarding Spinoza's attempted return to premodern theoretical conceptions of God or contemplation, however, this narrative is at best qualified. While the philosophical horizon has indeed radically changed, Spinoza remains an ambiguous figure—he stands on the border of modernity. The question this chapter attempts to answer is not Is Strauss a Spinozist? but rather Can Spinoza, in Strauss's terms, serve as a transmitter of premodern thought? I believe both (1) that the answer is yes, and (2) that we have reason to believe that Strauss was aware of this.

Because my argument turns on the claim that Strauss's Spinoza preserves the tripartite scheme of "argument/action/argument of the action," I believe that a restatement and development of this scheme in Strauss's "What is Political Philosophy?" is appropriate. In construing the essay as a kind of Platonic dialogue, I emphasized two aspects concerning how it ought to be understood—that is, the speech/content and the deed/form. In the context of the audience, these two aspects in fact constitute two separate reading experiences—that is, the nonphilosophical and the potentially philosophical. I now wish to expand on these two ways of reading in order to show how they lead to the aforementioned *inter-action* between the two. It is this third, *inter-active* experience that, for Strauss, amounts to the reorigination of Jerusalem and Athens as fundamental alternatives to the theological-political problem.

The *first* experience focuses on the "what" or the content, of the argument being made. In this context, "What Is Political Philosophy?" amounts to a set of speeches concerning the problem of political philosophy and its two historical responses—premodern (classical) and modern. Construed thus, Strauss is simply (1) defining and explaining the term *political philosophy* and (2) showing the relative merits of its classical version and the pitfalls of its modern counterpart. The *second* experience focuses on the "how" or the form in which the argument is embedded. The question implicit in this reading is: what is the deed of Strauss's essay that makes manifest the aforementioned argument of the essay? In this context, "What Is Political Philosophy?" amounts to a possible theoretical restoration of political philosophy, and thus Athens, within the context of Jerusalem. Differently stated, Strauss is bringing Athens *to* Jerusalem (and thus, restoring the Jerusalem/Athens distinction) in a manner similar to Socrates, or the Athenian Stranger. The context is characterized by attentiveness to Strauss's prologue as addressing the fact that the essay has a determinate narratival context (Hebrew University) and that Strauss is speaking to different audiences simultaneously. Construed thus, the listener/reader sees Strauss providing the first experience to nonphilosophers while simultaneously raising questions about the fundamentality of the Jerusalem/Athens distinction. This experience requires a more active, attentive, and careful stance on the part of the reader.

The *third* experience (the *successful* understanding of which admits of *no* guarantee) occurs when the speech/content and the deed/form of the lectures are viewed *inter-actively*. This *inter-action* constitutes the "argument of the action" of Strauss's essay. This would be the *properly philosophical* experience of the lecture. In this context, "What Is Political Philosophy?" amounts to an actual reorigination of the Jerusalem/Athens distinction in the souls of those who have already understood the insight of the second experience. Differently stated, the properly philosophical moment of "What Is Political Philosophy?" amounts to *an undergoing of philosophy as a way of life.* This means that, in bringing Athens to Jerusalem (in the immediate context of the essay), Strauss is also bringing Jerusalem to his subsequent potentially philosophical (i.e., Athenian) readers. The distinction between Jerusalem and Athens is therefore crucial not only for Jerusalem, but for Athens as well. Strauss's statement quoted earlier (from "Progress or Return?") bears repeating: "No one can be both a philosopher and a theologian . . . [b]ut every one of us can be and ought to be one or the other, the philosopher open to the challenge of theology or the theologian open to the challenge of philosophy" (JPCM, 116). Strauss is thus calling for the potential philosopher and potential theologian to "live that conflict" (JPCM, 270). For Strauss, the philosopher will realize that Athens—as much if not more than Jerusalem—is always already in the position of having to justify itself. This means that Strauss's imperative (contained in Strauss's prologue) to "never forget Jerusalem and what it stands for" *is a philosophical imperative.* In the bringing of Athens (that which is "spoken about") together with Jerusalem (that which is "never forgotten"), the listener/reader sees the significance and "mutual influence" of the two. This "seeing" has the character of an intellectual undergoing—that is, it is not passive, but neither is it discursively or instrumentally active either. In the terminology discussed in chapter 3, this "seeing" is an experience directed toward the "mysterious whole" of Strauss's essay; and the figure whom the reader is tacitly directed toward, is Maimonides.

Having illustrated the relation between argument, action, and argument of action in Strauss's essay, readers may have noticed that each term (taken here as an experience of reading) also correlates with a specific mode of comprehension (Spinoza refers to it as a type of knowing). The speech/content-experience (the argument) involves a type of learning characterized essentially by the passive reception of information in the manner of words, signs, and images. It, therefore, correlates with the reader's capacity for *imagination.* The deed/form-experience (the action) involves a more active participation on the part of the potentially philosophical audience; that is, this experience involves being able to conceptualize the difference between the content and form (and, therefore, between the nonphilosophers and themselves). Insofar as this experience is conceptual/discursive, it correlates with the capacity for *reason.* The third, properly philosophical, experience (the argument of the action) involves an immediate comprehension that is not simply ideational but affective as well—that is, this experience is characterized both by an intuitive seeing and by an affective undergoing. Insofar as this experience is immediate and intuitive, it correlates with the capacity for *intellect/understanding.* The threefold structure of argument, action, and argument of the action finds a mirror image in the three premodern types of knowing: *imaginatio*, *ratio*, and *intellectus* (in Spinoza's terms).

To say that this triad is premodern is to immediately raise a doubt about my claim concerning Strauss's Spinozan lens: Why draw the inference to Spinoza rather than to Plato, Aristotle, Plotinus, Augustine, Farabi, Averroes, or for that matter, Maimonides? As stated above, I give the following answer: that Spinoza carries this triadic distinction into a modern context means that he effectively operates as a mode of transmission for premodern thought. In light of Strauss's claim that a radical break exists between premodern and modern thought, all the other figures would suffer the same obscure fate if there were no "modern" representative of the imagination/reason/intellect triad. One might ask, however, why Maimonides should *need* a transmitter given that his thought, as philosophy, is transhistorical. For Strauss, it is not *Maimonides* who suffers from a possible lack of comprehension—it is *we* who do. Differently stated, the very possibility of recovering the premodern triad of *imagination*, *ratio*, and *intellectus* depends on our ability to *see* an alternative to the ideology of our own conceptual horizon or historical moment. Philosophers have no need for such transmission; but philosophers are also not stuck in the cave below the natural Cave. Until we are sure that we have emerged from the second cave, we are in need of a modern link to the premodern—or differently stated, we are momentarily in need of the distinction between the premodern and the modern in order to make the ascent to the fundamental philosophical problems. Whether or not one believes Strauss to have needed a transmitter depends largely on whether or not one believes Strauss to have been a philosopher from the beginning of his career. Given the changes that accompany his successive readings of both Maimonides and Spinoza, it is not implausible to suggest that Strauss, too, benefitted from such transmission.

I hold that Spinoza is *the* Early Modern representative of this premodern triad. What about Descartes and Leibniz? While a full discussion of their thought exceeds the parameters of this study, I hold that both thinkers are in fact early instances of the modern de-emphasis of intellect/understanding in favor of reason (the most explicit formulation of which occurs in Kant's subordination of

Verstand to *Vernunft* in the *Critique of Pure Reason*). For Descartes, this de-emphasis can be seen in the need for intuition to attain epistemological grounding in the form of clear and distinct ideas (as exemplified in *Meditations on First Philosophy*). For Leibniz, it can be seen in his prioritizing of hypothetical construction over perception of actuality (as exemplified in the *Discourse on Metaphysics*).[9] Therefore, if there is a last medieval thinker who is *simultaneously* an inaugural modern, I hold, with Strauss, that it is Spinoza.

In order to bear out the suggestion of a Spinozan lens for Strauss's Maimonides, we need to consider Strauss's *Persecution an the Art of Writing* as a whole. Nowhere is Strauss's discussion of esotericism more pronounced and developed than in this collection of essays. Moreover, it is a text that accomplishes in deed that which it presents in speech. Differently stated, by observing the argument of the action of *Persecution* generally—and the Spinoza essay in particular—one learns quite a bit about how Strauss construes the argument, action, and argument of the action in Spinozan terms. Given Spinoza's place on the border of the Ancients and Moderns, my claim is that his thought both acts as a lens for viewing premodern thought as well as transmits such thought to individuals living in modernity. The best place to begin is on the surface of Strauss's text. In addition to the aforementioned preface, Introduction and title essay (all of which serve a somewhat programmatic function), *Persecution* contains three essays, each dealing with a close readings of a specific thinkers text: "The Literary Character of the *Guide for the Perplexed*" (Maimonides), "The Law of Reason in the *Kuzari*" (Judah Halevi), and "How to Study Spinoza's *Theological-Political Treatise*." If one considers the volume as a whole, Maimonides occupies the center of the text (depending on whether one includes the un-numbered preface) while Spinoza occupies the beginning (i.e., the reference to him in the preface) and the end. Each of these essays fulfills a double function: they both provide information *about* exotericism and function as examples *of* exotericism (whether in the context of a Platonic dialogue or otherwise).[10] While the present chapter cannot discuss all aspects of Strauss's text, it is not unreasonable to wonder whether one might find out something about the argument/action/argument of the action distinction by attending to this text (particularly the essays dealing with Maimonides, Halevi, and Spinoza).

These remarks, however, only deal with the overall geography of the text. Where does one find anything remotely like the distinction between *imaginatio*, *ratio*, and *intellectus* in the actual content of the text? Further, what leads me to believe that such a distinction is operative both at the level of speech and deed? In fact, on reading *Persecution*, one finds different distributions of these words—and their linguistic correlates—throughout the essays. In short, one can say that the largest distribution of words relating to *imagination* (i.e., imagination, imaginative, image) occurs in the Maimonides essay, that of *ratio* (i.e., reason, rational, irrational) in the Halevi essay, and that of *intellectus* (i.e., intellect, intellectual, understand, understanding) in the Spinoza essay.[11] Is this distribution simply an accident? It would be difficult to supply an affirmative answer to this question given that the collection in which these distributions occur is the very one most likely to supply a performance of writing between the lines. If one answers in the negative, the question then becomes how to understand the distribution. That Maimonides would be associated with imagination, for Strauss, might be explainable given Strauss's interest in the political function of the prophets (which involves different levels of imagination). That Halevi would be associated with reason, for Strauss, might be explainable given Strauss's interest Halevi as a proponent of Kalam. But why would Strauss privilege Spinoza with respect to intellect/understanding? Why, moreover, would the total number of words referencing this triad be similarly favored in his Spinoza essay?[12]

The beginning of an answer to the first question comes in a relatively straightforward manner. In 1958, on receiving David Savan's seminal essay "Spinoza and Language," Strauss writes the following to Savan: "I began my understanding of the *Ethics* with reflections on 'intuitive knowledge.'"[13] Thus, Strauss is certainly not unaware of the importance of intellect (or in the language of the *Ethics*, the "third kind of knowing") for Spinoza. The second question can be answered by implication from answering the first: if Strauss is aware of the importance of intellect for Spinoza, by definition he would have to be aware of the importance of the other two terms as well. This is so for two reasons: (1) intellectual perception necessarily refers to perception of the whole (which includes lesser modes of perception), and (2) insofar as intellect is the mode of cognition characteristic of philosophers, the question immediately arises as to what the nonphilosophical types of cognition are. I hold that Strauss's focus on this triad in Spinoza shows his awareness of the fact that this triad, while often taken for granted in premodern thought, is quite unique within the context of modern thought. Thus, Spinoza functions as a special case, for Strauss, of a modern who attempts to preserve the contemplative life (which introduces the triadic structure of presentation) in a modern context. I will discuss this further in my specific treatment of Strauss's Spinoza essay.

First, however, another perhaps more basic question might leap out at readers about these terms put forth in Spinoza's *Ethics* (E) and *Treatise on the Emendation of the Intellect* (TdIE): Why would Strauss make use of them when he focuses on the *Theological-Political Treatise* (TTP) which does not appear to emphasize them? With respect to *this* question, it is helpful to note that Strauss does acknowledge the "reasonable presumption" that Spinoza's *Ethics* is exoteric—the "geometric fashion" acting as a form of cover rather than clarity (PAW, 186). Moreover, in making the case that Spinoza is an exoteric writer, Strauss references the TdIE (he translates it as the *Treatise on the Improvement of the Understanding*) (PAW, 177). Strauss's Spinoza essay is, therefore, not simply about the TTP;[14] it is about Spinoza's thought in general. Before we turn to the role of intellect/understanding in Strauss's Spinoza essay, however, it is important to gain a sense of how imagination and reason function respectively in the Maimonides's and Halevi's essays. This will allow readers to see the unique character of the Spinoza essay more clearly both in specificity as well as within the whole of *Persecution*.

Certainly the whole of *Persecution* can be understood as an illustration of the following statement from the introduction: "The issue of traditional Judaism versus philosophy is identical with the issue of Jerusalem versus Athens" (PAW, 20). Understood thus, the entire volume amounts to a series of portraits in which different thinkers allow Jerusalem and Athens to come to light. Already this bodes well for Spinoza's thought (at least in comparison to the thought of subsequent modern thinkers) insofar as the TTP remains in proximity to Jerusalem and Athens. Maimonides's thought, in sharp contrast, was not simply in proximity to Jerusalem and Athens—it was, in a sense, constituted by Jerusalem and Athens. His utter exposure to the distinction or opposition between Jerusalem and Athens led him, in Strauss's account, to compose different books for different audiences: "We conclude: The *Mishneh Torah* [Code of Law] is primarily addressed to the general run of men, while the *Guide* is addressed to the small number of people who are able to understand by themselves" (PAW, 94).[15]

The distinction between the "general run of men" and "the small number of people who are able to understand by themselves" bears greatly on the question of the political function of prophecy and, therefore (in Strauss's Maimonides essay), on the relation between imagination and intellect. The prophet, for Strauss's Maimonides, is the one who is able to communicate truth (gained by means of intellect) in a manner in which the general run of men can comprehend; he is able to combine (theoretical) truth and (practical) presentation in the service of politics. For Strauss, this description of the prophet amounts to both the speech and the deed of Maimonides's *Guide*: "The prophet . . . is a man who not only has attained the greatest knowledge . . . but who is able to perform the highest political function. A similar combination of theoretical and political excellence is required for the *understanding* of the secret teaching of the prophets. Since the *Guide* is devoted to the interpretation of that secret teaching, Maimonides will also have imitated, in some manner or other, the way of the prophets. To be sure, the prophet is enabled to perform his political function of governing the 'people of the earth' and of teaching them by the power of his *imagination,* i.e., by his capacity of representing the truth to the vulgar by means of *images* or parables" (PAW, 90–91; my emphases). Readers should note that imagination here refers to the practical question of presentation and teaching, where intellect/understanding refers to theory or, rather, contemplation. For both the Biblical prophet and for Maimonides (in his "prophetic capacity"), imagination is the political and pedagogical bridge between the few and the many. The imaginative presentation aims at preserving peace and order, while the intellectual content of that presentation is left for the potential philosophers to discover.

While Strauss's Maimonides seems to leave little room for an overall intellectual improvement among "the general run of men," he does decisively leave the door open for individual improvement (i.e., although he is pessimistic as to the intellectual fortunes of *all* humans or *every* human, he is not similarly pessimistic about *any* human). In a discussion of the last chapter heading of the *Guide*—dealing with "the word 'wisdom'" (PAW, 89)—Strauss illustrates this potential improvement: "'wisdom,' if rightly *understood*, indicates something absolutely superior to '*image*'; a man who *understands* the word wisdom according to its true meaning has overcome, or is on the way to overcoming, his *imaginary* views" (PAW, 90; my emphasis). Correct understanding, for Strauss's Maimonides, means ascending from an imaginary view to an intellectual perception. The possibility of this kind of ascent depends largely on the capacity of the one who seeks to understand. The nonphilosopher may, in fact, believe the word "wisdom" to be synonymous with the word "image." The potential philosopher may wonder whether an image, which is always particularly spatially and temporally located, can ever even approximate wisdom (which, for the premoderns always refers to an expression of the whole). Correctly understood, wisdom has a deeper kinship, if not identity, with intellect than with imagination. For present purposes, however, it is enough to reiterate that Maimonides presents imagination and intellect as distinct modes of perception that can be coordinated for pedagogical and political ends.

The first indication one gets as to the importance of reason for Strauss's Halevi occurs in the title: "The Law of Reason in the *Kuzari*." Halevi's book tells the story of the how the king of the Khazars converted to Judaism and, ostensibly, made Judaism the official religion of his kingdom. The book is presented largely as a dialogue between the king and a Jewish scholar; as such, it imitates the actual structure of a Platonic dialogue. Given that the Jewish scholar is communicating to a king (who may or may not be philosophically inclined), one might wonder why reason is emphasized to such an extent (as opposed to imagination). What emerges from Strauss's treatment of Halevi is that reason becomes necessary in order to achieve the universally practical aims of preserving peace and order based on images of divine authority. Insofar as images are neither universal nor self-justifying, imagination is in need of reason and rational argumentation in order to compel people to obey the law: "the *rational nomoi* have not been 'invented' [in a manner akin to images] to satisfy a passing need of a particular man or group, but, being emphatically '*rational*,' they have been set up by the philosophers with a view to the unchanging needs of man as man; they are codes fixing the political or other conditions most favorable to the highest perfection of man" (PAW, 116; my emphasis). Nonphilosophers are not simply in need of *imaginative* presentation of *intellectual* truth/wisdom; they are also in need of *rational* demonstration or persuasion as to why this *imaginative* presentation is correct. Put differently, reason functions as the deed that adds force to the argument made by the imagination. The "rational deed," in this case, presents to nonphilosophers the ordered societal structure that makes comprehensible the image of divine authority on which such a structure is based. The nonphilosophical and potentially philosophical comprehension of these rational laws, of course, differs: "[The scholar] *understands* then by *rational nomoi* the sum of rules which describe the indispensible minimum of morality required for the preservation of any society" (PAW, 127; my emphasis). Insofar as the Jewish scholar is not a fanatic (and, for Strauss, he is not [PAW, 141]), he comprehends the laws as they function within the political whole rather than according to a particular image (of divinity): "It is this social, or governmental, part of the Law of *Reason* which the scholar calls the Law of *Reason* and which he identifies with the Natural Law: the *rational nomoi* which he accepts, are purely governmental. He acts as if he were blind to the non-governmental part of the Law of *Reason*, or to the aim which it is destined to serve: he deliberately disregards that non-governmental part, or its aim, which is assimilation to 'the God of Aristotle'" (PAW, 138; my emphasis).

Differently stated, the scholar puts reason in service of the image of divine authority in order to serve the governmental aspect of the laws—he explicitly connects reason to imagination; in sharp contrast, he is, in this context, silent about the connection between reason and intellect/understanding. Why? Emphasizing the ascending connection between reason and intellect might lead to replacing the image of divine authority with the "God of Aristotle." What is the "God of Aristotle"? Simply put, it is *pure activity*.[16] But pure activity—and its naturally partial instantiation in philosophers—is unable to provide a legitimate basis for either law or morals: "if the philosophers are right in their appraisal of natural morality, of morality not based on Divine revelation, natural morality is, strictly speaking, no morality at all: it is hardly distinguishable from the morality essential to the preservation of a gang of robbers . . . Halevi could find a sign for the necessity of the connection between morality and revelation in the fact that the same philosophers who denied the Divine lawgiver, denied the obligatory character of what we would call the moral law" (PAW, 140–141). For this reason, Halevi's scholar, in Strauss's account, makes the exoteric connection between imagination and reason while leaving the connection between reason and intellect open for the potential philosophers (who presumably realize that the philosophical acceptance of "the God of Aristotle" would be harmful to law and morality). "Exoteric literature," Strauss tells us (in the title essay), "presupposes that there are basic truths which would not be pronounced in public by any decent man, because they would do harm to many people who, having been hurt, would naturally be inclined to hurt in turn him who pronounces the unpleasant truths" (PAW, 36). For the sake of nonphilosophers *as well as* potential and genuine philosophers, therefore, the reasoned ascent to the understanding of "the God of Aristotle" must be kept between the lines.

As discussed earlier, Strauss by no means holds that there are no ways to lead people from a lower to a higher level of comprehension (simply that the people in question must be philosophically inclined). Concerning writing between the lines, David Janssens makes this point explicitly: "if truth consists in the persistence of certain fundamental problems [e.g., the relation of the philosopher to the city], and if philosophy consists in becoming aware of these problems, we must wonder whether the primary objective of the art of writing is not instrumental in triggering and fostering this awareness."[17] Exotericism would be a practice with the objective to foster (among those who are able) the awareness of fundamental problems. Put differently, one *can* ascend from imagination to reason. Similarly, one *can* ascend from reason to understanding. There is *never* any *guarantee* that this ascent will be successful. In addition to the question concerning the capacity of the student, such an ascent is always, to a certain extent, up to chance.

Everything said up to this point concerning the triad of imagination/reason/intellect is common knowledge about the premoderns. I have suggested, however, that, for Strauss, the Ancients/Moderns distinction is not fundamental, but rather, historical. This suggests that the thought of a "modern" philosopher (one, in any case, able to transcend the modern horizon) might similarly appreciate this triadic structure. In this case, the philosopher under consideration is Spinoza. But this judgment about the Ancients/Moderns distinction can only be made retrospectively—that is, one can only see in hindsight, after an ascent is made, that the Ancients/Moderns distinction lacks philosophical substance. The question concerning how transmission of philosophy from a premodern to a modern context happens *such that one can see the historical for what it is*—that is, the question concerning *philosophical ascent*—is an important, if not fundamental, question. For Strauss, Spinoza is the site of this question: How can transmission happen even in conditions that do not favor it?[18] In asking this question, I can now discuss Strauss's Spinoza essay.

For Strauss, in Maimonidean and Spinozan fashion, there first needs to be the *desire* for understanding: "[The modern interpreter] presupposes . . . from the very outset . . . that Spinoza's whole position as Spinoza presented it and *understood* it, is untenable . . . he lacks then the strongest incentive for attempting to *understand* Spinoza's teaching as Spinoza himself *understood* it, that incentive being the suspicion that Spinoza's teaching is *the* true teaching" (PAW, 151–152; my emphasis except for the final noun marker). This "incentive"—that is, the suspicion that Spinoza's thought is simply true—does not operate on the level of mere cognitive judgment; rather, it carries an affective force with it. Put differently, the incentive for truth is a compulsion—be it construed as Platonic *eros* (love) or Spinozan *conatus* (desire to persevere in being). Strauss repeats this (perhaps for effect) two pages later: "If we reject Spinoza's view *a limine*, we will never be able to understand him because we will lack the necessary incentive for attempting to understand him properly [i.e., as he understood himself—meaning, as true]. On the other hand, if we open our minds, if we take seriously the possibility that he was right, we can understand him" (PAW, 154). The orientation toward understanding is, therefore, the affective compulsion for seeking the truth. I have thus far been focusing on the term "incentive" in these passages; if one now views understanding in the Spinozan sense of *intelligere*—immediate intuition—one finds that Strauss is also indicating to the reader that rejection of the view based on faulty comprehension (i.e., imagination or, worse, disinclined reason) occludes the affective disposition that allows for the possibility of attaining intellect. In contrast, the affective disposition that provides a rationally *open* stance does allow for the possibility of immediate understanding (which, as it is not a temporal, discursive, and thus partial cognition, is a cognition of a whole).

In Strauss's terms, the problem philosophy faces when confronted by imagination is not nearly as insidious as the one philosophy faces when confronted by disinclined reason (e.g., the modern conceit of disimpassioned philosophical progress): "According to Spinoza, the natural obstacle to philosophy is man's imaginative and passionate life, which tries to secure itself against its breakdown by producing what Spinoza calls superstition. The alternative that confronts man by nature is then that of a superstitious account of the whole on the one hand, and of the philosophical account on the other . . . Philosophy finds itself in its natural situation as long as its account of the whole is challenged only by superstitious accounts and not yet by pseudo-philosophies. Now, it is obvious that that situation does not exist in our time" (PAW, 156). Differently stated, modern philosophy, with its emphasis on disinclined and disaffected reason, undermines its own foundations in rejecting the very possibility of the truth of the whole. This situation is what Strauss (in "What is Political Philosophy?") calls "the self-destruction of reason" by accepting a pseudo-philosophy that simply rejects truth and the possibility of cognition of the whole. Imaginative superstition is a *natural* impediment to philosophy; self-destroying pseudo-philosophy (occluding its basis in faith by adopting the myth of disinclined reason) is a second, historical impediment to philosophy. In a move analogous to Heidegger's claim about the forgetting of the forgetting of the question of being, Strauss holds that modern thought is characterized by a forgetting of the rejection of premodern thought. *This* situation Strauss refers to as the "second cave." I hold that, in Strauss's terms, Spinoza is a legitimate heir to Maimonides insofar as he seeks to preserve the contemplative life even in a historical context characterized by the rhetoric of disinclined reason.

At this point, some might suspect that I am making too much of what I take to be the hints contained in Strauss's *Persecution*. True, the reading I am giving of Strauss's views on Spinoza is unconventional when viewed in the broader context of Strauss commentary. And I am making use of his procedure of reading between the lines in order to illustrate my claim. There is nothing *prima facie* problematic with this. Strauss is quite open about the provisional and propaedeutic character of reading between the lines: "Considerations of this kind are necessarily somewhat playful. But they are not so playful as to be incompatible with the seriousness of philosophy" (LSMM, 411). That reading between the lines is not the final moment of philosophy in no way forecloses its necessary character for philosophy. In this respect, Strauss indicates not only the import of such reading for philosophy but also its limits. One sees this in Strauss's response to the epistemological criticism reading between the lines: it neither leads to complete agreement between scholars nor provides absolute interpretive certainty. But neither do alternative interpretive methods (PAW, 30; WIPP, 231). Moreover, this practice of reading needs to be understood within the context of interpretive practice more generally. In keeping with the "irretrievably occasional character"[19] of interpretation, the activity of reading between the lines is motivated by the concern with emphatically uncovering something that is currently occluded. Strauss makes a remarkable claim to this effect in his review of a book by David Grene: "today it is perhaps better thus to overstate Plato's thesis regarding the disproportion between philosophy and politics than to follow the beaten path by failing to see a problem in the relation between philosophy and politics" (WIPP, 302). The activity of interpretation, which involves reading between the lines, has the function of providing emphasis where it has hitherto been lacking. In other words, interpretation is not the same as intellection (which would amount to an exact knowledge of the material under study); it is rather a remedy to past or current obscurantism. In this vein, I claim that my reading aims at emending a one-sided (but by no means simply incorrect) reading of the place occupied by Spinoza in Strauss's thought. And given that the repetition of words is, for Strauss, not simply accidental, I have a difficult time believing that Strauss's usage of the terms "imagination," "reason" and "understanding/intellect" (in *Persecution*) are simply accidental. This is so even granting the fact that the essays comprising *Persecution* were all (in some form or other) published separately prior to their collection in Strauss's volume.

Hints aside, however, why do I conclude that Strauss *knowingly affirms* Spinoza's thought to transmit a premodern sensibility into modernity? Ironically, Strauss encounters a *zetetic* character to Spinoza's prudential treatment of philosophy and the Bible, which is analogous to Maimonides's prudential treatment of philosophy and revealed law; and as Maimonides is concerned about the "vulgarity" of certain sages, so Spinoza worries about the theologians: "Spinoza considers the teaching of the Bible partly more rational and partly less rational than that of traditional theology. In so far as it is more rational, he tries to *remind* traditional theology of a valuable heritage which it has *forgotten*; in so far as it is less rational, he indicates to the more prudent readers the precarious character of the very basis of all actual theology" (PAW, 193–194; my emphasis). As Maimonides desires to preserve Jerusalem and Athens by means of recollection, Spinoza desires to recover this premodern distinction by means of recollection. The differences between the two, on this score, appear to be historical rather than philosophical. Differently stated, the divergence between the two thinkers concerns their modes of presentation more than the content of their thought. In this context, Strauss makes a remarkable claim supporting the distinction between historical presentation and philosophical thought (as it applies to Spinoza): "[Spinoza's] plea for 'the freedom of philosophizing,' and therefore for 'the separation of philosophy from theology,' is linked to its time in the first place because the time lacked that freedom and simultaneously offered reasonable prospects for its establishment. In another age, or even in another country, Spinoza would have been compelled by his principle of caution to make entirely different proposals for the protection of philosophy, *without changing in the least his philosophical thought*" (PAW, 192; my emphasis). Simply put, the unchanging character of philosophical thought means that the problem of transmission is only a problem from the perspective of historical context; as long as there are individuals who exhibit intellectual freedom, philosophy can occur. The problem of transmission is a problem, first and foremost, relating to historical context; it leads to the more fundamental problem of whether, in a given historical context, there are any intellectually free individuals.

In summary, *Persecution* gives readers three different pictures concerning the activity of knowing. In Strauss's account, (1) Maimonides shows the function of the imagination in presenting ideas to the nonphilosophical multitude, (2) Halevi shows the function of reason in demonstrating or compelling the nonphilosophical multitude to adopt the way of life set down by the imagined presentation of ideas, and (3) Spinoza shows the deep proximity between philosophical understanding of the whole and the desire for truth (i.e., the relation between intellect and affect). In the context of the whole of *Persecution*, it is Spinoza who supplies the greatest discussion of intellect—that is, of philosophical cognition. Careful readers might wonder, at this point, what constitutes, the argument, action, and argument of the action of Strauss's *Persecution*. While this topic would itself merit a separate study, I believe I can summarize it as follows: The argument of the text deals with (as Strauss says) the relation of philosophy and politics—that is, the need for premodern philosophers to write between the lines as a result of the theological-political problem of the Middle Ages (and its responses in the forms of Jerusalem and Athens). The action of the text intends to awaken wonder in potential philosophers as to why a modern figure (who, ostensibly, is atheistic) is placed at the end of a volume of medieval and ostensibly religious thinkers. The argument of the action intends to indicate that the whole of *Persecution* consists in showing (1) the fundamentality of the theological-political problem and Jerusalem and Athens; (2) the thought of Spinoza as a mode of transmission for (and possible recovery of) premodern thought (both in terms of the triad of cognition and the triad of presentation); and (3) the awareness that the question of transmission, seen retrospectively, is ultimately not an issue for philosophy.

That Strauss accords Spinoza the pride of place in all this suggests that he believes Spinoza to have transmitted a premodern conception of philosophy to people living in modernity. For Spinoza, the philosophical life contains no more of a guarantee concerning its successful adoption than it does for Maimonides—that is, the result is largely a matter of chance. Spinoza is unmistakably clear about this point in the autobiographical account contained in his *Treatise on the Emendation of the Intellect*: "after I had considered the matter a little [i.e., whether or not to adopt the philosophical life], I . . . found that, if I devoted myself to this new plan of life, and gave up the old, I would be giving up a good by its nature uncertain [i.e., the pursuance of wealth, honor, and sensual pleasure] . . . for *one uncertain* not by its nature (for I was seeking a permanent good) but *only in respect to its attainment*."[20] As Strauss's Maimonides exists on the border of Jerusalem and Athens, Strauss's Spinoza exists on the border of premodernity and modernity.

But what *is* this premodern conception of philosophy that Strauss puts forth as Maimonides (as transmitted through Spinoza)? What, in other words, does it mean to be on the borders of Judaism, philosophy, and history? I will now discuss this in relation to the work of two important readers of Strauss who, I claim, do not read him as a "border figure."

Defending the Borders Against (but also with) Meier and Vatter

What could it mean to be a citizen of Athens on the border of Jerusalem—that is, to be a philosopher who rejects the claims of revelation but acknowledges the necessity of (and even the need for) Jerusalem? Is such a thing possible? Is there an inevitable slide into religion the moment one is "open to the challenge" of Jerusalem? If Jerusalem and Athens are ways of life, corresponding to human desires, it seems as if affirming the efficacy of one necessarily leads to denying that of the other. Even remaining indecisive—in a manner akin to Buridan's Ass—would be impossible, since the very desires in question are fundamental needs of the human soul. Either one lives a life determined by obedience to a code of justice and peace, or one lives a life determined by free human inquiry. Insofar as there is no third realm between the two, what can existence on this border actually mean?[21]

This is the fundamental thrust of Heinrich Meier's reading of Strauss as a political philosopher. To my mind, no one has argued more strongly and persuasively that Strauss *understood himself* to have *refuted* revelation by showing that, in the words of Seth Benardete, "the Athens side comprehends the Jerusalem side."[22] For Meier, Jerusalem is necessary for Athens only insofar as it "deepens the insight into the conditions of [the philosopher's] existence and the presuppositions of his happiness, and this insight in turn drives the movement of reflection onward in such a way that he is in a position to think and to affirm in its necessity the fundamental alternative that negates the philosophical life without succumbing to or falling prey to that alternative in his thinking."[23] For Meier, the fundamental alternative to Strauss's political philosophy occurs in Carl Schmitt's political theology. This (in Meier's account) is one of the reasons why their "secret dialogue" is so important for an understanding of both thinkers.[24] To Schmitt's affirmations of "authority, revelation, and obedience"[25] as fundamentally and decisively based on a leap of faith, Strauss counters with an explanation of the ideas underlying faith in revelation that is "able to trace them back to their . . . necessities and to grasp them in light of their developmental possibilities."[26] What makes Meier's interpretation of Strauss so revolutionary is his claim that Strauss both grasps (via genealogical reason) the underlying ideas of revelation and nonetheless permits revelation to stand insofar as it allows philosophy to better recognize its own activity. Thus, the exoteric presentation of philosophy is not simply a result of persecution; it is additionally a result of philosophy's own dialectical need: "Does philosophy not become a conscious way of life solely insofar as it must assert itself against an authoritative objection?"[27] While Meier does not describe it in this way, it is not (I believe) unreasonable to suggest that his reading of Strauss weds Hegelian recognition with Nietzschean genealogy, thereby producing a radically modern Strauss (albeit one, like Laurence Lampert's, that oftentimes makes use of ancient and medieval figures in order to present his philosophy).

Within the context of a manuscript and notes for Strauss's 1948 lecture (delivered at the Hartford Theological Seminary) titled "Reason and Revelation," Meier emphasizes that, for Strauss, "Philosophy and revelation are connected by the fact that each in its own way insists on truth contrary to myth."[28] It is a matter, then, of showing that revelation is somehow connected (or at least is closer than philosophy) to myth: "On the other hand, myth and revelation belong together insofar as the critical-skeptical spirit has no predominance for them. Whereas what is common to myth and philosophy is that morality possesses no predominance for them. These delimitations and classifications . . . are enough for Strauss to show that the philosophical explanation of revelation is by no means forced to pass over the 'essential difference between myth and revelation,' but, on the contrary, is able to take account of the difference if it knows how to begin correctly."[29] In critically assessing and explaining the differences between myth and revelation, philosophy shows that it is farther apart from both myth and revelation than either is from each other.

The critical space opened up between philosophy, on the one hand, and myth and revelation, on the other, concerns the status of both morality and history: "The philosophical explanation of revelation requires, in other words, that the gulf separating myth and revelation be closed by means of a genealogical reconstruction that is oriented towards morality, or that the transition from nature to historicity, the derivation of the asserted singularity from intelligible necessity, be achieved."[30] Whereas revelation attempts to trump myth through its assertion of historical uniqueness (while preserving the former's inclination toward morality), the transhistorical and contemplative character of philosophy discloses the fundamental kinship between the former two. In being able to explain and comprehend revelation, philosophy "would demonstrate its superiority not only in the determination of the limits of what is possible. Philosophy would prove at the same time to be the judge of the articulation of revelation in human reality."[31] This would amount to a rhetorical win for philosophy (in defining the grounds on which the struggle is fought) as well as a dramatic reversal of the prosecutorial character of premodern philosophy (where philosophy had always to prove itself in the court of revealed law).

Meier holds that, in a series of eleven steps, Strauss lays out the genealogy that rationally comprehends the necessary grounds, possibilities, and limitations of revelation insofar as the latter is akin to myth. According to Meier, Strauss accomplishes this by fusing together the question of revealed *law* with that of revelation *as such*. Put differently, Meier's Strauss seeks not to critique the Christian *inheritance* of revelation (which would itself amount simply to a historical critique), but the very conditions for the possibility of all revelation: "The task that [Strauss] puts to the philosopher goes beyond a genealogical reconstruction. It consists in combining two ideas . . . two kinds—the species of divine laws and the species of divine revelations—with one another in such a way that the sequence of their historical appearance can be not only followed but also (through the demonstration of the logic on which the transformation of both ideas is based) *understood*."[32] In this way, the historical uniqueness of revelation is encapsulated within a philosophical description that can account for all possible future permutations in Jerusalem as well as those that have occurred in the past. In circumscribing the possibilities and limits of revelation,[33] therefore, Meier's Strauss accomplishes the following three tasks: (1) he affirms philosophy as the less limited way of life, (2) he negates or critiques revelation as the more limited way of life, and (3) he both preserves the necessity of the struggle between philosophy and revelation as the highest struggle of humankind and as necessary for the self-recognition of philosophy. While he does nothing to destroy revelation for the masses of people who might require it, Meier's Athenian Strauss (albeit an Hegelian-Nietzschean Athenian) ultimately and clearly affirms philosophy over revelation.

It would be a tremendous mistake to assert that Miguel Vatter's reading of Strauss is as far away from Meier's as one can possibly get; in fact, Vatter's reading appears to be a direct response to Meier's. For Vatter, Strauss's thought amounts to a political theology of revelation in which (and only in which) political philosophy comes to sight. For Vatter's Strauss, the contemplative life occurs literally and straightforwardly within the context of the practical, moral-political life—*this* is the profound meaning of Strauss's statement from *Philosophy and Law* to the effect that it is only within the context of authorization by law that philosophers are free to "aristotlize": "Toward the end of *Philosophy and Law*, Strauss says that all Jewish and Arabic medieval philosophers, in spite of their professed adherence to some form of Aristotelianism, are actually Platonists because they accept 'the primacy of inquiry about the good, about the right life,' whereas Aristotle stands for the 'primacy of interest in the contemplation of that which is and in knowledge of being.' Maimonides, in particular, is secretly a Platonist because he always remained faithful to the difference between the God of Israel and the God of Aristotle . . . The freedom of the philosopher stands lower than the sovereignty of the law. Strauss's medieval Plato turns Socratic tyrannical teaching on its head."[34] The justification of philosophy before the bar of law, for Vatter's Strauss, amounts to an unproblematic affirmation of the "facticity of law over its validity."[35] Unlike Schmitt (for whom the rule of law has a substantive legitimacy in addition to its historical actuality), therefore, Strauss turns out to be the genuine political realist.

When Strauss (in the same text) holds that Platonic philosophy is "*fulfilled* in the age of belief in revelation" (PL, 132–133), Vatter understands this literally: "the validity . . . of classical political philosophy becomes a function of the situation in which philosophy comes to find itself in relation to the happening of revelation. Plato is ultimately vindicated in so far as his thought 'calls for' divine revelation, and Platonism in general (understood as a discourse which posits the existence of a sphere of absolute validity) acquires its transhistorical validity only once it is factically situated by the event of divine revelation."[36] To the extent that Platonic political philosophy ascends from the factical historical context of revelation, it simultaneously testifies to that context as ultimate: "Platonic political philosophy is a preface, an intuition, into political theology."[37] Plato's thought is not itself sufficient for the movement from philosophy to faith, but it *does* (in the language of Strauss's *Thoughts on Machiavelli*) indicate the way while leaving readers to travel the rest of the distance by themselves. Thus, Vatter generates the remarkably paradoxical conclusion that "The novelty and provocation of Strauss's return to Plato consists in uncovering Plato as *the fundamental philosophical ally of the standpoint of Jerusalem*, which rejects the project of a philosophical or scientific foundation of ethics in favor of its foundation in divine revelation as law."[38]

As the concern over the contemplative life appears to motivate Meier's interpretation, so an interestingly Kantian concern over the moral life appears to motivate Vatter's. Insofar as it emphasizes moral duty as the ground of the political, it shows a kinship with the thought of Kant. Insofar as it posits divine authority as the ground of the moral (accessible through faith), it shows a kinship with Kierkegaard and Schmitt. Picking up on Strauss's insight that the absolute legitimation of law can only be guaranteed by reference to divine authority (i.e., the realm of the religious and moral as opposed to the contemplative), Vatter holds that "The political must be affirmed (as a moral duty) because only its permanence guarantees the perdurance of the possibility of deciding in an absolute sense between good and evil."[39] If the ability to make moral decisions lies in the absolute sense between good and evil, then lawful society (which inevitably operates by means of this distinction) is grounded in divine authority: "The ground of morality [for Strauss] is faith in the justice of the divine commandment: the authentic moral viewpoint understands that a command is just in virtue of its being commanded by God and not that God commands it because it is just."[40] Almost as a mirror image to Meier's reading, Vatter's reading presents a Strauss who shows that Athens comes to light always in the space opened and legitimated by Jerusalem. It is Jerusalem that determines the fundamental possibilities of Athens, not the other way around: "it is only faith in the historical happening of divine revelation that grants validity to Platonism, where Platonism is understood as the project of philosophically posing the question concerning what is the just life. The function of Platonism is to keep this question open in every historical period, but Platonism as such can never answer it."[41] If Meier's Strauss is a paradoxically Hegelian-Nietzschean Athenian, Vatter's is an equally paradoxical Kantian-Kierkegaardian-Schmittian Jerusalemite.

What might an alternative interpretation of Strauss on Jerusalem and Athens look like? What would a Maimonidean-Spinozan Strauss who presents an alternative construal of modernity amount to? Is the relation between Jerusalem and Athens exhausted by the "either/or" formulations that Meier and Vatter have given to it? Further, is it possible to affirm both Jerusalem and Athens without either expressing undue optimism about their mutual relation or falling into the trap of attempting to synthesize them?

While neither Meier nor Vatter affirms a Strauss who is situated on the border of Jerusalem and Athens, both of them provide helpful resources that allow a "Strauss on the border" to come to sight. In my view, Meier gives due weight both to Strauss's rejection of belief in revelation as well as to his untiring attempt to philosophically comprehend Jerusalem. He also raises the figure of the "Athenian Strauss" to a level hitherto unseen in his dialectically situating philosophy's need of revelation for its own self-recognition. Vatter, in turn, is correct in emphasizing both Strauss's lifelong interest in the relation between law and justice as well as his acknowledgment that the absolute legitimation of law can only come through being based on divine authority. Put differently, Meier and Vatter help us discern the contours of the Jerusalem/Athens relation. They err, in my view, by adopting one side of the debate to the virtual exclusion of the other. This is *not* to say that one could, in Strauss's terms, be a citizen of both Jerusalem and Athens. Rather, it is to acknowledge that interest in the other city is not—from the outset—heierarchically determined.

Meier's interpretation of Strauss holds to the primacy of Athens insofar as Athens defines the terrain in which Jerusalem comes to sight. Michael Zuckert has raised the important question as to whether this construal runs the risk of begging the question insofar as it fails "to disprove that revelation is a superhuman or miraculous event."[42] Additionally, however, one might ask what Meier's reading implies about Strauss's construal of philosophy and of morality. Certainly the philosopher is not a "decent" person (in the sense of the Aristotelian gentleman), but this does not mean that he or she has no concern over morality (however complex such a concern may be). The philosopher may theoretically reject revelation, but he or she cannot simply reject morality insofar as (1) it practically provides for the very survival of the philosopher and (2) it provides the alternative answer to the question that political philosophy never ceases to ask: what is the best/most just life? But morality is grounded, for Strauss, in (the belief in) the authority of divine law. Revelation, therefore, is an inevitable feature of engaging the philosophical question of the just life. That this question preoccupies both the Athenian and the Jerusalemite means that the philosopher will have to recognize, or be open to, the importance of the religious answer *even as he or she simultaneously chooses the alternative to that answer.*

Vatter's interpretation of Strauss holds to the primacy of Jerusalem insofar as Jerusalem opens the space in which Platonic political philosophy asserts both the primacy of the city and the necessity of the philosopher returning to the Cave to educate the nonphilosopher. In making this claim, Vatter appears to assert, for Strauss, the primacy of the practical over the theoretical *as such*. Does Strauss do the same? In his Halevi essay, Strauss states that "It is only on the basis of the assumption of the superiority of practical life to contemplative life that the necessity of revelation in general, and hence the truth of a given revelation in particular can be demonstrated" (PAW, 114). The practical context—the horizon of revelation and morality—in which the philosopher finds him- or herself—is, to use Vatter's term, the *factical* situation. I am compelled, however, to ask whether there is not more than one way to live out that situation. While it is clear that Strauss provides *resources* for construing Platonic political philosophy within the horizon of revelation, it is unclear whether he simply *advocates* for those resources or not. Certainly the philosopher cannot simply rest content with a view of the world that he or she believes to be theoretically problematic.

These specific points indicate my overall concern with both Meier's and Vatter's interpretations: in emphasizing the primacy of either the theoretical or the practical life, they risk taking a reductively modern course, either in the form of a rationalism (*a la* Hegel) or a "decisionist" (*a la* Kierkegaard), that demotes the other city in advocating one's own. In this way, they fall somewhat short of Strauss's preference for love of the good over love of one's own. But Jerusalem and Athens are not only two aspects of the whole; they are also aspects of one's soul. As such, a reduction of one to the other risks obscuring the subtlety of the whole/soul which Strauss attempts to illustrate. It is one thing to affirm a form of life as one's own, and Strauss never for a moment suggests that such an affirmation is wrong; it is another thing to depreciate the value (or even, for some, the desirability) of the alternative. I do not see, in Strauss, be it a Jerusalemite or Athenian Strauss, the depreciation of the given alternative. That the success of this nonreductive relation to both Jerusalem and Athens is largely due to chance does not for a moment suggest, to Strauss, that it is an unworthy a pursuit. Whichever city one belongs to, Strauss holds to a Maimonidean line by viewing Jerusalem in terms of divine law and morality and Athens in terms of contemplation. This is the substance of Strauss's being an Athenian on the border of Jerusalem—that is, of being a philosopher "open to the challenge" of revelation. And the fact that Strauss is able to bring articulation to both Jerusalem and Athens is (I claim) a philosophical virtue present in modernity given adequate voice by Spinoza (in his *Treatise on the Emendation of the Intellect*): in adopting the philosophical form of life, Spinoza holds that one must "know as much of the nature of things as is necessary . . . to conclude rightly from it the differences, agreements and oppositions of things."[43] This nonreductive modern appropriation of premodern philosophy (which holds good for the argument, the action, and the argument of the action of a text) amounts to Strauss's presentation of Maimonides through a Spinozan lens.

At this point the reader might notice that my reading of Strauss is in close proximity to Kenneth Hart Green's presentation in his recent volume of Strauss's collected writings on Maimonides. This proximity, however, does not foreclose the possibility of differences in emphasis. At the end of his "Editor's Introduction," he too presents a nonreductive relation between Jerusalem and Athens in Strauss: "The Messiah is the hope—proclaimed as not unreasonable by Maimonides, and as a matter eminently worthy of serious consideration by Strauss—that someday this harmony may be fully achieved, while not doing away with the very fundamental tension which both acknowledged for so long as history is not yet completely redeemed" (LSM, 87). One might playfully express Green's statement by simply saying "This year in Athens, next year in Jerusalem." Green is careful to qualify his statement with respect to Strauss; the fact that Strauss considers this hope worthy of consideration, in fact, renders it at least as philosophical as religious; and certainly the question-worthiness of this hope is distinct from its blanket affirmation. However, Strauss is not simply affirmative with respect to Jerusalem and Athens—he is also very aware of the limitations and excesses of both cities as well.[44] In "Restatement of Xenophon's *Hiero*," Strauss notes that philosophy involves a "radical detachment from human beings as such" (WIPP, 122) and draws the analogy between the philosopher and the tyrant (WIPP, 122). In the same essay, Strauss also notes that sectarianism involves the overwhelming of fundamental questions by the "'subjective certainty' of a solution" (WIPP, 116). While Strauss refers to this problem within the context of dogmatic philosophy, it serves equally as well as a diagnosis of religious fanaticism. In addition to Strauss's *affirmatively* nonreductive treatment of Jerusalem and Athens, therefore, I maintain that his thought also contains a critically nonreductive treatment of the potential tyranny of philosophy and religion. Put differently, Strauss not only has a two-sided account of the theological-political problem, he also has a two-sided critique of the twin bases of political idolatry. While Strauss does not use this language, his critique of political idolatry paradoxically resembles nothing so much as Theodor Adorno's political construal of the Jewish ban on images. Although Strauss does not go as far as Adorno's statement to the effect that "[t]he mere thought of hope is a transgression against [the ban],"[45] he does indicate that the excesses of Jerusalem and Athens point to the same political problem—tyranny.[46]

Concluding Remarks

In sum, the Strauss I have tried to present here is one who (1) recollects the premodern understanding of the theological-political problem and Jerusalem and Athens, (2) appreciates the eminently philosophical stance of being a citizen of one city while remaining on the border of the other city, and (3) attempts to recover and reoriginate these two philosophical stances through practices of reading, writing, and showing how they are in fact possible today. In so doing, he has shown readers an alternative construal of modernity—one that steadfastly refuses to reduce Jerusalem, Athens, premodernity, or modernity to static and neutral Weberian "ideal types." What ultimately comes from construing Strauss in this manner? I can, at present, think of at least two things: *First*, it might lead us to question the very historical designations that we initially depend on when considering the context for a thinker's philosophy. Put differently, it may be that Strauss's overall discourse about the Ancients and the Moderns, when pursued to its conclusion, undermines that very distinction in favor of a properly philosophical perspective.[47] From this perspective, thought-worthy questions (i.e., questions found in the works of thinkers such as Plato, Spinoza, Farabi, Kant, Nietzsche, Aristotle, Heidegger, and the Biblical authors) can now be viewed in terms of the intellectual trajectories they initiated. Philosophers are, in an important respect, contemporaneous with one another rather than products simply of the historical context in which they first arise. *Second*, it presents a model for what it means to engage in a nondogmatic construal of philosophy: given the permanent relation between Jerusalem and Athens, perception of the whole would be identical with the awareness of the limitations of reason and faith. This is only a problem if we construe philosophy as, at bottom, an instrumental task rather than as a way of life. Taking philosophy in the latter sense would allow us to be more cognizant of the political whole in which philosophy, itself, occurs.

NOTES

Introduction

1. I would like to acknowledge the similarity of my conception of Strauss's "nondogmatic" philosophical practice with the conception articulated by Robert Howse in the conclusion of his 2014 *Leo Strauss: Man of Peace* (Cambridge, UK: Cambridge University Press). I thank Howse for making the uncorrected page proofs of this text available to me during the completion of my own study.
2. While there were philosophical schools in antiquity, they did not occur in or as institutions. In modernity, analogously, philosophy is most visible as an institutional discipline.
3. Concerning the relation of poetry and philosophy, Plato's use of poetry shows that the former is subordinate to the latter: "Philosophy as philosophy is unable to persuade the nonphilosophers or the multitude; it is unable to charm them. Philosophy needs, then, poetry as its supplement . . . nothing which is admirable in poetry is lost if poetry is understood as ministerial [to philosophy]" (see Leo Strauss, *The Rebirth of Classical Political Rationalism: Essays and Lectures by Leo Strauss*, ed., Thomas L. Pangle [Chicago: University of Chicago Press, 1989], 171; hereafter RCPR.) Concerning the gentleman: "The gentleman is not identical with the wise man. He is the political reflection, or imitation of the wise man. Gentlemen have this in common with the wise man, that they 'look down' on many things which are highly esteemed by the vulgar or that they are experienced in things noble and beautiful. They differ from the wise because they have a noble contempt for precision [and] because

they refuse to take cognizance of certain aspects of life" (see Leo Strauss, *Natural Right And History* [Chicago: University of Chicago Press, 1965], 142; hereafter NRH).

4. Leo Strauss, "The Spirit of Sparta or the Taste of Xenophon," *Social Research* 6.4 (1939), 535.
5. This is the significance of Glatzer's remark to Strauss (which I discuss in chapter 2) to the effect that, for the Jewish people, losing Maimonides as a believing Jew would be like depriving Judaism of its root (GS, 3, 549–550).
6. Cf. Michael Zuckert, "Straussians," in the *Cambridge Companion to Leo Strauss*, ed., Steven B. Smith (Cambridge, UK: Cambridge University Press, 2009), 263–286; Catherine and Michael Zuckert, *The Truth About Leo Strauss: Political Philosophy and American Democracy* (Chicago: University of Chicago Press, 2006). The Zuckerts make an important addition to the already established Straussian "geography" by adding the category of "Midwest Straussianism." Since it is not yet clear to me that this category has a distinct position on the question of Jerusalem and Athens, I leave it for now.
7. See, for example, Heinrich Meier, *Leo Strauss and the Theological-Political Problem*, trans., Marcus Brainard (Cambridge, UK: Cambridge University Press, 2006), 43.
8. Leora Batnitzky, *Leo Strauss and Emmanuel Levinas: Philosophy and the Politics of Revelation* (Cambridge, UK: Cambridge University Press, 2006), xxi.
9. Leo Strauss, *What Is Political Philosophy? And Other Studies* (Chicago: University of Chicago Press, 1959), 155; hereafter WIPP.
10. See, for example, Theodor Adorno, *Negative Dialectics*, trans., E. B. Ashton (New York: Continuum Books, 2003), 402.
11. Given Strauss's critique of historicism, as well as his imperative to "understand authors as they understand themselves," this approach functions sometimes as a presupposition and sometimes as an explicit theme. For an instance of the latter, see Alan Udoff, "On Leo Strauss: An Introductory Account," in *Leo Strauss' Thought: Towards a Critical Engagement*, ed. Alan Udoff (Boulder, CO: Lynne Reinner Publishers, 1991), 1–29.
12. Michael Zank, "Jewish Philosopher of the Hour?" *The Review of Politics* 71.4 (Fall 2009), 667–668.

13. I explore this issue in more detail in my "The Theological-Political Problem in Leo Strauss's Moses Mendelssohn-Writings," in the *Journal of Jewish Thought and Philosophy* 22:2 (2014), 191–215.
14. Leo Strauss and Hans-Georg Gadamer, "Correspondence Concerning *Wahrheit Und Methode*," *Independent Journal of Philosophy* 2 (1978), 6.
15. Seth Benardete's forward to Leo Strauss, *On Plato's Symposium* (Chicago: University of Chicago Press, 2001), ix.
16. I was unable to locate any transcript of Strauss's lectures. However, the Hebrew University announcement of the lectures (provided to me by Ofer Tzemach) shows that they were structured in the same manner—with the same three subheadings—as the essay "What Is Political Philosophy?" (in the book of the same name). For this reason, I believe that it is reasonable to assume that an equivalence exists.

    There exists, in the Strauss archives (Leo Strauss Papers, Box 5, Folder 18), a three-page set of Henry M. Magid's typed notes from Strauss's January 30, 1954 lecture (given at the Graduate Faculty Alumni Association of the New School for Social Research) titled "What Is Political Philosophy?" The contents of these notes loosely and schematically resemble some of the material contained in the Hebrew University lectures (and ultimately the published article).
17. I qualify my statement with the word "appears" insofar as I have not come across any account that states positively that Strauss did not give the third and final lecture (as advertised by the Hebrew University [thanks go to Ofer Tzemach for providing me with the initial advertisement of the lectures]). My claim is based on the following information: (1) there exist, in the Strauss archives and on the Strauss Center's website, two audio files that provide the first two lectures (analogous to the first two sections of "What is Political Philosophy?"), and (2) the person who introduced Strauss (at the beginning of the first lecture) mentions that Strauss will give two lectures—not three [thanks go to Nitzan Lebovic for assistance with the Hebrew of the introducer]), and (3) the original 1957 published version of "What Is Political Philosophy" (used as the basis for the Hebrew translation of the essay in the journal *Iyyun* two years before) does not

contain the third section of the essay (as the version in Strauss's volume of the same name does). Therefore, while an aura of uncertainty still hovers around my claim, I believe that there is enough justification to make use of it as a working assumption.

18. The version of "What is Political Philosophy?" published in Review of Politics (19: 3 [August 1957], 343-368) is something of a transitional text that manifests aspects of the lectures and aspects of the final version. Most importantly for the present purposes (and unlike either the lectures or the final version of the essay), it lacks Strauss's crucial first paragraph that (as I argue in chapter 3) functions as a prologue for the entire piece. A full comparision between the two published versions is beyond the scope of the present project. Since the more complete and influential one is the version in Strauss's book of the same name (published during Strauss's lifetime), it is that version that I address in this study.
19. I discovered the audio files of Strauss's lectures on the Leo Strauss Center's website very late into my project. For this reason, I am unable to give a completely comprehensive account of the differences between the lectures and the essay except for how they affect my overall argument in chapters 3 and 4 of the present work. My hope is that this inaugural treatment of the differences will lay the groundwork for subsequent research into this fascinating year in Strauss's career. My reproduction of parts of the lectures is in accordance with the principle of fair use as outlined by the Leo Strauss Estate. The audio files are available at The Leo Strauss Center website under the heading Occasional Lectures.

Chapter 1

1. Stanley Rosen, *Hermeneutics as Politics* (New Haven: Yale University Press, 1987), 17.
2. Ibid., 112.
3. Ibid., 112.
4. Ibid., 110.
5. Leo Strauss, *Jewish Philosophy and the Crisis of Modernity: Essays*

and Lectures in Modern Jewish Thought, ed. Kenneth Hart Green (Albany: State University of New York Press, 1997), 380; hereafter JPCM. See also Rosen, 112.

6. Cf. Rosen, 19–49. For a critique of Rosen's interpretation, focusing on the question of "will," with which I am sympathetic, see Christopher A. Colmo, "Reason and Revelation in the Thought of Leo Strauss," *Interpretation* 18:1 (Fall 1990), 145–160.
7. As Richard Velkley has persuasively shown in *Heidegger, Strauss, and the Premises of Philosophy: On Original Forgetting* (Chicago: University of Chicago Press, 2011), 27–42. See also, Laurence Lampert, *Leo Strauss and Nietzsche* (Chicago: University of Chicago Press, 1996), 138–141. In this respect, Gourevitch is correct in his assertion about the "cathartic" character of Strauss's emphasis on return. See Victor Gourevitch, "Philosophy and Politics II," *Review of Metaphysics* 22 (1968), 323.
8. It should be noted that Rosen modifies his thesis in this direction somewhat in "Leo Strauss and the Quarrel Between the Ancients and the Moderns"—see Stanley Rosen, *Essays in Philosophy: Ancient*, ed., Martin Black [South Bend, IN: St. Augustine's Press, 2013], 300. Finally, the focus of Rosen's reading of Strauss appears to shift from Kant to Hegel in *The Idea of Hegel's Logic* (Chicago: University of Chicago Press, 2014), 1, 51–52, 58, 63. For a critique of the "decisionist" reading of Strauss similar to my own, see chapter 3 of Robert Howse's *Leo Strauss: Man of Peace.*
9. Tertullian, *The Prescription Against Heretics*, in *Ante-Nicene Fathers: vol. 3*, edited by Alexander Roberts, James Donaldson, and A. Cleveland Coxe (Buffalo, NY: Christian Literature Publishing Co., 1885), 9.
10. Saint Augustine, *City of God*, trans. Henry Bettenson (New York: Penguin Books, 2003), part 2, book 15, chapter 1, 595.
11. Ibid., part 2, book 15, chapter 2, 596.
12. Leo Strauss to Eric Voegelin, 10.12.50 in *Faith and Political Philosophy: The Correspondence Between Leo Strauss and Eric Voegelin, 1934–1964*, trans. and ed. Peter Emberley and Barry Cooper (University Park, PA: Pennsylvania State University Press, 1993), 75; hereafter, FPP.
13. Hannah Arendt, *The Life of the Mind*, one-vol. ed. (New York: Harcourt, 1978), part 2, 84.

14. Saint Augustine, *Confessions*, trans. Henry Chadwick (Oxford, UK: Oxford University Press, 1998), 7.15, 123.
15. Ibid., 7.16, 123.
16. "Crucial" both in the sense of "important" and in the sense of "referring to the Cross."
17. Saint Augustine, *Confessions*, 7.14, 121–122.
18. Compare JPCM, 118.
19. Matthew Arnold, *Culture and Anarchy*, edited by Samuel Lipman (New Haven: Yale University Press, 1994), 108. See also Daniel Tanguay, *Leo Strauss: An Intellectual Biography*, translated by Christopher Nadon (New Haven, CT: Yale University Press, 2007), 145.
20. Ibid., 109.
21. Ibid., 87.
22. Ibid., 88. In his review of Jacob Talmon's *The Nature of Jewish History—Its Universal Significance*, Strauss cites Talmon to the effect that "the idea of 'the chosen people' as of a 'holy nation' or 'a people of priests' expresses what Matthew Arnold called the Jewish passion for right acting as distinct from the Greek passion for right seeing and thinking " (JPCM, 411). We similarly find Strauss employing the Arnoldian distinction in his preface to Isaac Husik's *Philosophical Essays*. JPCM, 257–258. See also Tanguay, 145–146.
23. In this respect, see JPCM, 377–379.
24. Leo Strauss, *Philosophy and Law: Contributions to the Understanding of Maimonides and His Predecessors*, trans. Eve Adler (Albany: State University of New York Press, 1995), 138n2; hereafter PL.
25. Lev Shestov, *Athens and Jerusalem*, trans. Bernard Martin (New York: Simon and Schuster, 1968). See also Tanguay, 145.
26. Hans Kohn, *The Idea of Nationalism: A Study in Its Origins and Background* (New Brunswick, CT: Transaction Publishers, 2005).
27. Erich Auerbach, *Mimesis: The Representation of Reality in Western Literature*, trans. Willard R. Trask (Princeton, NJ: Princeton University Press, 2003).
28. Shestov, 59. Cf. Tanguay, 145.
29. Ibid., 442.

30. Ibid., 443.
31. Kohn, 31–32.
32. Auerbach, 23.
33. Kohn, 60.
34. See JPCM, 411.
35. Concerning Augustine in general, and *City of God* in particular, see Strauss's 1958 Kant Seminar (particularly, May 7, lecture 12). Cf. NRH, 144; JPCM, 335; Leo Strauss, *Persecution and the Art of Writing* (Chicago: University of Chicago, 1988), 35; GS, 3: 240, 439. Additionally, Timothy Burns related to me a discussion with Ernest Fortin where, on being asked about whether Strauss was familiar with Augustine, Fortin replied that he absolutely was. I thank Burns for sharing this information with me.
36. It would not be unreasonable to wonder whether the formulation of Strauss's 1924 question concerning the relation of Jews to Europe—"What Has Europe to Do with Us as Jews!"—is related to Tertullian's famous question. See Leo Strauss "On the Argument with European Science," in *Leo Strauss: The Early Writings (1921–1932)*, trans. and ed. Michael Zank (Albany: State University of New York Press, 2002), 108; hereafter EW. Regarding Strauss's more general familiarity with Tertullian, see Leo Strauss, *Spinoza's Critique of Religion*, trans., E. M. Sinclair (Chicago: University of Chicago Press, 1997), 277n30; hereafter, SCR.
37. Although, as Rémi Brague points out, he could not have been familiar with it at the time of his first formulation of the distinction (in the 1940s). See Rémi Brague, "Athens, Jerusalem, Mecca: Leo Strauss's 'Muslim' Understanding of Greek Philosophy," *Poetics Today* 19.2 (1998), 236.
38. Leo Strauss, "Farabi's Plato," in *Louis Ginzberg Jubilee Volume* (New York: American Academy for Jewish Research, 1945), 377; hereafter FP. See also Alfarabi, *The Political Regime*, trans. Fauzi M. Najjar in *Medieval Political Philosophy*, ed. Ralph Lerner and Muhsin Mahdi (Ithaca, NY: Cornell University Press, 1963), 37.
39. See David Janssens, "The Philosopher's Ancient Clothes: Leo Strauss on Philosophy and Poetry," in *Modernity and What Has*

Been Lost: Considerations on the Legacy of Leo Strauss, ed. Paweł Armada and Arkadiusz Górnisiewicz (South Bend, IN: St. Augustine's Press, 2011), 71.

40. See in this context Alan Udoff, "'After Such Knowledge, What Forgiveness?' On Jankélévitch and the Question of Repentance," in *Vladimir Jankélévitch and the Question of Forgiveness*, ed. Alan Udoff (Lanham, MD: Lexington Books, 2013), 192–193.
41. At this point, readers might wonder whether any relation exists between Strauss's Jerusalem/Athens distinction and Nietzsche's Apollonian/Dionysian distinction as presented in *The Birth of Tragedy*. While a full treatment of this issue would require nothing less than a separate monograph, I can at least outline the relevant questions for such a project:
(1) Is the form-giving, image-making, dream-creating capacity of the Apollonian equivalent to the religious narrative underpinning the order-bestowing capacity of Jerusalem? (2) Is the intoxicating, self-dissolution characteristic of the Dionysian equivalent to the divine madness and intellectual freedom characteristic of Athens? (3) Is the Apollonian/Dionysian distinction legitimately thought beyond its aesthetic contours in Nietzsche—that is, do the two terms express or illustrate fundamental ways of life? And (4) is Jerusalem/Athens a tragic distinction? My initial thought is this: even if (1) and (2) are the case (which I doubt), (3) and (4) would not hold. Differently stated, the Jerusalem/Athens distinction describes capacities and ways of life that exceed the construal of life as a work of art. At any rate, for Nietzsche, the Apollonian/Dionysian distinction arises prior to the advent of Socrates/Socratism—it is therefore "pre-Socratic." That Socrates is the figure who, in Nietzsche's view, attempts to do away with this distinction and replace it with a rational and scientific practice leads Strauss to claim that Nietzsche's treatment of Socrates (in *The Birth of Tragedy)* seems to assume (in contradistinction to al-Razi's suggestion) that the early and later Socrates are involved in the same activity (see Leo Strauss, *Socrates and Aristophanes* [Chicago: University of Chicago Press, 1966], 8, 314; hereafter, SA).
42. Insofar as "Jerusalem" and "Athens" refer to potencies of the human soul—and not to historical or geographical places—it seems as if (qua language) they could be interchangeable with

other names. This interchangeable character, however, would always have to be justified in the tribunal of common recognizability. For this reason, it does not seem, for example, that terms could be interchangeable with each other.

43. Leo Strauss, "Some Remarks on the Political Science of Maimonides and Farabi," trans. Robert Bartlett, in *Leo Strauss on Maimonides: The Complete Writings*, ed., Kenneth Hart Green (Chicago: University of Chicago Press, 2013), 305; hereafter, LSM. On the philosopher's wandering in the desert, see Judah Halevi, *Kuzari*, 3.37 (the central paragraph of the central section of the text). For a modern analogue to this, see Jean-Jacques Rousseau, *The Reveries of the Solitary Walker*, trans., Charles E. Butterworth (Indianapolis, IN: Hackett Publishing Company, 1992), 95.
44. It would be tempting, for the purposes of alluding to the dangers of religious fanaticism, to suggest that, while Athens has a center and a periphery, Jerusalem has (so to speak) a center that is everywhere and a periphery that is nowhere. However, for Strauss, both Jerusalem and Athens have a center and a periphery. Both Socrates and Jeremiah are located at the respective peripheries of their metaphorical cities. This is not to suggest, however, that the *relation between* center and periphery looks the same in each city—compare Cicero, *Laws*, iii. 19 (Marcus Tullius Cicero, *On the Republic and on the Laws*, trans., David Fott [Ithaca, NY: Cornell University Press, 2014], 188).
45. In this respect, compare Strauss's discussion concerning the need to go through the stage in which justice appears identical with "citizen-morality" (NRH: 150n24) and his discussion of the "spiritual hell" that Halevi went through before he left philosophy and "returned to the Jewish fold" (PAW, 109).
46. This, in turn, raises another interesting issue (which cannot be pursued in the present context): if the very distinction between Jerusalem and Athens were to be acknowledged as a legitimate distinction only by Athens, then—viewed from the standpoint of the entirety of the theological-political problem—"Jerusalem and Athens" would function (in the terminology of Seth Benardete) as an indeterminate dyad.
47. While it is true that (for Strauss) Platonic political philosophy begins and moves in the realm of *doxa* (opinion), it is not for

that reason simply irrational. In its attempt to replace opinion with knowledge, it operates as rational *zeteticism*. In its telling of noble lies, its operates as rational exotericism.

48. Warren Zev Harvey, "The Seventy Languages of Shem and Japeth," unpublished presentation in Bologna, June 2009.
49. In addition to Tanguay and Velkley, see Adi Armon, "Just Before the 'Straussians': The Development of Leo Strauss's Political Thought from the Weimar Republic to America," *New German Critique* 37. 3 (Fall 2010), 173–198; Leora Batnitzky, *Leo Strauss and Emmanuel Levinas: Philosophy and the Politics of Revelation* (Cambridge, UK: Cambridge University Press, 2006); David Janssens, *Between Athens and Jerusalem: Philosophy, Prophecy, and Politics in Leo Strauss's Early Thought* (Albany: State University of New York Press, 2008); Laurence Lampert, "Strauss's Recovery of Esotericism," in *The Cambridge Companion to Leo Strauss*, ed. Steven B. Smith (Cambridge, UK: Cambridge University Press, 2009), 63–92; Benjamin Lazier, *God Interrupted: Heresy and the European Imagination Between the World Wars* (Princeton, NJ: Princeton University Press, 2008); Heinrich Meier, "How Strauss Became Strauss," in *Enlightening Revolutions: Essays in Honor of Ralph Lerner*, ed. Svetozar Minkov (Lanham, MD: Lexington Books, 2006), 363–382; Heinrich Meier, *Leo Strauss and the Theological-Political Problem*, trans. Marcus Brainard (Cambridge, UK: Cambridge University Press, 2006); Samuel Moyn, "From Experience to Law: Leo Strauss and the Weimar Crisis of the Philosophy of Religion," *History of European Ideas*, 33, 2007, 174–194; Jerry Muller, "Leo Strauss: The Political Philosopher as a Young Zionist," *Jewish Social Studies* 17: 1, Fall 2010, 88–115; Eugene R. Sheppard, *Leo Strauss and the Politics of Exile: The Making of a Political Philosopher* (Waltham, MA: Brandeis University Press, 2006); Steven Benjamin Smith, "Leo Strauss's Discovery of the Theologico-Political Problem," *European Journal of Political Theory* 12:4 (October 2013), 388–408; Steven B. Smith, *Reading Leo Strauss: Politics, Philosophy, Judaism* (Chicago: University of Chicago Press, 2006); Benjamin Aldes Wurgaft, "Culture And Law in Weimar Jewish Medievalism: Leo Strauss's Critique of Julius Guttmann, *Modern Intellectual History* 11:1 (2014), 119–146; Martin D. Yaffe, "Interpretive Essay" in *Leo Strauss on Moses Mendelssohn*, trans., ed., and

with an interpretive essay by Martin D. Yaffe (Chicago: University of Chicago Press, 2012), hereafter LSOMM; Michael Zank, "Introduction" to EW.

50. See Moyn, 178–90 and Sheppard, 13, 26. For an account of the ambivalence that the early Strauss felt over this movement from his Orthodox upbringing to philosophy, see Hans Jonas, *Memoirs*, trans. Krishna Wilson, ed. Christian Wise (Waltham, MA: Brandeis University Press, 2008), 49. One might assume that Hannah Arendt's 1954 remark to Karl Jaspers that Strauss "is a convinced orthodox atheist" refers to precisely this movement and conflict. See *Hannah Arendt-Karl Jaspers—Correpsondence: 1926–1969*, trans. Robert and Rita Kimber, ed. Lothar Kohler and Hans Saner (New York: Harcourt, Brace & Company, 1992), 244.
51. Rémi Brague, "Athens, Jerusalem, Mecca," 246.
52. Hermann Cohen, *Religion of Reason Out of the Sources of Judaism*, trans. Simon Kaplan (Atlanta: Scholars Press, 1995); hereafter, ROR.
53. See Sheppard, 31 and 33.
54. "More Early Writings by Leo Strauss from the *Jüudische Wochenzeitung füur Cassel, Hessen und Waldeck*," ed. Thomas Meyer, trans. Michael Zank, *Interpretation* 39.2, 2012, 116–117; hereafter MEW.
55. GS, 3, 414; Velkley, 47.
56. Ibid.
57. Meier, 7, 9.
58. This despite the fact that Lessing may have meant his reticence for Mendelssohn's own good.
59. Concerning the relation of neo-Orthodoxy in this context, Strauss notes that "The Judaism to which [Rosenzweig] returned was not identical with the Judaism of the age prior to Moses Mendelssohn" (JPCM, 151).
60. Ahad Ha'am, *Selected Essays of Ahad Ha-'am*, trans. Leon Simon (New York: The Jewish Publication Society of America, 1962), 187 and 194.
61. Achad ha'Am, *The Supremacy of Reason (To the Memory of Maimonides)*, trans. Leon Simon (London: The Zionist, 1917), 1–48. See also Aryeh Leo Motzkin, "On the Interpretation of Maimonides," *Independent Journal of Philosophy* 2 (1978), 39–46;

Warren Zev Harvey, "The Return of Mamonideanism," *Jewish Social Studies* 42: 3–4 (Summer-Autumn 1980), 251.

62. See Hermann Cohen, *Ethics of Maimonides*, trans. Almut Sh. Bruckstein (Madison, WI: University of Wisconsin Press, 2004), 61–62. Cf. PL, 21, 79.

63. Immanuel Kant, *Critique of Pure Reason*, trans. and ed. Paul Guyer and Allen W. Wood (Cambridge, UK: Cambridge University Press, 1997), 396 (A314/B370). For Strauss's critiques of this interpretive principle, see WIPP, 66–67, 76 and PAW, 143.

64. One gets a sense of Strauss's conflicted philosophical attitude toward Cohen if one considers together Strauss's statement that his study of Maimonides has occurred "in the course of about twenty-five years of frequently interrupted but never abandoned study," with his statement (in the introduction to Cohen's *Religion of Reason*) that "it is more than forty years since I last studied or even read the *Religion of Reason*, and within the last twenty years I have only from time to time read or looked into some of his other writings." See, respectively, Strauss's "How to Begin to Study *The Guide of the Perplexed*," in Moses Maimonides, *The Guide of the Perplexed: Volume One*, trans. Shlomo Pines (Chicago: University of Chicago Press, 1963), xi, and JPCM, 267.

65. Hartwig Wiedebach (in personal correspondence) provides a qualification to this statement by holding that Cohen's discussion of God's virtues refers by implication to prophetic mission.

66. He does, however, refer to Jeremiah 29 in select places. See Hermann Cohen, *Werke: Band 15—Kleinere Schriften 4: 1907–1912*, ed., Hartwig Wiedebach (Hildescheim, Germany: Georg Olms Verlag, 2009), 145, 611; Hermann Cohen, *Werke: Band 17—Kleinere Schriften 6: 1916–1918*, ed., Hartwig Wiederbach (Hildesheim, Germany: Georg Olms Verlag, 2002), 123, 251. Readers should note that the final reference in 17:6 occurs in Cohen's "Antwort auf Martin Buber (1916)."

67. Martin Buber, *On the Bible: Eighteen Studies*, ed. Nahum N. Glatzer (Syracuse, NY: Syracuse University Press, 2000), 156; hereafter, OTB.

68. This is a lacuna in Susan Orr's otherwise wonderful treatment of Strauss's 1967 lecture. See Susan Orr, *Jerusalem and Athens:*

Reason and Revelation in the Works of Leo Strauss (Lanham, MD: Rowman and Littlefield, 1995).

69. Martin Buber and Hermann Cohen, "A Debate on Zionism and Messianism," trans. M. Gelber and S. Weinstein, in *The Jew in the Modern World: A Documentary History*, ed. Paul Mendes-Flohr and Jehuda Reinharz (Oxford, UK: Oxford University Press, 2011), 651–655; hereafter, JMW.
70. Martin Buber, *Between Man and Man*, trans. Ronald Gregor-Smith (New York: Routledge, 2004), 162. See also Martin Buber, "Autobiographical Fragments," in *The Philosophy of Martin Buber*, ed., Paul Arthur Schlipp and Maurice Friedman (La Salle, IL: Open Court, 1967), 12.
71. Hermann Cohen, *Reason and Hope: Selections from the Jewish Writings of Hermann Cohen*, trans. Eva Jospe (Cincinnati, OH: HUC Press, 1993), 87.
72. Immanuel Kant, "Perpetual Peace: A Philosophical Sketch," in Immanuel Kant, *Political Writings*, trans. H. B. Nisbett, ed. Hans Reiss (Cambridge: Cambridge University Press, 1991), 115.
73. Leo Strauss, Seminar on Kant, 1958, lecture 11 (May 5).
74. I am grateful to the University of Chicago Hillel, as well as its then-rabbi Daniel Libenson, for allowing me access to the recording of "An Evening with Martin Buber."

Chapter 2

1. Gotthold Ephraim Lessing, "Nathan the Wise," trans. Bayard Quincy Morgan in *Nathan the Wise, Minna Von Barnhelm, and Other Plays and Writings*, ed., Peter Demetz (New York: Continuum, 1995, 181.
2. LSM, 425–426. Cf. Ralph Lerner, "Dispersal by Design," in *Reason, Faith, and Politics: Essays in Honor of Werner J. Dannhauser*, ed. Arthur M. Melzer and Robert P. Kraynak (Lanham, MD: Lexington Books, 2008), 39.
3. The question of "access," "transferability," or "transmissibility" will be dealt with in chapter 5. Mentioning it here suffices as a "hinge" between Strauss's critique of modern Jewish thought and philosophy (as discussed chapter 1) and the recovery of

Maimonides (to be discussed in this chapter). In this light, the above epigrams are meant to highlight that Strauss's Maimonides understood precisely what the modern Jewish thinkers (as discussed in chapter 1) did not: the significance of the theological-political problem.

4. Leo Strauss GS, 3, 549–550 as cited in LSTPP: 23–24n32; translation modified.
5. See, in this context, Leora Batnitzky, *How Judaism Became a Religion* (Princeton, NJ: Princeton University Press, 2001).
6. Moyn, 190–194.
7. A possible qualification to this statement might be the fact that Strauss only appears to mention Rawidowicz in his correspondence rather than engage his work in publications or lectures (see GS, 3, 436, 485, 522, 524–525, 711, 721. Regarding Cohen, see LSM: 174–222, JPCM, 267–282 (esp. 270–272, 274, 278), and the entirety of PL; for Husik, see JPCM: 235–264 (esp. 249–253); for Wolfson, see LSM: 101, 115, 405–406; for Baron, see LSM: 355n46 and 48; for Altmann, see LSM: 347n15, 357n56, 372n95.
8. Leopold Zunz, "On Rabbinic Literature," trans., A. Schwartz, in *The Jew in the Modern World: A Documentary History,* 3rd ed., ed., Paul Mendes-Flohr and Judah Reinharz (Oxford, UK: Oxford University Press, 2011), 247.
9. Leo Strauss, *Thoughts on Machiavelli* (Chicago: University of Chicago Press, 1984), 173; hereafter, TM.
10. Martina Urban, "Persecution and the Art of Representation: Schocken's Maimonides Anthologies of the 1930s," in *Maimonides and His Heritage*, ed., Idit Dobbs-Weinstein, Lenn E. Goodman, and James Allan Grady (Albany: State University of New York Press, 2009), 154. The figure and thought of Maimonides, therefore, was a privileged site of battle and resistance in pre–World War II German intellectual circles. Since the present section of this chapter constitutes an exercise in intellectual history, mention should be made of three other similar intellectual battle sites—Plato, Hobbes, and Spinoza. All four sites help us appreciate (at the very least) Strauss's originality within, as well as distinction from, his intellectual climate. Regarding Plato, see Simona Forti, "The Biopolitics of Souls: Racism, Nazism, and Plato," *Political Theory* 34. 9 (2006), 9–32;

for Hobbes, see John P. McCormick, "Fear, Technology, and the State: Carl Schmitt, Leo Strauss, and the Revival of Hobbes in Weimar an National Socialist Germany," *Political Theory*22.4 (1994), 619–652, and Lazier, 111–132; for Spinoza, see Michael A. Rosenthal, "Spinoza and the Crisis of Liberalism in Weimar Germany," *Hebraic Political Studies* 3. 1 (Winter 2008), 94–112, and Lazier, 67–110.

11. Urban, 154.
12. Ibid., 155.
13. Ibid., 157–159.
14. Ibid.
15. Ibid., 171. I do not claim that Strauss published *Philosophy and Law* with Schocken for reasons reducible to the contexts supplied by Schocken or by the modern Maimonides commentators. Meier may well be correct, that is, that it was not Strauss's intention to publish his text with Schocken Verlag in order to celebrate the Maimonides anniversary (see "How Strauss Became Strauss," 364). It nonetheless remains the case that Strauss was aware of the importance of Maimonides for the Jewish community (as his aforementioned reference to Glatzer's remark makes clear) and took this into account, and even addressed this issue in subsequent writings on Maimonides (LSM, 541).
16. Harry Wolfson, "Maimonides and Halevi: A Study in Typical Jewish Attitudes Towards Greek Philosophy in the Middle Ages," *The Jewish Quarterly Review*, New Series, 2.3 (January 1912), 306.
17. Ibid., 307.
18. Ibid., 314.
19. Ibid., 315.
20. Julius Guttmann, *Philosophies of Judaism: The History of Jewish Philosophy from Biblical Times to Franz Rosenzweig*, trans., David W. Silverman (New York: Holt, Reinhart, and Winston, 1964), 182.
21. Isaac Husik, *A History of Mediaeval Jewish Philosophy* (New York: Dover Publications, 2002), 236–311.
22. Cohen, *Ethics Of Maimonides* 23; translation modified. See also, Hermann Cohen, *Werke: Band 15: Kleinere Schriften IV—1907–1912,* ed., Hartwig Wiedebach (Hildescheim, Germany: George Olms Verlag, 2009).

23. Ibid., 52.
24. Ibid., 53; translation modified.
25. Ibid., 50.
26. Ibid., 192; translation modified.
27. Alexander Altmann, "Maimonides' *Guide of the Perplexed*," trans. Edith Erlich and Leonard H. Ehrlich in Alexander Altmann, *The Meaning of Jewish Existence: Theological Essays 1930–1939*, ed., Alfred L. Ivry (Waltham, MA: Brandeis University Press, 1991), 67.
28. Ibid., 70.
29. Salo W. Baron, "The Historical Outlook of Maimonides," *Proceedings of the American Academy for Jewish Research* 6 (1934–1935), 5–113.
30. Ibid., 12.
31. See Kenneth Hart Green, *Leo Strauss and the Rediscovery of Maimonides* (Chicago: University of Chicago Press, 2013), 52.
32. Guttmann, 152.
33. Ibid., 153.
34. Readers should recall that the first four chapters of Maimonides's *Eight Chapters* are, in large measure, a recapitulation (in a vastly different context) of material from Aristotle's *Nicomachean Ethics.* See Maimonides, *Ethical Writings of Maimonides*, ed. Raymond L. Weiss and Charles Butterworth (New York: Dover Publications, 1975), 60–74.
35. Husik, 236.
36. Ibid., 239.
37. Ibid., 300; my emphasis. Paradoxically, despite Huisk's critique of idealizing interpretation (as Strauss reads him [JPCM, 256]), he still *appears* to be a practitioner of it.
38. Simon Rawidowicz, "On Interpretation," *Proceedings of the American Academy for Jewish Research* 26 (1957), 85.
39. Ibid., 101.
40. Ibid., 101. For a nearly identical stance, regarding Maimonides's thought, see Isadore Twersky, *Introduction to the Code of Maimonides (Mishneh Torah)*, (New Haven, CT: Yale University Press: 1980), 96.
41. The following recapitulation, therefore, comes from Brague, "Leo Strauss and Maimonides," 93–97.

42. Meier, "How Strauss Became Strauss," 364.
43. In this context, mention should also be made of Strauss's second companion essay on Abravanel (from 1937), "Abravanel's Critique of Monarchy," which also deals interestingly with Maimonides. See *Reorientation: Leo Strauss in the 1930s,* ed. Martin Yaffe and Richard Ruderman (New York: Palgrave Macmillan, 2015), 267–268.
44. Meier, 367–368.
45. Ibid., 366.
46. Ibid., 369. For the January 20, 1938 letter to Klein comparing Maimonides and Nietzsche, see GS, 3, 545; Laurence Lampert, "Strauss's Recovery of Esotericism," in *Cambridge Companion*, 63.
47. Kenneth Hart Green argues that the difference between Strauss's second and third periods is primarily stylistic and therefore not substantial enough to justify their separation into distinct periods. See Kenneth Hart Green, *Jew and Philosopher: The Return to Maimonides in the Jewish Thought of Leo Strauss* (Albany: State University of New York Press, 1993), 222n15. In contrast, Steven Lenzner seems to argue that the difference is more substantial. See Steven Lenzner, "A Literary Exercise in Self-Knowledge: Strauss's Two-Fold Interpretation of Maimonides," *Perspectives on Political Science* 31. 4 (Fall 2002), 230.
48. Alexander Altmann, "Leo Strauss: 1899–1973," *Proceedings of the American Academy for Jewish Research* 41–42 (1975), xxxvi, as cited in Green, *Leo Strauss and the Rediscovery of Maimonides*, 140.
49. Theodor W. Adorno, "Late Style in Beethoven," in Theodor W. Adorno, *Essays On Music,* ed. Richard Leppert, trans. Susan Gillespie (Berkeley, CA: University of California Press, 2002), 566–567; my emphasis.
50. In this respect, see Aryeh Tepper, *Progressive Minds, Conservative Politics: Leo Strauss's Later Writings On Maimonides* (Albany: State University of New York Press, 2013).
51. GS, 3, 711; Meier, "How Strauss Became Strauss," 380.
52. Ibid., 650; 380.
53. See Strauss's November 17, 1972 letter to Gershom Scholem, GS, 3, 765.

54. *The Correspondence of Walter Benjamin and Gershom Scholem: 1932–1940)*, ed. Gershom Scholem, trans. Gary Smith and Andre Lefevere (Cambridge, MA: Harvard University Press, 1989), 156.
55. Cited in Thomas Meyer, "Leo Strauss's Religious Rhetoric (1924–1938)," unpublished paper.
56. GS, 3, 545; Lampert, "Leo Strauss's Recovery of Esotericism," 64.
57. Ibid.
58. GS, 3, 716; Meier, "How Strauss Became Strauss," 378.
59. Meier, *Leo Strauss and the Theological-Political Problem*, 24n32. Readers should note that Strauss paradoxically expresses this concluding thought about the relation between Xenophon and Maimonides as a *kal v'homer* (*a fortiori* argument)—a prominent mode of Talmudic argumentation.
60. Lazier, 123.
61. Ibid., 110.
62. GS, 3, 751.
63. GS, 3, 740–741.
64. *Ethical Writings of Maimonides*, 75, 81.
65. Or, as Leora Batnitzky calls it, "co-ordinated." See, for example, Leora Batnitzky, *Leo Strauss and Emmanuel Levinas: Philosophy and the Politics of Revelation* (Cambridge: Cambridge University Press, 2006), 11.
66. Leo Strauss to Seth Benardete, Nov. 15, 1967 (Leo Strauss Papers, Box 4, File 18). I have not been able to locate Benardete's original letter to which Strauss's is the reply.
67. Velkley; Gregory Bruce Smith, *Between Eternities: On the Tradition of Political Philosophy, Past, Present and Future* (Lanham, MD: Lexington Books, 2008), 239.
68. Tanguay, 68; Meier, "How Strauss Became Strauss," 367.
69. Rémi Brague, "Leo Strauss and Maimonides," in *Leo Strauss's Thought: Towards a Critical Engagement*, 93.
70. Leo Strauss, *Studies in Platonic Political Philosophy*, ed. Thomas Pangle (Chicago: University of Chicago Press, 1983).
71. Alfred L. Ivry, "The Jerusalem of Medieval Jewish Philosophy," in *Gladly to Learn and Gladly to Teach: Essays on Religion and Political Philosophy in Honor of Ernest L. Fortin, A. A.*, eds. Michael P. Foley and Douglas Kries (Lanham, MD: Lexington Books, 2002), 47.

72. Ernest L. Fortin, "Why I Am not a Thomist," in Ernest L. Fortin, *Ever Ancient, Ever New: Ruminations on the City, the Soul, and the Church*, ed. Michael P. Foley (Lanham, MD: Rowman & Littlfield, 2007), 180.
73. Velkley, 142–155.
74. Compare PAW, 105n29 and 117 in this regard.
75. Even if it were so, such transparency would also be in need of legitimation. "Transparency itself," as Halbertal notes, "is never transparent." See Moshe Halbertal, *Concealment and Revelation: Esotericism In Jewish Thought and Its Philosophical Implications*, trans., Jackie Feldman (Princeton, NJ: Princeton University Press, 2007), 165.
76. Compare TM, 334n68.
77. Compare:

    1. "He gouged her just where the wristbone joins the palm and immortal blood came flowing quickly from the goddess, the ichor that courses through their veins, the blessed gods—they eat no bread, they drink no shining wine, and so the gods are bloodless, so we call them deathless." (Homer, *Iliad*, trans. Robert Fagels [New York: Penguin Books, 1990], 175)
    2. "The gods are called deathless (*athanatoi*) because they are bloodless (*anaimones*), for to be bloodless (*ambrotoi*) is to be immortal (*ambrotoi*). Men give a name to the gods (*athanatoi*) that replaces an explanation (*ambrotoi*) with a description. They have therefore ceased to be aware of what really makes for the difference between the gods and themselves. Diomedes' wounding of Aphrodite restores that awareness. It is a necessary step in freeing the heroes from the illusion that their likeness to the gods has fostered." (Seth Benardete, *The Argument of the Action: Essays on Greek Poetry and Philosophy*, eds., Ronna Burger and Michael Davis [Chicago: University of Chicago Press, 2000], 56).
    3. *Image [selem]* . . . People have thought that in the Hebrew language image denotes the shape and configuration of a thing. This supposition led them to the pure doctrine of the corporeality of God, on account of His saying: *Let us make man in our image, after our likeness.* For they thought

> that God has a man's form, I mean his shape and configuration. The pure doctrine of the corporeality of God was a necessary consequence to be accepted by them . . . [They] deemed that if they abandoned this belief, they would give the lie to the biblical text; that they would even make the deity to be nothing at all unless they thought that God was a body provided with a face and a hand, like them in shape and configuration. However, He is, in their view, bigger and more resplendent than they themselves, and the matter of which He is composed is not flesh and blood. The term *image* [unlike the term *to'ar*, which is the term the multitude use for "form" when it denotes "shape" and/or "configuration"] . . . is applied to the natural form, I mean to the notion in virtue of which a thing is constituted as a substance and becomes what it is . . . [It] would follow that *image* is an equivocal or amphibolous term applied to the specific form and also to the artificial form and to what is analogous to the two in the shapes and configurations of the natural bodies. That which was meant in the scriptural dictum, *let us make man in our image*, was the specific form, which is intellectual apprehension, not the shape and configuration. (Moses Maimonides, *The Guide of the Perplexed: Volume One*, trans., Shlomo Pines [Chicago: University of Chicago Press, 1963], 21–22)

I would like to thank Alan Udoff for his discussion with me concerning the Homeric reference and terminology contained in Strauss's letter to Benardete.

78. Cf. Martin Heidegger, *Schelling's Treatise on the Essence of Human Freedom*, trans., Joan Stambaugh (Athens, OH: Ohio University Press, 1985), 13.
79. The term *political theology* occurs specifically within the context of Strauss's essay on Halevi: "Plato's *Laws* were known in Halevi's period as Plato's rational *nomoi* . . . The ambiguity of the term 'rational *nomoi*,' [in Halevi's *Kuzari*] *viz*., that it might designate an essentially political code, such as that suggested in Plato's *Laws*, which contains a political theology, and an essentially apolitical rule of conduct destined for the guidance of the

philosopher alone, would at any rate be easily understandable on the basis of Plato's own teaching" (PAW, 116).

80. Cf. Strauss's remark on Socrates in PAW, 138.
81. Readers should also note that Strauss makes use of this phrase in "Farabi's Plato" in the context of a passing reference to Maimonides. See "Farabi's Plato," 382.
82. One might extend this Aristotelian reflection by noting that Strauss's essay from *Persecution* also contains an instance of the phrase "[those] who understand *of* themselves" (LSM, 377; my emphasis). Might this be Strauss's rearticulation of the Aristotelian distinction between a thing's existence being "by nature," as opposed to simply being "of nature"?
83. See also PAW, 114–117.
84. See, in this context, PAW, 113.
85. See Corine Pelluchon, *Leo Strauss and the Crisis of Rationalism: Another Reason, Another Enlightenment,* trans., Robert Howse (Albany: State University of New York Press, 2014), 212; Leo Strauss, *The Political Philosophy of Hobbes: Its Basis and Its Genesis*, trans. Elsa M. Sinclair (Chicago: University of Chicago Press, 1984), 143–146, 153; Thomas L. Pangle, *Leo Strauss: An Introduction to His Thought and Intellectual Legacy* (Baltimore, MD: Johns Hopkins University Press, 2006), 138n20.
86. I here follow Roslyn Weiss's interpretation of Maimonides's construal of the "apples of gold" image. See Roslyn Weiss, "Four Parables About *Peshat* as Parable," *CCAR*, 4/2008, 3–19.

Chapter 3

1. I would like to thank Ofer Tzemach of the Hebrew University Archives for providing me with an image of the announcement of Strauss's lectures.
2. Steven B. Smith, *Reading Leo Strauss*, 16.
3. In a certain respect, I am calling attention to the converse of what Joshua Parens addresses in his wonder over the inclusion of "Maimonides's Statement on Political Science" alongside the more general and "programmatic" pieces in *What Is Political Philosophy?* See Joshua Parens, "Strauss on Maimonides's Secretive

Political Science," in *Leo Strauss's Defense of the Philosophical Life: Reading* What Is Political Philosophy?, ed. Rafael Major (Chicago: University of Chicago Press, 2013), 116–117.

4. Jonathan Cohen, *Philosophers And Scholars: Wolfson, Guttmann, and Strauss on the History of Jewish Philosophy*, trans. Rachel Yarden (Lanham, MD: Lexington Books, 2007), 284.
5. Leo Strauss, "On a New Interpretation of Plato's Political Philosophy," *Social Research,* 13 (September 1946), 328; hereafter NIPPP.
6. Thanks go to Ofer Tzemach for providing me with this information.
7. Laurence Lampert, "Nietzsche's Challenge to Philosophy in the Thought of Leo Strauss," *Review of Metaphysics* 58: 3 (March 2005), 605.
8. Steven B. Smith, "Introduction: Leo Strauss Today," in *Cambridge Companion*, 19–24.
9. GS, 3, 718, 720. See also Smith, "Introduction," 34–35.
10. As Tanguay puts it, "even if Strauss perceived the limits of the Zionist solution, he remained faithful to certain aspects of Zionist thought." See Tanguay, 14–15.
11. As stated above, sight (for Strauss) is the philosophical sense par excellence. In this context, see NRH, 86–88; Leo Strauss "On Collingwood's Philosophy of History," *Review of Metaphysics* 5.4 (June 1952), 571–572; Leo Strauss, *On Tyranny: Including the Strauss-Kojève Correspondence*, eds. Victor Gourevitch and Michael Roth (New York: Free Press, 1991), 74 (hereafter, OT); Leo Strauss, "The Re-Education of the Axis Countries Concerning the Jews," *Review of Politics* 69 (2007), 538; David Janssens, "The Philosopher's Ancient Clothes: Leo Strauss on Philosophy and Poetry," 71; Genesis 3:5–7; Job 19:26–27. On the opposite of such seeing, cf. PL: 26. One is reminded, here of Strauss's experience on hearing Heidegger's 1922 lectures on Aristotle (Leo Strauss, *The Rebirth of Classical Political Rationalism*, 27–28; JPCM, 458). On this issue, see Rodrigo Chacón, "Reading Strauss from the Start: On the Heideggerian Origins of 'Political Philosophy,'" *European Journal of Political Theory* 9.3 (2010), 287–307.
12. Martin Gilbert, *Israel: A History* (New York: Harper, 2008), 297. While there are many fine histories of Israel, I use Gilbert's

insofar as it details events happening around the time period of Strauss's visit.

13. Ibid., 291.
14. Ibid., 301.
15. Benjamin Harshav, *Language in Time of Revolution* (Berkeley: University of California Press, 1993), viii.
16. Gilbert, 300.
17. Yairah Amit, "The Study of the Hebrew Bible in Israel—Between Love and Knowledge," *Jewish History* 21 (2007), 203.
18. Gilbert, 299–300.
19. In this context, we might wonder about whether a parallel exists between the status and usage of the Hebrew Bible in Israeli education and Homer's *Iliad* and *Odyssey* in ancient Athens.
20. Tali Tadmor Shimony, "Teaching the Bible as a Common Culture," *Jewish History* 21 (2007), 162.
21. Gershom Scholem, *On the Possibility of Jewish Mysticism in Our Time and Other Essays*, trans., Jonathan Chipman, ed. Avraham Shapira (Philadelphia, PA: The Jewish Publication Society, 1997), 27–28.
22. Compare PAW, 101.
23. Nasser Behnegar, "Reading *What Is Political Philosophy?*" *Perspectives on Political Science* 39.2 (April–June 2010), 66.
24. This suggests that Strauss's lecture can be understood as an instance of what he refers to (in "Classical Political Philosophy") as the "transferable" character of political science—that is, its relevance and significance is not limited to the initial place and context of its delivery (WIPP, 82).
25. Leo Strauss to Peter H. Odegard, April 2, 1953 (Leo Strauss Papers, University of Chicago, Box 4, Folder 14).
26. Thanks to Alan Udoff for suggesting this image to me. See also RCPR, 125. For an insightful discussion concerning the *conflation* of these two oppositions, see Alan Udoff, "Retracing the Steps of Franz Rosenzweig," in Franz Rosenzweig, "*The New Thinking*," ed. and trans. Alan Udoff and Barbara Galli (Syracuse, NY: Syracuse University Press, 1999), 204–205.
27. See also PAW, 155–156; EW, 215; cf. Friedrich Nietzsche, *Beyond Good and Evil: Prelude to a Philosophy of the Future*, in *Basic Writings of Nietzsche*, ed. and trans. Walter Kaufmann (New York: Modern Library, 2000), 419.

28. See, in this context, Nathan Tarcov, "Philosophy and History: Tradition and Interpretation in the Work of Leo Strauss," *Polity* 16.1 (Autumn 1983), 5–29.
29. While this claim is not identical to Strauss's other claim that (for the Ancients) philosophy seeks to replace opinions with knowledge, it is not exclusive to it either. It may, in fact, be the case that the limits of human knowledge (political or otherwise) extend to fundamental problems. As Strauss acknowledges, this is still better than "blindness or indifference" to such questions (WIPP, 11).
30. By making this conjunction, I do not mean to deny the enormous differences existing between *immortal* Greek divinities (who still bear a relation to the world of mortals) and the radically other eternal God of monotheism. See Hannah Arendt, *The Human Condition* (Chicago: University of Chicago Press, 1998), 17–21.
31. RCPR, 143.
32. While I view the "object" of Strauss's indirect communication in these lectures to be chiefly the Jerusalem/Athens distinction rather than, as Laurence Lampert claims, the distinction between love of one's own and love of the good, I do recognize a profound sympathy between his interpretation of the lectures and my own. See Laurence Lampert, "The Argument of Strauss's 'What Is Political Philosophy?'" *Modern Age* 22 (Winter 1978), 45–46.
33. Leo Strauss, NIPPP, 35. See also, PAW, 100–101, 112–113, 119; Aryeh Motzkin, "Halevi's Kuzari as a Platonic Dialogue," *Interpretation* 9 (1980), 111–124.
34. Seth Benardete, "Strauss on Plato," in AA, 409.
35. Ibid., 409.
36. Jacob Klein, *A Commentary on Plato's Meno* (Chicago: University of Chicago Press, 1989), 18; hereafter, CPM.
37. Benardete, 409.
38. Seth Benardete, "Memorial Speech for Leo Strauss," in Seth Benardete, *The Archaeology of the Soul: Platonic Readings of Ancient Poetry and Philosophy*, ed. Ronna Burger and Michael Davis (South Bend, IN: St. Augustine's Press, 2012), 376.
39. See also RCPR, 164. For an interesting discussion concerning the influence of Heidegger on Strauss's conception of the

"mysterious character of the whole," as well as the corrective offered by Strauss, see Velkley, 121–132.

40. Leo Strauss, "The Three Waves of Modernity," in Leo Strauss, *Introduction to Political Philosophy*, ed. Hilail Gildin (Detroit, MI: Wayne State University Press, 1989), 81–98. This does not mean that no interesting differences exist anyway with respect to the content of the two pieces. In "Three Waves" Strauss spends far less time on Locke than he does in "What is Political Philosophy?" Alternatively, he spends more time on Marx in the former essay than he does in the latter one. Because these disparities fall outside the scope of my project, I can do no more than mention them here.
41. Cf. Stanley Rosen, *Plato's Symposium* (New Haven, CT: Yale University Press, 1987), 10.
42. See also RCPR, 178, 180. Without wishing to push the similarity between Plato's and Maimonides's literary styles too far, it should be noted that Maimonides's *Guide* is (according to Strauss) essentially a "substitute for conversations or speeches" (PAW, 47)"—thus, a text which maintains an "oral" character—which also contains a prologue in the form of an "epistle dedicatory" to Maimonides's student Joseph (PAW, 49); cf. Plato's *Laws*, 722d–723b.
43. I would like to thank Warren Zev Harvey for the aforementioned informed speculation provided to me in private correspondence. At any rate, Yeshayahu Leibowitz's encounter with Strauss in 1954–1955 was apparently more than speculation. As Harvey recounts, Leibowitz (until this time an anti-Maimonidean) was so outraged at Strauss's continual reference to Maimonides as a philosopher (and only exoterically as a believing Jew) that he adopted exactly the opposite position to Strauss's. See Yeshayahu Leibowitz, "Maimonides—The Abrahamic Man," trans. Elvin Kose, *Judaism*, 6.2 (1957), 149; Yeshayahu Leibowitz, "*Lishmah* and Not-*Lishmah*," trans. Yoram Navon, in Yeshayahu Leibowitz, *Judaism, Human Values, and the Jewish State*, ed., Eliezer Goldman (Cambridge, MA: Harvard University Press, 1992), 68.
44. This is in marked contrast to the courses Strauss taught, during this year, which were only open to Faculty and Students: (1) Political Philosophy: A Historical Analysis of Primary Issues

(class), (2) Aristotle's *Politics* and *The Laws* of Plato (class), and (3) Machiavelli and Spinoza (seminar). Thanks go again to Ofer Tzemach of the Hebrew University Archives for this information. Eva Shorr, editor of the journal *Iyyun*, was also able to track down a note in the April 1955 issue (6.2) which makes mention of two other lectures Strauss delivered at the Beit Hillel (Hillel House) at Hebrew University: (1) "Genesis," and (2) "Genesis of Philosophy."

45. Laurence Lampert, "Nietzsche's Challenge," 605.
46. See also, Laurence Berns, "The Relation Between Philosophy and Religion: Reflections on Leo Strauss's Suggestion Concerning the Source and Sources of Modern Philosophy," *Interpretation* 19.1 (Fall 1991), 52.
47. My emphasis. All scriptural references come from *Tanakh: A New Translation of the Holy Scriptures According to the Traditional Hebrew Text* (Philadelphia, PA: The Jewish Publication Society, 1985).
48. See also CM, 1.
49. Niccolò Machiavelli, *The Prince,* trans. Harvey Mansfield (Chicago: University of Chicago Press, 1998), 61.
50. Martin Buber, *Kingship of God*, trans. Richard Scheimann (New York: Humanity Books, 1967).
51. I recognize that, in asserting this, I am open to the charge of ignoring the possible exoteric significance of a paraphrase or a change of words. Those who level this charge would, then, have to explain (1) the significance of the different formulations, (2) the significance of Strauss's usage of the term "forgetting" in his final published essay, and (3) which version exhibits the exotericism in question. I do not believe that this difference is an instance of exotericism.

Chapter 4

1. On the subject of Ideas as problems, see Hilail Gildin, "Leo Strauss on the Understanding of the Politically Better and Worse," *Interpretation* 35.1 (2006), 7; Stanley Rosen, "Leo Strauss and the Possibility of Philosophy," *Review of Metaphysics* 53 (March 2000), 563.
2. See also Leo Strauss, OT: 277; Jeremy Mhire, "What Is Really

Different About *What Is Political Philosophy?*" *Perspectives on Political Science* 40.1 (January–March 2011), 54–57.

3. See Lampert, "Nietzsche's Challenge to Philosophy," *The Review of Metaphysics* 58.3 (March 2005), 585–619; Laurence Lampert, *Leo Strauss and* Nietzsche (Chicago: University of Chicago Press, 1996), 136–145; William H. F. Altman, *The German Stranger: Leo Strauss and National Socialism* (Lanham, MD: Lexington Books, 2011), 2011), 403–444. Lampert's treatments are sober, thoughtful extensions of his Nietzschean-Platonic interpretation of Strauss. Altman's excited treatment (which emphasizes Hegel and Heidegger) transcends philosophy in the direction of Homeric poetry. In this respect Lampert's revisions to his essay on WIPP (in his most recent volume) travel a certain distance in the direction of Altmann. See Laurence Lampert, *The Enduring Importance of Leo Strauss* (Chicago: University of Chicago Press, 2013), 227–247.
4. In order to aid readers interested in what I take to be the overall structure of the final essay (interpolating the place where, and dates when, they were advertised to be delivered), I here provide a brief "roadmap":

"What Is Political Philosophy?":
Lectures Delivered at the Faculty of Law (Ratisbone Building) at the
Hebrew University of Jerusalem, 1954–1955 Academic Year

Lecture/Section I.
"The Problem of Political Philosophy"
(delivered Thursday December 23, 1954)

Paragraph 1: Prologue to the Entire Set of Lectures/Entire Essay
Paragraphs 2–6: Introduction to Lecture/Section 1
Paragraphs 7–15: Definitions
Paragraphs 16–26: Social Science, Positivism, Relativism

Lecture/Section II.
"The Classical Solution" (delivered Thursday, December 30, 1954)

Paragraphs 27–29: Introduction to Lecture/Section 2

Paragraphs 30–38: The Character of Classical Political Philosophy
Paragraphs 31–33: Digression on Wine and the Athenian Stranger
Paragraphs 39–43: Objections to Classical Political Philosophy

Lecture/Section III.
"The Modern Solutions" (supposed to be delivered Thursday, January 6, 1955)

Paragraph 44: Introduction to Lecture/Section 3
Paragraphs 45–57: First Wave of Modernity: Machiavelli
Paragraphs 58–59: First Wave of Modernity: Hobbes, Locke, Montesquieu
Paragraphs 60–65: Second Wave of Modernity
Paragraph 66: Third Wave of Modernity

As discussed in chapter 3, while the prologue to the entirety of the lectures occurs at the beginning of the first lecture, its breadth and comprehensive character indicates that it is meant to serve as the beginning of the whole.

If my articulation is correct, there are a few things worthy of note. First, Strauss's digression (which he subsequently indicates with the phrase, "But let us return after this long story to . . ." [WIPP, 33]) is located near the center (paras. 31–33) of the central lecture (i.e., 2) of "What Is Political Philosophy?" Second, except for one mention of the word *Decalogue* (para. 53), all particular references having to do with Jerusalem drop out after lecture 2. Third, unlike lecture 2, lecture 3 adopts a narrative and developmental (i.e., historical) presentation. Fourth, the presence of Machiavelli in lecture 3 cannot be overemphasized. Out of the entire twenty-three paragraphs comprising lecture 3, thirteen of them are dedicated to Machiavelli (Altman, *The German Stranger*, 424). The discussion of Machiavelli not only dwarfs in size the rest of the historical discussion of modern political philosophy, it is also the largest single section in the entirety of "What Is Political Philosophy?" I will address this more specifically during my discussion of lecture three.

5. Altman holds that the "subject matter/function" distinction present in "What is Political Philosophy?" is different than the one in "On Classical Political Philosophy," where "political philosophy designates not so much a subject matter as a manner of

treatment" (WIPP, 93). From this he infers that one needs to read the Hebrew University lectures in the light of "On Classical Political Philosophy" in order to see that Strauss is reading between the lines (Altman, 404–405). On further consideration, one might wonder if the two passages are as distinct as Altman would have the reader believe. The statement from "On Classical Political Philosophy" occurs near the end of the essay, thus suggesting that the politic treatment of philosophy is, *in the last analysis*, more about "leading the qualified citizens, or rather their qualified sons, from the political life to the philosophical life." In "What is Political Philosophy?", Strauss's statement occurs near the beginning, thus suggesting that one initially understands political philosophy to comprise of two (perhaps) equal parts—subject matter and function. Far from reading "What is Political Philosophy?" *in the light of* "On Classical Political Philosophy," it seems as that reading the two essays in the order of their published presentation (in Strauss's book) would allow readers to appreciate the dual character of political philosophy *as well as* the changed viewpoint that the different characters presuppose. In this respect, Strauss's indication that political philosophy refers to "the political, or popular, treatment of philosophy" (WIPP, 93) would amount to the same thing as his statement about the function of political philosophy having to do with its relevance to political life.

6. Aristotle, *Nicomachean Ethics*, trans. Robert C. Bartlett and Susan D. Collins (Chicago: University of Chicago Press, 2011), 117 (1139b4–6).
7. There is a break in the recording of the lectures at the corresponding point in the essay where Strauss begins to discuss "political ideas." The recording picks up again immediately afterwards. It is reasonable to assume that this lacuna is the result of a tape-flip and that his Hebrew University audience was privy to his quotation.
8. John Locke, *An Essay Concerning Human Understanding*, ed., Peter H. Niddich (Oxford, UK: Oxford University Press, 1979), 47 (I.1.8). Locke's actual phraseology is "*Phatnom, Notion, Species*, or whatever it is, which the Mind can be employ'd about in thinking."
9. In the lectures, Strauss quotes Hillel's statement in the original

Hebrew and only references the 3rd chapter of Spinoza's text.

10. Leo Pinsker, "Auto-Emancipation: An Appeal to His People by a Russian Jew," trans. David Blondheim, in *The Zionist Idea: A Historical Analysis and Reader*, ed. Arthur Herzberg (Philadelphia: The Jewish Publication Society, 1997), 198.
11. Readers should recall, in this context, that in the early 1950s, Israel's Prime Minister David Ben-Gurion started a campaign to have the ban on Spinoza (imposed by the Amsterdam Jewish community in the seventeenth century) lifted. Yirmiyahu Yovel, *Spinoza and Other Heretics: The Marrano of Reason* (Princeton, NJ: Princeton University Press, 1989), 202. Yovel rightly raises the question as to who today would actually be authorized to lift the ban? (Yovel, 203).
12. A more literal rendering of Spinoza's statement occurs in Martin Yaffe's translation of the text: "I would absolutely believe that, unless the foundations of their religion were to make their spirits effeminate, they will someday, given the occasion—as human affairs are changeable—erect their imperium once more" (*Spinoza's Theological-Political Treatise*, trans. Martin Yaffe [Newburyport, MA: Focus Publishing, 2004], 42).
13. I owe this formulation to Warren Zev Harvey (given in private correspondence). Concerning the necessity of giving voice to both sides of the argument (in this case, the Mutakallimun and the Aristotelians), see Maimonides, *Guide: Volume One*, 179, 181–182. See also Warren Zev Harvey, "Why Maimonides Was Not a Mutakallimun," in *Perspectives On Maimonides: Philosophical and Historical Studies*, ed. Joel Kraemer (Oxford, UK: The Littman Library of Jewish Civilization, 2008), 105–114.
14. As this concerns the relation between Maimonides and Spinoza, see Joshua Parens, "Prudence, Imagination, and Determination of Law in Alfarabi and Maimonides," in *Enlightening Revolutions*, 46.
15. See Heinrich Meier, *Carl Schmitt And Leo Strauss: The Hidden Dialogue*, trans. J. Harvey Lomax (Chicago: University of Chicago Press, 1995). Schmitt had also helped Strauss secure his Rockefeller Grant that allowed him to find employment outside of Germany.
16. Nitzan Lebovic, "The Jerusalem School: The Theopolitical Hour," *New German Critique*, 35. 3 (Fall 2008), 97–120. In

this context, see also Buber's own reflections on his presence at Hebrew University in his draft letter to Hans Blüher (January 15, 1955). Martin Buber, *The Letters of Martin Buber: A Life of Dialogue*, eds. Nahum Glatzer and Paul Mendes-Flohr, trans. Richard and Clara Winston and Harry Zohn (Syracuse, NY: Syracuse University Press, 1996), 590–591.

17. Lebovic, 108. See also, 109–115.
18. Carl Schmitt, *Political Theology: Four Chapters on the Concept of Sovereignty*, trans., George Schwab (Chicago: University of Chicago Press, 2005), 5, 36.
19. Ibid., 36–37.
20. Carl Schmitt, *The Concept of the Political*, trans., George Schwab (Chicago: University of Chicago Press, 2007), 26.
21. Heinrich Meier picks up on this as well. Chapter 3 of his book *The Lessons of Carl Schmitt* is titled "Revelation, Or He That Is Not with Me Is Against Me." The present reading of Schmitt is deeply informed by Meier's interpretation. See Heinrich Meier, *The Lesson of Carl Schmitt: Four Chapters on the Distinction Between Political Theology and Political Philosophy*, trans. Marcus Brainard (Chicago: University of Chicago Press, 2011).
22. Carl Schmitt, *The* Nomos *of the Earth*, trans. G. L. Ulmen (New York: Telos Press Ltd., 2003), 59–60.
23. In this context, see also Carl Schmitt, "Three Possibilities for a Christian Conception of History," trans. Mario Wenning, *Telos* 147 (2009), 169. For an example of the *katechon* in the form of a personage, see Carl Schmitt, "A Pan-European Interpretation of Donoso Cortés," trans. Mark Grzeskowiak, *Telos* 125 (2002), 100–115.
24. See Meier, *The Lesson of Carl Schmitt*, 66; Meier, *Carl Schmitt and Leo Strauss*, 68, 83. Perhaps in contradistinction to Meier, I would argue that Schmittian political theology is *specifically* Christian insofar as it is premised on faith in the *event* of revelation (as opposed to revealed *law*). In this context, see Corine Pelluchon, "Strauss and Christianity," trans. unknown, *Interpretation*, 33.2, 185–203.
25. Carl Schmitt, "Three Possibilities," 169–170.
26. Martin Buber, *Between Man and Man*, 87, 89.
27. Martin Buber, *Kingship of God*, 58.
28. Martin Buber, "Renewal of Judaism," trans. Eva Jospe, in Martin

Buber, *On Judaism*, ed., Nahum Glatzer (New York: Schocken Books, 1995), 55.

29. See Michael Fishbane's introduction to Buber's *Moses*. Martin Buber, *Moses: The Revelation and the Covenant*, trans. unknown (Amherst, NY: Humanity Books, 1998), 7, 9, 11.
30. Ibid., x; my emphasis.
31. Schmitt, *The Concept of the Political*, 34; my emphasis. See also Meier, *The Lesson of Carl Schmitt*, 26–65.
32. Ibid., 30.
33. I realize that, on making this claim, I am open to the hue and cry of those who wish to suggest that Strauss also doesn't present both sides of positions (as supposedly evidenced in his exoteric practice). The difference, in my view, is this: I do not believe (as Altman does) that Strauss is attempting to undermine the foundations of liberal democracy. Hence, his exoteric practice has a pedagogical rather than political-ideological function. Strauss is attempting to preserve a space within the polis for the philosophical way of life. This (on his own account) requires both concealing the radicality of that activity (i.e., the fact that philosophical ideas amount to fundamental problems admitting of no worldly solution) from nonphilosophers and simultaneously awakening a desire to pursue that activity in the souls of potential philosophers. In short, I am compelled by Velkley's treatment of this issue in *Heidegger, Strauss*.
34. Martin Buber, *Kingship of God*, 14.
35. Jacob Taubes, *From Cult to Culture: Fragments Toward a Critique of Historical Reason*, ed., Charlotte Elisheva Fonrobert and Amir Engel (Stanford, CA: Stanford University Press, 2010), 3–9.
36. Buber, *Kingdom of God*, 57.
37. Buber, *Moses*, 186.
38. Martin Buber, *The Prophetic Faith*, tran. unknown (New York: Collier Books, 1977), 126–154. See also Lebovic, 100–106.
39. Buber, *The Prophetic Faith*, 152.
40. Ibid.
41. Ibid., 148.
42. Ibid., 146; my emphasis.
43. Strauss's text is appended to Schmitt's *Concept of the Political*. See *The Concept of the Political*, 119.
44. Ibid., 122.

45. Ibid.
46. It might be that Strauss also has in mind a passage from Hegel's *Phenomenology of Spirit* as an earlier ("second wave") instance of the same problem:

> The manner of study in ancient time is distinct from that of the modern world, in that the former consisted in the cultivation of and the perfecting of the natural mind. Testing life carefully at all points, philosophizing about everything it came across, the former created an experience permeated through and through by universals. In modern times, however, an individual finds the abstract form ready made . . . Hence, nowadays, the task before us consists not so much in getting the individual clear of the stage of sensuous immediacy, and making him a substance that thinks and is grasped in terms of thought, but rather the very opposite: it consists in actualizing the universal, and giving it spiritual vitality, by the process of breaking down and superseding fixed and determinate thoughts.

G. W. F. Hegel, *The Phenomenology of Mind*, trans. J. B. Baillie (New York: Harper Torchbooks, 1967), 94 as cited in Alan Udoff, "Levinas and the Question of Friendship," *Levinas Studies: An Annual Review*, vol. 1 (Pittsburgh, PA: Duquesne University Press, 2005), 195n36. I thank Alan Udoff for sharing with me the information that Strauss was apparently so impressed by this particular passage of Hegel (in Baillie's translation) that he typed it up on a separate sheet of paper; it has been preserved, according to Udoff, in the Strauss archives in Chicago.
47. This is, in no way, meant to deny the enigmatic character of Strauss's reference to Whitehead (which reference falls outside the scope of the present study).
48. Gershom Scholem, "Reflections on Modern Jewish Studies (1944)," in Gershom Scholem, *On the Possibility of Jewish Mysticism for Our Time*, 60. Cf. Gershom Scholem, "The Science of Judaism—Then and Now," trans. Michael A. Meyer (New York: Schocken Books, 1971), 307: "We have only one task left: to give the remains of Judaism a decent burial."

49. See Leo Strauss, "The Spirit of Sparta or the Taste of Xenophon," *Social Research* 6.4 (November 1939), 531; WIPP, 125.
50. Leo Strauss, "Restatement," Critical Edition, ed., Emmanuel Patard, *Interpretation* 36.1 (Fall 2008), 77–78.
51. Cf., NRH, second epigraph. See also Richard Kennington, "Strauss's *Natural Right and History*, in Udoff, *Leo Strauss's Thought: Towards a Critical Engagement*, 244.
52. Thanks to Warren Zev Harvey for this information.
53. See also Susan Shell, "'To Spare the Vanquished and Crush the Arrogant': Leo Strauss's Lecture on 'German Nihilism,'" in *Cambridge Companion to Leo Strauss*, 189. Cf. PAW, 96.
54. RCPR, 29.
55. See also NRH, 136.
56. See also Tanguay, 195.
57. Readers may be interested to note the divergence between the very end of the second section of "What is Political Philosophy" and the end of the second Hebrew University lecture. I here reproduce them both: "It [Philosophy] is the highest form of the mating of courage and moderation. In spite of its highness or nobility, it could appear as Sisyphean or ugly, when one contrasts its achievement with its goal. Yet it is necessarily accompanied, sustained and elevated by *eros*. It is graced by nature's grace" (WIPP: 40); "Pascal has said that 'we know too little to be dogmatists and too much to be skeptics.' He believed that this true and beautiful sentence constitutes a refutation of philosophy. But according to Socrates or Plato, this sentence supplies the only possible legitimation of philosophy. Knowledge of ignorance does not legitimate reason's disavowal of reason. It only legitimates the resolve to continue in the quest for clarity or in investigation. Pascal's resolve would appear, in the eyes of Plato or Socrates, as softness of the soul. Not softness, abandon, or despair is called for by man's nature and his condition as we know it, but the endurance, courage or manliness which is necessarily accompanied and sustained by eros. *Sapare aude* [dare to know]."
58. The clearly Husserlian references in these statements support the view (made by Velkley, Bruce Smith, and Lampert among others) that Strauss's advocacy of classical philosophy is a

recovery of classical philosophy, and thus takes its own point of departure from modern philosophical premises.

59. The italicization of "e.g.," here is Strauss's and deserves some discussion. I believe the italicized emphasis, in this case, to refer to the fact that Aristotle's *Politics* had an apparent influence on the medieval Christian thinkers, but not the Jewish or Islamic ones. Insofar as medieval Jewish and Islamic thought lacked access (for whatever reason) to Aristotle's *Politics*, they did not study it (except, perhaps, for Farabi). For Strauss, the lack of Aristotle's *Politics*—coupled with the placement of Plato's *Republic* as the successor book to Aristotle's *Nicomachean Ethics*—is of fundamental importance for understanding the difference between medieval Christian and medieval Islamic and Jewish thought (PAW, 8–9; SR, 5–6, 24; see also LSM, 580–582; Ernest L. Fortin, "The Political Thought of St. Thomas Aquinas," and "Politics and Philosophy in the Middle Ages: The Aristotelian Revolution," respectively, in Ernest L. Fortin, *Classical Christianity and the Political Order: Reflections on the Theologico-Political Problem*, ed., J. Brian Benstad (Lanham, MD: Rowman and Littlefield Publishers, 1996), 151–155, 179–180.
60. Leo Strauss, "What Is Liberal Education?" in Leo Strauss, LAM, 6. For an important medieval articulation of this thought, see Joseph Albo, *Book of Roots*, trans. Ralph Lerner in *Medieval Political Philosophy*, 1st ed., 252.
61. Maimonides, "Logic," trans. Muhsin Mahdi, in *Medieval Political Philosophy*, 2nd ed., 182; my emphasis.
62. For a significant medieval articulation of a consequence of this new situation, see Joseph Albo in *Medieval Political Philosophy*, 1st ed., 248. See also Tanguay, 175–176; JPCM, 397–398.
63. See Strauss to Eric Voegelin, December 10, 1950, in FPP, 75. Cf. Karl Reinhardt, "Philosophy and History Among the Greeks," *Greece & Rome*, Second Series, 1:2 (June 1954), 82–90.
64. Cf., TM, 297.
65. See also TM, 202–203.
66. Compare NRH, 160.
67. Cf., TM, 173, 218–219.
68. For a similar formulation of this question, see Jeffrey A. Bernstein, "'With a Friend Like This' or How to Begin to Read

William H. F. Altman," *Interpretation* 39:2 (Spring/Summer 2012), 210.

69. See NRH, 158.
70. Maimonides, *The Guide of the Perplexed: Volume Two*, 510–511.
71. For an alternative take on the relation between theory and politics/practice in Maimonides, see Janssens, *Between Athens and Jerusalem*, 58–60. In making this claim, I mean to suggest neither that Strauss's view of Maimonides was uncontroversial at the time he developed it, nor that it is uncontroversial today. In this context see Moshe Halbertal's and Avishai Margalit's discussion of Maimonides's interpretation of the ban on divine imagery as divergent from its Biblical and Rabbinic construals (Moshe Halbertal and Avishai Margalit, *Idolatry*, trans. Naomi Goldblum [Cambridge, MA: Harvard University Press, 1992], 45–47). Warren Zev Harvey notes that Strauss's overall interpretation of Maimonides's exotericism is predicated on an ambivalence toward such a strong stance. Harvey holds that, while Strauss had a deep respect for Maimonides as a philosopher, "[Strauss] also . . . loved Jerusalem and feared prejudicing the case against her. For while he was convinced that Maimonides had chosen Athens, he was not, perhaps, altogether convinced that the choice was wise" (Warren Zev Harvey, "The Return of Maimonideanism," *Jewish Social Studies* 42: 3–4 (Summer/Autumn 1980), 255.

Chapter 5

1. *Averroes on Plato's* Republic, trans. Ralph Lerner (Ithaca, NY: Cornell University Press, 1974), 4.
2. EW, 217.
3. While the pairing of Maimonides and Spinoza has been a theme familiar to many commentators, it is in no way shared by all. For a recent commentary that decisively rejects such a pairing (on grounds provided by Strauss) see Joshua Parens, *Maimonides & Spinoza: Their Conflicting Views of Human Nature* (Chicago: University of Chicago Press, 2012). For my response to Parens's reading, see Jeffrey A. Bernstein, "Rethinking the Relation

Between Maimonides and Spinoza," *Interpretation* 40.1 (2013), 79–103.

4. Shlomo Pines argues that Farabi makes use of a paraphrase or summary of the *Politics*. See Shlomo Pines, "Aristotle's *Politics* in Arabic Philosophy," *Israel Oriental Studies* V (1975), 150–160.
5. One place where Strauss provides a clear statement of what this entails is in his Introduction to Mendelssohn's *Morning Hours* and *to the Friends of Lessing:* "to be sure, [Spinoza] granted 'thinking' (*cogitatio*) to the infinite substance, but denied 'understanding' (*intellectio*) . . . Spinoza, though granting to the infinite substance the two attributes of thought and extension in an equal manner, nevertheless in fact claimed priority for extension over thought and so arrived at materialistic consequences" (LSMM, 91–92).
6. Miguel Vatter, "Natural Right and State of Exception in Leo Strauss," in *Crediting God: Sovereignty and Religion in the Age of Global Capitalism*, ed. Miguel Vatter (New York: Fordham University Press, 2011), 206.
7. In this context, see Pelluchon, *Leo Strauss and the Crisis of Rationalism*, 244.
8. Strauss's subsequent relation to Maimonides (from this point in his philosophical career) has been the subject of much discussion. One recent interpretation (based on a June 22, 1952 letter to Gershom Scholem) holds that Strauss viewed his interest in Maimonides as a "Thomistic detour" on the way to the more extreme rationalism of Plato. On this reading, Maimonides becomes, for Strauss, simply a derivation of the more genuine thought expressed in Plato's own political philosophy. For this reading, see Michael Zank, "Arousing Suspicion Against a Prejudice: Leo Strauss and the Study of Maimonides' *Guide of the Perplexed*," in *Moses Maimonides (1138–1204): His Religious, Scientific, and Philosophical* Wirkungsgeschichte *in Different Cultural Contexts*, ed. Göge K. Hasselhoff and Otfried Fraisse, in *Ex Oriente Lux: Rezeptionen Und Exegesen Als Traditionskritik, Band 4,* ed., Almut Sh. Bruckstein, Navid Kermani, Angelika Neuwirth, and Andreas Pflitsch (Würzburg: Ergon Verlag, 2004), 551n10, 571; Michael Zank, "The Heteronomy of Jewish Philosophy," *The Journal of Jewish Thought and Philosophy,* 20.1

(2012), 117n15. It should be noted that "Thomistic detour" is not a phrase that occurs in the 1952 letter but, rather, a paraphrase. Marcus Brainard's translation of the passage in question runs as follows: "I have moved, so to speak, contrary to G[uttmann]'s moderate rationalism, on the path via a Jewish Thomism to radical 'rationalism,' am now on the right wing (for the right is the truth, the left is sinister, as no one knows better than you), whereas I stood on the left wing in *Philosophy and Law*: Guttmann ever in the middle" (Meier, "How Strauss Became Strauss," 379n29; GS, 3, 765).

There would be much to say about this passage in terms of its "politics" and its "humor." In the present context, however, I emphasize that Strauss simply claims to have traveled on a path and changed places. That this amounts to a substantive detour on the path *away* from Maimonides, in the manner claimed, is in need of further demonstration. Maimonides remains the one figure about whom Strauss wrote throughout his entire career. While it is true that Strauss's position on Maimonides changes after *Philosophy and Law* (as I have discussed in chapter 2), to change direction or position is not simply to have made a detour. Underlying this reading of Strauss's relation to Maimonides is an interpretation holding that Strauss's interest in Judaism is simply exoteric. The alternative, presumably, would be to take religious belief in God "seriously." In my discussion of Meier's work (in the present chapter), I claim that this set of alternatives amounts to a false dichotomy. This is so not only for Strauss's thought, but additionally for Judaism per se. As a religion based on law, Judaism is as much a political community as it is a "faith" community. The question for Strauss (as discussed in chapter 1) is: how can he *philosophically* find a way to live without belief. While Strauss's "movement from the left to the right" can very well be understood as a movement from Jerusalem to Athens, to pose that distinction as one between Maimonides and Plato is insufficiently dialectical: Strauss had a Socratic, Platonic, Farabian, and Nietzschean Maimonides (perhaps among others); the fact that the figure of Maimonides is present throughout his entire philosophical trajectory ought to compel readers to ask the question (which the present study attempts to answer):

what is it *about Maimonides* that makes him worthy of being a permanent philosophical interlocutor for Strauss? Philipp von Wussow presents a cogent alternative interpretation: the "radical naturalism," of which Strauss speaks, is not simply a non-Maimonidean Platonic rationalism. It refers instead to the philosopher who accepts religion for the sake of society. Strauss, therefore, left "Jewish Thomism" behind because (in Strauss's reading) Maimonides no longer functioned as a key authority for *Jewish* thought. In this context, see PAW, 8–9. I thank von Wussow for sharing his insights on this issue with me.

9. The classic text dealing with the general modern deemphasis on understanding in favor of reason is David R. Lachterman, *The Ethics of Geometry: A Genealogy of Modernity* (New York: Routledge, 1989).
10. For a clear discussion of this aspect of *Persecution*, see Michael S. Kochin, "Morality, Nature, and Esotericism in Leo Strauss's *Persecution and the Art of Writing*," *Review of Politics* 64. 2 (Spring 2002), 261–283.
11. By my count, the breakdown per essay of words dealing with *imaginatio*, *ratio*, and *intellectus* runs as follows:

	imaginatio	*ratio*	*intellectus*
1. Introduction	1	10	5
2. Title essay	0	4	8
3. Maimonides	19	13	55
4. Halevi	0	191	8
5. Spinoza	4	72	138

12. Again by my count: Introductory essay (16), title essay (12), Maimonides essay (87), Halevi essay (199), and Spinoza essay (214). While PAW is a collection of essays (and not properly a "book," it nonetheless was prepared and arranged by Strauss. It is, therefore, not unreasonable to assume that the structure of PAW expresses his intention.
13. Leo Strauss, correspondence with David Savan, November 25, 1958 (Leo Strauss Papers, Box 4, Folder 17). Also of note in the letter is Strauss's admission that he "studied Spinoza with intensity in the 1920's and in the 1940's." Strauss's assessment of

Spinoza's influence on his own thought amounts to something like a mean between the influences of Cohen and Maimonides, respectively.

14. One final point may be worthy of note: The Maimonides and Spinoza essays are the only ones in *Persecution* that make reference to those people who are able to "understand by [himself]/themselves." This (set of) formulation(s) occurs three times in the Maimonides essay and once in the Spinoza essay (during a brief discussion of Maimonides). Spinoza would, then, appear to be the modern recipient of the contemplative life more prevalent in Maimonides's time.
15. While I have (in previous chapters) cited "The Literary Character" essay from LSM, in this chapter I have cited it from PAW in order (1) to keep continuity with the rest of the chapter in that text and (2) to ease the facility of reference for the reader.
16. I do not here take a stand on whether this is identical (in Aristotelian terms) with *noesis noesos*. I simply mean to distinguish between Aristotle's God (whatever it is) and the personal God of the Hebrew Bible. In this connection, see Markus Gabriel, "God's Transcendent Activity: Ontotheology in *Metaphysics* 12," *Review of Metaphysics* 25 (December 2009), 385–414.
17. David Janssens, "The Philosopher's Ancient Clothes," 67.
18. This is, I claim, a distant philosophical relative to the question concerning the best way of life and whether/under what circumstances it can be attained.
19. Strauss and Gadamer, "Correpsondence," 6.
20. Benedict Spinoza, *The Collected Works of Spinoza: Volume I*, tran., Edwin Curley (Princeton, NJ: Princeton University Press, 1985), 8; my emphasis.
21. For an interesting attempt at construing a third realm in Strauss's account of Jerusalem and Athens, see Sharon Portnoff, *Reason and Revelation Before Historicism: Strauss and Fackenheim* (Toronto: University of Toronto Press, 2011), 211.
22. Seth Benardete, *Encounters and Reflections: Conversations with Seth Benardete*, ed. Ronna Burger (Chicago: University of Chicago Press, 2002), 176.
23. Heinrich Meier, *Leo Strauss and the Theological-Political Problem*, 43.

24. See Meier's discussions in *Carl Schmitt and Leo Strauss* and *The Lesson of Carl Schmitt*, respectively.
25. Meier, *Leo Strauss*, 87.
26. Ibid., 41.
27. Ibid., 28.
28. Ibid., 31.
29. Ibid., 31–32.
30. Ibid., 32.
31. Ibid.
32. Ibid., 33–34.
33. Compare with Strauss's account of Aristophanes on justice in SA, 312.
34. Miguel Vatter, "Natural Right," 205.
35. Ibid.
36. Ibid.
37. Ibid., 204.
38. Ibid., 203; my emphasis. Vatter makes essentially the same point in his reading of *Natural Right and History*: if, in light of his discussion of Aristotle, there is nothing "natural" in classical natural right, the only possibility left is to ground such natural right in a "fundamental distinction between friend and enemy that overlaps a theologically grounded distinction between good and evil" (ibid., 200).
39. Miguel E. Vatter, "Taking Exception to Liberalism: Heinrich Meier's *Carl Schmitt and Leo Strauss: The Hidden Dialogue*," *Graduate Faculty Philosophy Journal* 19–20.2–1 (1997), 333.
40. Ibid., 334.
41. Vatter, "Natural Right," 206.
42. Michael Zuckert, "Straussians," *The Cambridge Companion to Leo Strauss*, 269.
43. Curley, 15; translation slightly modified.
44. For a formulation of this point sympathetic to my own construal, see Alan Udoff, "On Leo Strauss: An Introductory Account," in *Leo Strauss's Thought*, 11–12.
45. Theodor Adorno, *Negative Dialectics*, trans. E. B. Ashton (New York: Continuum Books, 2003), 402.
46. In this context, it is relevant to note Robert Howse's fascinating portrayal of the middle and later period Strauss as performing a

philosophical *t'shuvah* (return, repentance) for his early flirtation with illiberal politics, thus enacting a kind of internal coordination of Jerusalem and Athens. See the Introduction to Howse's 2014 *Leo Strauss: Man of Peace*, (Cambridge, UK: Cambridge University Press).

47. Compare Stanley Rosen, "Straussian Hermeneutics" (Stanley Rosen, *Essays in Philosophy: Ancient*, ed., Martin Black [South Bend, IN: St. Augustine's Press, 2013]), 37; and Stanley Rosen, *The Ancients and the Moderns* (New Haven, CT: Yale University Press, 1989), 3.

BIBLIOGRAPHY

Achad ha'Am. *The Supremacy of Reason (To the Memory of Maimonides)*, translated by Leon Simon. London: The Zionist, 1917, pp. 1–48.

Adorno, Theodor. *Negative Dialectics*, translated by E. B. Ashton. New York: Continuum Books, 2003.

———. *Essays on Music*, translated by Susan Gillespie, edited by Richard Leppert. Berkeley, CA: University of California Press, 2002.

Ahad Ha'am. *Selected Essays of Ahad Ha-'am*, translated by Leon Simon. New York: The Jewish Publication Society of America, 1962.

Albo, Joseph. *Book of Roots*, translated by Ralph Lerner. In *Medieval Political Philosophy: A Sourcebook*, 1st ed., edited by Ralph Lerner and Muhsin Mahdi. Ithaca, NY: Cornell University Press, 1963.

Alfarabi. *The Political Regime*, translated by Fauzi M. Nijjar. In *Medieval Political Philosophy: A Sourcebook*, 1st ed., edited by Ralph Lerner and Muhsin Mahdi. Ithaca, NY: Cornell University Press, 1963.

Altman, William H. F. *The German Stranger: Leo Strauss and National Socialism*. Lanham, MD: Lexington Books, 2011.

Altmann, Alexander. *The Meaning of Jewish Existence: Theological Essays 1930–1939*, edited by Alfred L. Ivry. Waltham, MA: Brandeis University Press, 1991.

Amit, Yairah. "The Study of the Hebrew Bible in Israel—Between Love and Knowledge," *Jewish History* 21 (2007): 199–208.

Arendt, Hannah. *The Human Condition*. Chicago: University of Chicago Press, 1998.

Arendt, Hannah and Karl Jaspers. *Correspondence: 1926–1969*, edited by Lothar Kohler and Hans Saner and translated by Robert and Rita Kimber. New York: Harcourt, Brace and Company, 1992.

Aristotle. *Nicomachean Ethics*, translated by Robert C. Bartlett and Susan D. Collins. Chicago: University of Chicago Press, 2011.

Armon, Adi. "Just Before the 'Straussians': The Development of Leo Strauss's Political Thought from the Weimar Republic to America." *New German Critique* 37.3 (Fall 2010): 173–198.

Arnold, Matthew. *Culture and Anarchy*, edited by Samuel Lipman. New Haven: Yale University Press, 1994.

Augustine. *City of God*, translated by Henry Bettenson. New York: Penguin Books, 2003.

———. *Confessions*, translated by Henry Chadwick. Oxford, UK: Oxford University Press, 1998.

Auerbach, Erich. *Mimesis: Representations of Reality in Western Literature,* translated by Willard Trask. Princeton, NJ: Princeton University Press, 2003.

Averroes on Plato's Republic, translated by Ralph Lerner. Ithaca, NY: Cornell University Press, 1974.

Baron, Salo W. "The Historical Outlook of Maimonides." *Proceedings of the American Academy of Jewish Research* 6 (1934–35): 5–113.

Batnitzky, Leora. *How Judaism Became a Religion.* Princeton, NJ: Princeton University Press, 2011.

———. *Leo Strauss and Emmanuel Levinas: Philosophy and the Politics of Revelation.* Cambridge, UK: Cambridge University Press, 2006.

Behnegar, Nasser. "Reading *What Is Political Philosophy?*" *Perspectives on Political Science* 39.2 (April–June 2010): 66–71.

Benardete, Seth. *The Archaeology of the Soul: Platonic Readings of Ancient Poetry and Philosophy*, edited by Ronna Burger and Michael Davis. South Bend, IN: St. Augustine's Press, 2012.

———. *The Argument of the Action: Essays on Greek Poetry and Philosophy*, edited by Ronna Burger and Michael Davis. Chicago: University of Chicago Press, 2000.

———. *Encounters and Reflections: Conversations with Seth Benardete*, edited by Ronna Burger. Chicago: University of Chicago Press, 2002.

Benjamin, Walter and Gershom Scholem. *The Correspondence of Walter Benjamin and Gershom Scholem*, edited by Gershom Scholem, translated by Gary Smith and Andre Lefevere. Cambridge, MA: Harvard University Press, 1989.

Berns, Laurence. "The Relation Between Philosophy and Religion: Reflections on Leo Strauss's Suggestion Concerning the Source and Sources of Modern Philosophy." *Interpretation* 19.1 (Fall 1991): 43–60.

Bernstein, Jeffrey A. "Rethinking the Relation Between Maimonides and Spinoza." *Interpretation* 40.1 (2013): 79–103.

———. "The Theological-Political Problems in Leo Strauss's Moses Mendelssohn Writings." *Journal of Jewish Thought and Philosophy*, 22 (2014), 191–215.

———. "'With a Friend Like This' or How to Begin to Read William H. F. Altman." *Interpretation* 39.2 (Spring–Summer 2012): 195–212.

Brague, Rémi. "Athens, Jerusalem, Mecca: Leo Strauss's 'Muslim' Understanding of Greek Philosophy." *Poetics Today* 19.2 (1998): 235–259.

———. "Leo Strauss and Maimonides." In *Leo Strauss's Thought: Towards a Critical Engagement*, edited by Alan Udoff. Boulder, CO: Lynne Reinner Publishers, 1991.

Buber, Martin. *Between Man and Man*, translated by Ronald Gregor-Smith. New York: Routledge, 2004.

———. *Kingship of God*, translated by Richard Scheimann. New York: Humanity Books, 1967.

———. *The Letters of Martin Buber: A Life Of Dialogue*, edited by Nahum Glatzer and Paul Mendes-Flohr and translated by Richard and Clara Winston and Harry Zohn. Syracuse, NY: Syracuse University Press, 1996.

———. *Moses: The Revelation and the Covenant*, translator unknown. Amherst, NY: Humanity Books, 1998.

———. *On the Bible: Eighteen Studies*, edited by Nahum N. Glatzer. Syracuse, NY: Syracuse University Press, 2000.

———. *On Judaism*, edited by Nahum Glatzer. New York: Schocken Books, 1995.

———. *The Prophetic Faith*, translator unknown. New York: Collier Books, 1977.

Chacón, Rodrigo. "Reading Strauss from the Start: On the Heideggerian Origins of 'Political Philosophy,'" *European Journal of Political Theory*, 9.3 (2010); 287–307.

Cicero, Marcus Tullius. *On the Republic and on the Laws*, translated by David Fott. Ithaca, NY: Cornell University Press, 2014.

Cohen, Hermann. *The Ethics of Maimonides,* translated by Almut Sh. Bruckstein. Madison:: University of Wisconsin Press, 2004.

———. *Reason and Hope: Selections from the Jewish Writings of Hermann Cohen*, translated and edited by Eva Jospe. Cincinnati, OH: HUC Press, 1993.

———. *Religion of Reason out of the Sources of Judaism*, translated by Simon Kaplan. Atlanta, GA: Scholar's Press, 1995.

———. *Werke: Band 15—Kleinere Schriften 4: 1907–1912*, edited by Hartwig Wiedebach. Hildescheim, Germany: Georg Olms Verlag, 2009.

———. *Werke: Band 17—Kleinere Schriften 6: 1916–1918*, edited by Hartwig Wiederbach. Hildescheim, Germany: Georg Olms Verlag, 2002.

Cohen, Jonathan. *Philosophers and Scholars: Wolfson, Guttmann, and Strauss on the History of Jewish Philosophy*, translated by Rachel Yarden. Lanham, MD: Lexington Books, 2007.

Colmo, Christopher. "Reason and Revelation in the Thought of Leo Strauss," *Interpretation* 18.1 (Fall 1990): 145–160.

Emberley, Peter and Barry Cooper, eds. and trans. *Faith and Political Philosophy: The Correspondence Between Leo Strauss and Eric Voegelin.* University Park, PA: Pennsylvania State University Press, 1993.

Forti, Simona, "The Biopolitics of Souls: Racism, Nazism, and Plato." *Political Theory* 34.9 (2006): 9–32.

Fortin, Ernest L. *Classical Christianity and the Political Order: Reflections on the Theologico-Political Problem*, edited by J. Brian Benstad. Lanham, MD: Rowman and Littlefield Publishers, 1996.

———. *Ever Ancient, Ever New: Ruminations on the City, the Soul, and the Church*, edited by Michael P. Foley. Lanham, MD: Rowman and Littlefield, 2007.

Gabriel, Markus. "God's Transcendent Activity: Ontotheology in *Metaphysics* 12." *Review of Metaphysics* 25 (December 2009): 385–414.

Gilbert, Martin. *Israel: A History*. New York: Harper Publishers, 2008.

Gildin, Hilail. "Leo Strauss on the Understanding of the Politically Better and Worse," *Interpretation* 35.1 (2006): 3–10.

Gourevitch, Victor. "Philosophy and Politics II." *Review of Metaphysics* 22 (1968): 281–328.

Guttmann, Julius. *Philosophies of Judaism: The History of Jewish Philosophy from Biblical Times to Franz Rosenzweig*, translated by David W. Silverman. New York: Holt, Reinhart, and Winston, 1964.

Green, Kenneth Hart. *Jew and Philosopher: The Return to Maimonides in the Jewish Thought of Leo Strauss*. Albany: State University of New York Press, 1993.

———. *Leo Strauss and the Rediscovery of Maimonides*. Chicago: University of Chicago Press, 2013.

Halbertal, Moshe. *Concealment and Revelation: Esotericism in Jewish Thought and Its Philosophical Implications*, translated by Jackie Feldman. Princeton, NJ: Princeton University Press, 2007.

Halbertal, Moshe and Avishai Margalit. *Idolatry*, translated by Naomi Goldblum. Cambridge, MA: Harvard University Press, 1992.

Halevi, Judah. *The Kuzari: An Argument for the Faith of Israel*, translated by Hartwig Hirschfeld. New York: Schocken Books, 1964.

HaLevi, Rabbi Yehuda. *The Kuzari: In Defense of the Despised Faith*, translated by N. Daniel Korobkin. New York: Feldheim Publishers, 2009.

Harshav, Benjamin. *Language in a Time of Revolution*. Berkeley, CA: University of California Press, 1993.

Harvey, Warren Zev. "The Return of Maimonideanism." *Jewish Social Studies* 42.3–4 (Summer-Autumn 1980): 249–268.

———. "The Seventy Languages of Shem and Japeth," paper presented, Bologna, Italy, June 2009, unpublished paper.

———. "Why Maimonides Was Not a Mutakallimun," pp. 105–114. In *Perspectives on Maimonides: Philosophical and Historical Studies*, edited by Joel Kraemer. Oxford, UK: The Littman Library of Jewish Civilization, 2008.

Hegel, G. W. F. *The Phenomenology of Mind*, translated by J. B. Baillie. New York: Harper Torchbooks, 1967.

Heidegger, Martin. *Schelling's Treatise on the Essence of Human Freedom*, translated by Joan Stambaugh. Athens, OH: Ohio University Press, 1985.

Herzberg, Arthur, ed. *The Zionist Idea: A Historical Analysis and Reader.* Philadelphia: The Jewish Publication Society, 1997.

Homer. *Iliad*, translated by Robert Fagels. New York: Penguin Books, 1990.

Howse, Robert. *Leo Strauss: Man of Peace.* Cambridge, UK: Cambridge University Press, 2014.

———. "The Philosophy of Law and the Legal Status and Role of Philosophy: Reflections On Leo Strauss, *Philosophie Und Gesetz*," unpublished paper.

Husik, Isaac. *A History of Medieval Jewish Philosophy.* New York: Dover Publications, 2002.

Ivry, Alfred L. "The Jerusalem of Medieval Jewish Philosophy," pp. 29–52. In *Gladly To Learn, Gladly To Teach: Essays on Religion And Philosophy in Honor of Ernest L. Fortin, A.*, edited by Michael P. Foley and Douglas Kries. Lanham, MD: Lexington Books, 2002.

Janssens, David. *Between Athens and Jerusalem: Philosophy, Prophecy, and Politics in Leo Strauss's Early Thought.* Albany: State University of New York Press, 2008.

———. "The Philosopher's Ancient Clothes," pp. 53–71. In *Modernity and What Has Been Lost: Considerations on the Legacy of Leo Strauss*, edited by Armanda, Paweł, and Arkadiusz Górnisiewicz. South Bend, IN: St. Augustine's Press, 2011.

Jonas, Hans. *Memoirs*, translated by Krishna Wilson, edited by Christian Wiese. Waltham, MA: Brandeis University Press, 2008.

Kant, Immanuel. *Critique of Pure Reason*, translated and edited by Paul Guyer and Allen W. Wood. Cambridge, UK: Cambridge University Press, 1997.

———. *Political Writings*, translated by H. B. Nisbett and edited by Hans Reiss. Cambridge, UK: Cambridge University Press, 1991.

Kennington, Richard. "Strauss's *Natural Right and History*," pp. 227–252. In . *Leo Strauss's Thought: Towards a Critical Engagement*, edited by Alan Udoff. Boulder, CO: Lynne Reinner Publishers, 1991.

Klein, Jacob. *A Commentary on Plato's* Meno. Chicago: University of Chicago Press, 1989.

Kochin, Michael S. "Morality, Nature, and Esotericism in Leo Strauss's *Persecution and the Art of Writing*," *Review of Politics* 64.2 (Spring 2002): 261–283.

Kohn, Hans. *The Idea of Nationalism: A Study in Its Origins and Background.* New Brunswick, CT: Transaction Publishers, 2005.

Lachterman, David R. *The Ethics of Geometry: A Genealogy of Modernity.* New York: Routledge, 1989.

Lampert, Laurence. "The Argument of Strauss's 'What Is Political Philosophy?'" *Modern Age* 22 (Winter 1978): 38–46.

———. *The Enduring Importance of Leo Strauss.* Chicago: University of Chicago Press, 2013.

———. *Leo Strauss and Nietzsche.* Chicago: University of Chicago Press, 1996.

———. "Nietzsche's Challenge to Philosophy in the Thought of Leo Strauss," *Review of Metaphysics* 58.3 (March 2005): 585–619.

———. "Strauss's Recovery of Esotericism," pp. 63–92. In *The Cambridge Companion to Leo Strauss*, edited by Steven Smith. Cambridge, UK: Cambridge University Press, 2009.

Lazier, Benjamin. *God Interrupted: Heresy and the European Imagination Between the World Wars.* Princeton, NJ: Princeton University Press, 2008.

Lebovic, Nitzan. "The Jerusalem School: The Theopolitical Hour." *New German Critique* 35.3 (Fall 2008): 97–120.

Leibowitz, Yeshayahu. *Judaism, Human Values, and the Jewish State*, edited by Eliezer Goldman. Cambridge, MA: Harvard University Press, 1992.

———. Yeshayahu. "Maimonides—The Abrahamic Man," translated by Elvin Kose. *Judaism* 6.2 (1957): 148–154.

Lenzner, Steven. "A Literary Exercise in Self-Knowledge: Strauss's Two-Fold Interpretation of Maimonides." *Perspectives on Political Science* 31.4 (Fall 2002): 225–234.

Lerner, Ralph. "Dispersal by Design." In *Reason, Faith, and Politics: Essays in Honor of Werner J. Dannhauser*, edited by Arthur M. Melzer and Robert P. Kraynak. Lanham, MD: Lexington Books, 2008.

Lessing, Gotthold Ephraim. *Nathan the Wise, Minna Von Barnheim, and Other Plays and Writings*, edited by Peter Demetz. New York: Continuum, 1995.

Linker, Damon. "The Philosopher and Everyone Else." *The New Republic*, July 31, 2006.

Locke, John. *An Essay Concerning Human Understanding*, edited by Peter H. Niddich. Oxford, UK: Oxford University Press, 1979.

McCormick, John P., "Fear, Technology, and the State: Carl Schmitt, Leo Strauss, and the Revival of Hobbes in Weimar and National Socialist Germany." *Political Theory* 22.4 (1994): 619–652.

Machiavelli, Niccolò. *The Prince*, translated by Harvey Mansfield. Chicago: University of Chicago Press, 1998.

Maimonides, Moses. *Ethical Writings of Maimonides*, edited by Raymond L. Weiss and Charles Butterworth. New York: Dover Publications, 1975.

———. *The Guide of the Perplexed: Volumes One and Two*, translated by Shlomo Pines. Chicago: University of Chicago Press, 1963.

———. "Logic," translated by Muhsin Mahdi. In *Medieval Political Philosophy: A Sourcebook*, 2nd ed., edited by Joshua Parens and Joseph C. Macfarland. Ithaca, NY: Cornell University Press, 2011.

Major, Rafael, ed. *Leo Strauss's Defense of the Philosophical Life: Reading* What Is Political Philosophy? Chicago: University of Chicago Press, 2013.

Meier, Heinrich. *Carl Schmitt and Leo Strauss: The Hidden Dialogue*, translated by J. Harvey Lomax. Chicago: University of Chicago Press, 1995.

———. "How Strauss Became Strauss," pp. 363–382. In *Enlightening Revolutions: Essays in Honor of Ralph Lerner*, edited by Svetozar Minkov. Lanham, MD: Lexington Books, 2006.

———. *Leo Strauss and the Theological-Political Problem*, translated by Marcus Brainard. Cambridge, UK: Cambridge University Press, 2006.

———. *The Lesson of Carl Schmitt: Four Chapters on the Distinction Between Political Theology and Political Philosophy*, translated by Marcus Brainard. Chicago: University of Chicago Press, 2011.

Meyer, Thomas. "Leo Strauss's Religious Rhetoric (1924–1938)," unpublished paper.

Mendes-Flohr, Paul and Jehuda Reinharz, eds. *The Jew in the*

Modern World: A Documentary History, 3rd ed. Oxford, UK: Oxford University Press, 2011.

Mhire, Jeremy. "What Is Really Different About *What Is Political Philosophy?*" *Perspectives On Political Science* 40.1 (January–March 2011): 54–57.

Motzkin, Aryeh, "Halevi's *Kuzari* as a Platonic Dialogue." *Interpretation* 9 (1980): 111–124.

Motzkin, Aryeh Leo. "On the Interpretation of Maimonides." *Independent Journal of Philosophy* 2 (1978): 39–46.

Moyn, Samuel. "From Experience to Law: Leo Strauss and the Weimar Crisis of the Philosophy of Religion." *History of European Ideas* 33, 2007: 174–194.

Muller, Jerry, "Leo Strauss: The Political Philosopher as a Young Zionist." *Jewish Social Studies* 17.1 (Fall 2010): 88–115.

Nietzsche, Friedrich. *Basic Writings of Nietzsche*, translated and edited by Walter Kaufmann. New York: Modern Library, 2000.

Orr, Susan. *Jerusalem and Athens: Reason and Revelation in the Works of Leo Strauss*. Lanham, MD: Rowman and Littlefield, 1995.

Pangle, Thomas L. *Leo Strauss: An Introduction to His Thought and Intellectual Legacy*. Baltimore: Johns Hopkins University Press, 2006.

Parens, Joshua. *Maimonides and Spinoza: Their Conflicting Views of Human Nature*. Chicago: University of Chicago Press, 2012.

———. "Prudence, Imagination, and Determination of Law in Alfarabi and Maimonides," pp. 31–55. In *Enlightening Revolutions: Essays in Honor of Ralph Lerner*, edited by Svetozar Minkov. Lanham, MD: Lexington Books, 2006.

———. "Strauss on Maimonides's Secretive Political Science," pp. 116–136. In *Leo Strauss's Defense of the Philosophical Life: Reading* What Is Political Philosophy?, edited by Rafael Major. Chicago: University of Chicago Press, 2013.

Pelluchon, Corine. *Leo Strauss and the Crisis of Rationalism: Another Reason, Another Enlightenment*, translated by Robert Howse. Albany: State University of New York Press, 2014.

———. "Strauss and Christianity," translator unknown, *Interpretation* 33. 2 (2006): 185–203.

Pegis, Anton C., ed. *Introduction to St. Thomas Aquinas:* The Summa Theologica *and* the Summa Contra Gentiles. New York: Modern Library, 1948.

Pines, Shlomo. "Aristotle's *Politics* in Arabic Philosophy." *Israel Oriental Studies* V (1975): 150–160.

Plato. *The Laws*, translated by Thomas Pangle. Chicago: University of Chicago Press, 1980.

Portnoff, Sharon. *Reason and Revelation Before Historicism: Strauss and Fackenheim*. Toronto: University of Toronto Press, 2011.

Rawidowicz, Simon. "On Interpretation," *Proceedings of the American Academy for Jewish Research* 26 (1957): 83–126.

Reinhardt, Karl. "Philosophy and History Among the Greeks." *Greece & Rome*, Second Series 1. 2 (June 1954): 82–90.

Rosen, Stanley. *The Ancients and the Moderns: Rethinking Modernity*. New Haven, CT: Yale University Press, 1989.

———. *Essays in Philosophy: Ancient*, edited by Martin Black. South Bend, IN: St. Augustine's Press, 2013.

———. *Hermeneutics as Politics*, 2nd ed. New Haven, CT: Yale University Press, 2003.

———. *The Idea of Hegel's* Science of Logic. Chicago: University of Chicago Press, 2014.

———. "Leo Strauss and the Possibility of Philosophy," *Review of Metaphysics* 53 (March 2000): 541–564.

———. *Plato's Symposium*. New Haven, CT: Yale University Press, 1987.

Rosenthal, Michael A. "Spinoza and the Crisis of Liberalism in Weimar Germany," *Hebraic Political Studies* 3.1 (Winter 2008): 94–112.

Rousseau, Jean-Jacques. *The Reveries of the Solitary Walker*, translated by Charles E. Butterworth. Indianapolis, IN: Hackett Publishing Company, 1992.

Schlipp, Paul Arthur and Maurice Friedman, eds. *The Philosophy of Martin Buber*. La Salle, IL: Open Court, 1967.

Schmitt, Carl. *The Concept of the Political*, translated by George Schwab. Chicago: University of Chicago Press, 2007.

———. *The* Nomos *of the Earth*, translated by G. L. Ulmen. New York: Telos Press, 2003.

———. "A Pan-European Interpretation of Donoso Cortés," translated by Mark Grzeskowiak. *Telos* 125 (2002): 100–115.

———. *Political Theology: Four Chapters on the Concept of Sovereignty*, translated by George Schwab. Chicago: University of Chicago Press, 2005.

———. "Three Possibilities for a Christian Conception of History," translated by Mario Wenning. *Telos* 147 (2009): 167–170.

Scholem, Gershom. *The Messianic Idea in Judaism and Other Essays on Jewish Spirituality*. New York: Schocken Books, 1995.

———. *On the Possibility of Jewish Mysticism in Our Time and Other Essays*, translated by Jonathan Chipman and edited by Avraham Shapira. Philadelphia: The Jewish Publication Society, 1997.

Shell, Susan. "'To Spare the Vanquished and Crush the Arrogant': Leo Strauss's Lecture on 'German Nihilism,'" pp. 171à192. In *The Cambridge Companion to Leo Strauss*, edited by Steven Smith. Cambridge, UK: Cambridge University Press, 2009.

Sheppard, Eugene R. *Leo Strauss and the Politics of Exile: The Making of a Political Philosopher*. Waltham, MA: Brandeis University Press, 2006.

Shestov, Lev. *Athens and Jerusalem*, translated by Bernard Martin. New York: Simon and Schuster, 1968.

Shimony, Tali Tadmor. "Teaching the Bible as a Common Culture." *Jewish History* 21 (2007): 159–178.

Smith, Gregory Bruce. *Between Eternities: On the Tradition of Political Philosophy, Past Present and Future*. Lanham, MD: Lexington Books, 2008.

Smith, Steven, "Introduction: Leo Strauss Today," pp. 1–12. In *The Cambridge Companion to Leo Strauss*, edited by Steven Smith. Cambridge, UK: Cambridge University Press, 2009.

Smith, Steven. *Reading Leo Strauss: Politics, Philosophy, Judaism*. Chicago: University of Chicago Press, 2006.

Smith, Steven Benjamin. "Leo Strauss's Discovery of the Theological-Political Problem," *European Journal of Political Theory* 12. 4 (October 2013): 388–408.

Spinoza, Baruch. *Theological-Political Treatise*, translated by Martin Yaffe. Newburyport, MA: Focus Publishing, 2004.

Spinoza, Benedict. *The Collected Works of Spinoza: Volume 1*, translated and edited by Edwin Curley. Princeton, NJ: Princeton University Press, 1985.

———. *Opera*, 4 vols., edited by Carl Gebhardt. Heidelberg, Germany: C. Winter, 1925.

Strauss, Leo. *The Early Writings (1921–1932)*, edited and translated by Michael Zank. Albany: State University of New York Press, 2002.

———. "Farabi's Plato," *Louis Ginzberg Jubilee Volume*. New York: American Academy for Jewish Research, 1945.

———. *Gesammelte Schriften—Band 3: Hobbes' Politische Wissenschaft Und Zugehörige Schriften—Briefe*, Zweite Auflage, edited by Heinrich Meier and Wiebke Meier. Stuttgart, Germany: J. B. Metzler, 2008.

———. *Introduction to Political Philosophy*, edited by Hilail Gildin. Detroit: Wayne State University Press, 1989.

———. *Jewish Philosophy and the Crisis of Modernity: Essays and Lectures in Modern Jewish Thought*, edited by Kenneth Hart Green. Albany: State University of New York Press, 1997.

———. *Leo Strauss on Maimonides: The Complete Writings*, edited by Kenneth Hart Green. Chicago: University of Chicago Press, 2013.

———. *Leo Strauss on Moses Mendelssohn*, edited and translated by Martin D. Yaffe. Chicago: University of Chicago Press, 2012.

———. *Liberalism Ancient and Modern*. Chicago: University of Chicago Press, 1995.

———. "More Early Writings from the *Jüdische Wochenzeitung für Cassel, Hessen und Waldeck*," edited by Thomas Meyer, translated by Michael Zank, *Interpretation* 39.2 (2012): 109–137.

———. *Natural Right and History*. Chicago: University of Chicago Press, 1965.

———. "On Collingwood's Philosophy of History," *Review of Metaphysics* 5.4 (June 1952): 559–586.

———. "On a New Interpretation of Plato's Political Philosophy," *Social Research* 13 (September 1946): 326–367.

———. *On Plato's Symposium*, edited by Seth Benardete. Chicago: University of Chicago Press, 2001.

———. *On Tyranny*, edited by Victor Gourevitch and Michael S. Roth. Chicago: University of Chicago Press, 2000.

———. "Persecution and the Art of Writing." *Social Research* 8.1–4 (1941): 488–504.

———. *Persecution and the Art of Writing*. Chicago: University of Chicago Press, 1988.

———. *Philosophy and Law: Contributions to the Understanding of Maimonides and His Predecessors*, translated by Eve Adler. Albany: State University of New York Press, 1995.

———. *The Political Philosophy of Hobbes: Its Basis and Its Genesis*, translated by Elsa M. Sinclair. Chicago: University of Chicago Press, 1984.

———. *The Rebirth of Classical Political Rationalism: Essays and Lectures by Leo Strauss*, edited by Thomas L. Pangle. Chicago: University of Chicago Press, 1989.

———. "The Re-education of the Axis Countries Concerning the Jews," *Review of Politics* 69.4 (2007): 530–538.

———. *Reorientation: Leo Strauss in the 1930s*, edited by Martin D. Yaffe and Richard S. Ruderman. New York: Palgrave MacMillan, 2014.

———. "Restatement," Critical Edition edited by Emmanuel Patard, *Interpretation* 36.1 (Fall 2008): 3–100.

———. *Socrates and Aristophanes.* Chicago: University of Chicago Press, 1980.

———. *Spinoza's Critique of Religion*, translated by E. M. Sinclair. Chicago: University of Chicago Press, 1997.

———. "The Spirit of Sparta or the Taste for Xenophon," *Social Research* 6.1–4 (1939): 502–536.

———. *Studies in Platonic Political Philosophy*, edited by Thomas Pangle. Chicago: University of Chicago Press, 1983.

———. *Thoughts on Machiavelli.* Chicago: University of Chicago Press, 1984.

———. "What Is Political Philosophy?" *Journal of Politics*, 19.3 (August 1957), 343–368.

———. *What Is Political Philosophy? And Other Studies.* Chicago: University of Chicago Press, 1988.

Strauss, Leo, and Hans-Georg Gadamer. "Correspondence Concerning *Warheit Und Methode.*" *Independent Journal of Philosophy* 2 (1978): 5–12.

Tanakh: A New Translation of the Holy Scriptures According to the Traditional Hebrew Text. Philadelphia: The Jewish Publication Society, 1985.

Tanguay, Daniel. *Leo Strauss: An Intellectual Biography*, translated by Christopher Nadon. New Haven, CT: Yale University Press, 2007.

Tarcov, Nathan. "Philosophy and History: Tradition and Interpretation in the Work of Leo Strauss," *Polity* 16.1 (Autumn 1983): 5–29.

Taubes, Jacob. *From Cult to Culture: Fragments Toward a Critique of*

Historical Reason, edited by Charlotte Elisheva Fonrobert and Amir Engel. Stanford, CA: Stanford University Press, 2010.

Tepper, Aryeh. *Progressive Minds, Conservative Politics: Leo Strauss's Later Writings on Maimonides.* Albany: State University of New York Press, 2013.

Tertullian, *The Prescription Against the Heretics*, in *Anti-Nicene Fathers: Volume Three*, edited by Alexander Roberts, James Donaldson, and A. Cleveland Coxe. Buffalo, NY: Christian Literature Publishing Co., 1885.

Twersky, Isadore. *Introduction to the Code of Maimonides (Mishnah Torah).* New Haven, CT: Yale University Press, 1980.

Udoff, Alan. "After Such Knowledge, What Forgiveness? On Jankélévitch and the Question of Repentance," pp. 191–217. In *Vladamir Jankélévitch and the Question of Forgiveness*, edited by Alan Udoff. Lanham, MD: Lexington Books, 2013.

———. "Levinas and the Question of Friendship." *Levinas Studies: An Annual Review* 1 (2005): 139–155, 191–196.

———. "On Leo Strauss: An Introductory Account," pp. 1–29. In *Leo Strauss's Thought: Towards a Critical Engagement*, edited by Alan Udoff. Boulder, CO: Lynne Reinner Publishers, 1991.

———. "Retracing the Steps of Franz Rosenzweig," pp. 153–173, 192–213. In *Franz Rosenzweig's "The New Thinking,"* translated and edited by Alan Udoff and Barbara Galli. Syracuse, NY: Syracuse University Press, 1999.

Urban, Martina. "Persecution and the Art of Representation: Schocken's Maimonides Anthologies of the 1930s." In *Maimonides and His Heritage*, edited by Idit Dobbs Weinstein, Lenn E. Goodman, and James Allan Grady. Albany: State University of New York Press, 2009.

Vatter, Miguel. "Natural Right and State of Exception in Leo Strauss," pp. 190–206. In *Crediting God: Sovereignty and Religion in the Age of Global Capitalism*, edited by Miguel Vatter. New York: Fordham University Press, 2011.

Vatter, Miguel E. "Taking Exception to Liberalism: Heinrich Meier's *Carl Schmitt and Leo Strauss: The Hidden Dialogue.*" *Graduate Faculty Philosophy Journal* 19–20 (1997): 323–344.

Velkley, Richard. *Heidegger, Strauss, and the Premises of Philosophy: On Original Forgetting.* Chicago: University of Chicago Press, 2011.

Weiss, Roslyn. "Four Parables About *Peshat* as Parable," *CCAR* 4 (2008): 3–19.

Wolfson, Harry Austryn. "Maimonides and Halevi: A Study in Typical Jewish Attitudes Towards Greek Philosophy in the Middle Ages." *The Jewish Quarterly Review*, New Series 2.3 (January 1912): 297–337.

Wurgaft, Benjamin Aldes. "Culture and Law in Weimar Jewish Medievalism: Leo Strauss's Critique of Julius Guttmann." *Modern Intellectual History* 11.1 (2014): 119–146.

Yovel, Yirmiyahu. *Spinoza and Other Heretics: The Marrano of Reason*. Princeton: Princeton University Press, 1989.

Zank, Michael. "Arousing Suspicion Against a Prejudice: Leo Strauss and the Study of Maimonides' *Guide of the Perplexed*, pp. 549–571, in *Moses Maimonides (1138–1204): His Religious, Scientific, and Philosophical* Wirkungsgeschichte *in Different Cultural Contexts*, edited by Görge K. Hasselhoff and Otfried Fraisse, in *Ex Oriente Lux: Rezeptionen Und Exegesen Als Traditionskritik: Band 4*, edited by Almut Sh. Bruckstein, Navid Kermani, Angelika Neuwirth and Andreas Pflitsch. Würzburg, Germany: Ergon Verlag, 2004.

———. "The Heteronomy of Jewish Philosophy," *Journal of Jewish Thought and Philosophy* 20.1 (2012): 99–134.

———. "Jewish Philosopher of the Hour?" *Review of Politics* 71.4 (2009): 662–668.

Zuckert, Michael, "Straussians," in *The Cambridge Companion to Leo Strauss*, edited by Steven Smith, pp. 263–286. Cambridge, UK: Cambridge University Press, 2009.

Zuckert, Michael and Catherine Zuckert. *The Truth About Leo Strauss: Political Philosophy and American Democracy*. Chicago: University of Chicago Press, 2006.

INDEX

Abravanel, Isaac, 44, 181
Adorno, Theodor, xxiv, 27, 46, 163, 166, 181, 205
Ahad Ha'am, 23–24, 108, 175
Aksin, Benjamin, 79
Albo, Joseph, 18, 199
  Text:
  Book of Roots 18, 199
Altman, William H. F., 94, 191–193, 196, 200
Altmann, Alexander, xxvii, 35, 40–41, 43, 46, 178, 180–181, 191
Aquinas, Thomas, 95–96, 199, 215
Arendt, Hannah, 7, 27, 169, 175, 188
Aristophanes, 52, 172, 205
Aristotle, xxi, 16, 25, 37, 39–40, 42–43, 46, 49, 54, 56–57, 59, 71, 93, 99, 116, 122, 135–136, 142, 148–149, 158, 164, 180, 186, 190, 193, 199, 201, 204–205
Aristotelian, xxviii, 11–12, 37–39, 41–43, 49, 56–58, 60, 80, 122, 128, 136, 158, 161, 185, 194, 199, 204
  Aristotelize, 57, 158
  Texts:
  Nicomachean Ethics, 93, 180, 193, 199
  Politics, 122
Arnold, Matthew, xxvi, 7–8, 10–11, 170
  Text:
  Culture and Anarchy, 37, 170
Athenian Stranger, 65, 71, 140, 192
Athens. *See* Theological-Political Problem
Auerbach, Eric, xxvi, 8–11, 170–171
  Text:
  Mimesis, 8, 200
Augustine, 5–7, 10–11, 142, 169–172
  Texts:
  City of God, 5, 169, 171
  Confessions, 6, 170
Averroes, 16, 51, 131, 135–136, 142, 200
  Averroism, 127
  Text:
  On Plato's Republic, 135
Avicenna, 44
  Text:
  Divisions of the Rational Sciences, 44, 47, 51

Bacon, Francis, 120
Bar-Hillel, Yehoshua, 78
Baron, Salo, xxvii, 35, 40–41, 43, 48, 178, 180
Barth, Karl, 17–18, 107, 138
Batnitzky, Leora, xxii–xxiii, 166, 174, 178, 182
Beethoven, Ludwig von, 46, 181
Benardete, Seth, xxvii, 50, 54, 75–76, 155, 167, 173, 182–184, 204
Benjamin, Walter, 27, 47, 181
Bergmann, Samuel Hugo, 102
Bergson, Henri, 111
Bloom, Alan, xxii, 44
Brague, Rémi, 17, 44, 51, 171, 175, 180, 182
Buber, Martin, xxvii, 5, 25, 27–32, 65, 73, 78, 83–84, 92, 102, 104–110, 116, 176–177, 190, 195–196
  Texts:
  Kingship of God, 83, 190, 195–196
  Moses, 104–105, 196
  The Prophetic Faith, 104, 107, 196
  Buberian, 5, 25, 102, 108

Cohen, Geulah, 102
Cohen, Hermann, xxvii, 5, 17–19, 25–31, 35, 38–41, 43–44, 54, 56, 84, 92, 11–112, 138, 175, 179, 204
  Texts:
  Religion of Reason Out of the Sources of Judaism, 18, 26, 28, 175–176
  Ethics of Maimonides, 39, 176, 179, 210
  "The Social Ideal of Plato and the Prophets," 30
  Cohenian, 5, 25, 26, 56
Cropsey, Joseph, 22

De Lagarde, Paul, 17
Diachronic approach, xxiv–xxv, 50. *See also* Synchronic approach

Ebbinghaus, Julian, 17
Empedocles, 16

Farabi, 14, 16, 44, 51, 64, 131, 136, 142, 164, 171, 173, 185, 194, 199, 201
  Farabian, 46, 202
Freud, Sigmund, 17

Glatzer, Nahum, 34–35, 44, 50, 166, 176, 179, 195–196
Gogarten, Friedrich, 138
Green, Kenneth Hart, 162, 163, 169, 173, 180–181
Guttmann, Julius, 38–39, 41–43, 48, 57, 174, 179–180, 186, 202

Halevi, Judah, xxix, 37, 55, 136, 143–145, 147–149, 153, 161, 173, 179, 184, 188, 203
  Text:
  Kuzari, 173, 184, 188
Hebrew University of Jerusalem, xxvi–xxviii, 28, 44, 48, 63–65, 67, 70–73, 76–78, 80, 83, 85–86, 92, 98–99, 102, 104, 108, 110–112, 120, 130, 132, 140, 167, 185, 190–191, 195, 198
Hegel, Georg Friedrich Wilhelm, 25, 29, 55, 120, 125, 156, 158, 160, 162
  Hegelian, 29, 156, 158, 160
Heidegger, Martin, xxi, 4, 36, 51, 55, 90, 107, 109, 111–112, 116–117, 120, 151, 164, 169, 184, 186, 188, 191, 196
  Heideggerian, 186
Heraclitus, 75
Herzl, Theodore, 17, 98–100

Hesiod, 16
Hobbes, Thomas, xxi, 8, 19, 26, 35, 48, 96, 120, 125–126, 135, 137, 178–179, 185, 192
  Hobbesian, 125
Homer, 10, 50, 54, 183, 187
  Homeric, 10, 184, 191
Husik, Isaac, xxvii, 35, 39, 42–44, 57, 170, 178–180
Husserl, Edmund, 111
  Husserlian, 198

Israel, xxviii, 19, 29, 39–40, 42, 54, 56, 65–71, 79–81, 85, 102, 104, 106–107, 113–116, 118, 119, 130–131, 158, 186–187, 194, 201

Jabotinsky, Vladamir 'Ze'ev', 19, 65–66, 79
Jacobi, Friedrich Heinrich, 17, 21–22
Jaffa, Harry, xxii
Janssens, David, xxiv, 149, 171, 174, 186, 200, 204
Jerusalem. *See* Theological-Political Problem

Kalam, 15, 42, 54–55, 59, 144
Kant, Immanuel, xxi, 3–5, 16–17, 25–27, 29–31, 38, 85, 94, 99, 112, 120, 125, 142, 159, 164, 169, 171, 176–177
  Texts:
  "Perpetual Peace—A Philosophical Sketch," 30, 177
  Prolegomena to Any Future Metaphysics, 29
  Kantian, xxvii, 25–26, 29, 32, 159–160
Katechon, 103, 195
Kaufmann, Yehezikel, 78
Kendall, Willmoore, 67
Kierkegaard, 11, 107, 159–162
  Kierkiegaardian, 9, 102
Klausner, Joseph, 68
Klein, Jacob, xxvii, 33, 47–48, 181, 188
Kohn, Hans, xxvi, 8–11, 170–171
  Text:
  The Idea of Nationalism, 8, 170
Krüger, Gerhard, xxvii, 18, 47
Kuhn, Helmut, 49

Lampert, Laurence, 65, 79, 156, 169, 174, 181–182, 186, 188, 190–191, 198
Lebovic, Nitzan, 102, 167, 194–196
Leibniz, Gottfried Wilhelm, 142–143
Leibowitz, Nehama, 78
Leibowitz, Yeshayahu, 78, 116, 189
Lessing, Gotthold Ephraim, 20–21, 33, 175, 177, 201
Locke, John, 96–97, 120, 125, 189, 192–193
  Text:
  An Essay Concerning Human Understanding, 97
Löwith, Karl, xxvii, 47
  Text:
  Meaning in History, 103
Luther, Martin, 102

Machiavelli, Niccolò, xxi, 83, 96–99, 116, 120, 124, 126–128, 130–131, 137, 159, 178, 190, 192
  Text:
  The Prince, 83
Maimonides, Moses, xxi–xxii, xxvii–xxix, 14, 18, 24–25, 33–60, 63–64, 72, 74, 90–92, 116, 120–121, 123–124, 128–132, 135–139, 141–147, 151, 153–155, 158, 162, 166,

Maimonides (*continued*)
170, 173, 175–176, 178–182, 184–185, 189, 194, 199–204
Texts:
The Guide of the Perplexed, 18, 33, 40, 42, 45, 48–50, 53–54, 57–59, 64, 74, 129, 143, 146, 176, 180, 184, 189, 194
Eight Chapters, 50, 180
Mishneh Torah, 40, 45, 58–59, 146, 180
Maimonidean, xxi, xxix, 42, 132, 138, 150, 160, 162, 189, 200, 203
Marx, Karl, 120, 189
Meier, Heinrich, xxii-xxix, 14, 20, 45, 137–138, 155–161, 166, 174–175, 179–182, 194–196, 202, 204–205
Mendelssohn, Moses, 18, 20–22, 26, 167
Meyer, Thomas, 18, 175, 182

Nasser, Gamal Abdel, 68
Neo-Orthodoxy, xxi, 18–20, 34, 138, 175
Nietzsche, Friedrich, xxi, 4, 11, 17, 29, 45, 51, 120–121, 124, 138, 164, 169, 172, 181, 186, 187, 190–191
Text:
Thus Spoke Zarathustra, 45
Nietzschean, 9, 156, 158, 160, 191, 202
Nomos, nomoi, 86, 123, 128, 130, 147–148, 184
Nordau. Max, 17

Odegard, Peter H., 71, 187
Otto, Rudolph, 17

Parmenides, 16
Paul, 6
Pines, Shlomo, 45, 78, 116, 176, 184, 201, 214
Pinsker, Leo, 98–101, 194
Pinskerian, 99
Plato, xxi, 7, 14–17, 25, 27–28, 30, 40, 43, 45–46, 52, 57, 71–72, 74–75
Texts:
Euthyphro, 97
Laws, 45, 47, 51, 65, 184
Phaedrus, 57
Republic, 74, 135–136
Platonic, xxvii–xxix, 7, 11, 30, 49, 51–52, 56, 58–59, 60, 63–87, 92, 132, 135–139, 143, 147, 150, 152, 158–159, 161, 182, 188, 191, 202–203
Platonist/Platonism, 7, 40, 56, 159–160
Plotinus, 142
Political Theology, 55, 101–105, 108–109, 138, 155, 158–159

Rawidowicz, Simon, xxvii, 35, 42–43, 57, 178, 180
Rosen, Stanley, 3–4, 12–13, 94, 137, 168–169, 189–190, 206
Rosenzweig, Franz, xxi, 17–19, 69, 105, 109, 138, 175, 179, 187
Rotenstreich, Nathan, 78
Rousseau, Jean-Jacques, 120, 125, 173

Sartre, Jean-Paul, 107
Savan, David, 144, 203
Schelling, Friedrich Willhelm Joseph von, 55, 184
Schmitt, Carl, 12, 36, 55, 94, 101–109, 155–156, 158–159, 179, 194–196, 204–205
Texts:

The Concept of the Political, 101–102, 195
The Nomos of the Earth, 103, 195
Political Theology, 101–102, 195
"Three Possibilities for a Christian Conception of History," 103, 195
Schmittian, 102, 107–108, 160
Scholem, Gershom, xxvii, 35, 47–49, 64–65, 69–70, 78, 106, 112, 116, 181, 182, 187, 197, 201
Schopenhauer, Arthur, 17
Shestov, Lev, xxvi, 8–9, 11–12, 15, 170
Simon, Ernst, 47
Socrates, 9, 13, 25, 48, 51–53, 55, 57, 74, 81, 85, 140, 172–173, 185, 198
Socratic/Socratism, 43, 45, 57, 59, 76, 93–95, 97, 158, 172, 202
Sophocles, 97
Text:
Antigone, 97
Spinoza, Baruch, xxi, xxix, 8–9, 19, 26, 35–36, 44, 51, 74, 85, 98–100, 108, 135–139, 141, 145, 149–155, 160, 162, 164, 171, 178–179, 190, 194, 200–201, 203–204
Texts:
Ethics, 74, 145
Theological-Political Treatise, 99–100, 143, 145, 194
Treatise on the Emendation of the Intellect, 145
Spinozan, xxix, 95, 135, 138, 142–143, 150, 160, 162
Spinozist, xxix, 21, 139
Strauss, Leo
Texts:
"Cohen and Maimonides," 44, 204
"How to Begin to Study *The Guide of the Perplexed*," 45, 176
"How to Study Medieval Philosophy," 45
"How to Study Spinoza's *Theological-Political Treatise*,"143
"Introduction to Maimonides' *Guide of the Perplexed*," 45
"Jerusalem And Athens," 27
"The Law of Reason in the *Kuzari*," 143, 147
"The Literary Character of *The Guide for the Perplexed*," 45, 143
"Maimonides' Statement on Political Science," 45, 123
Natural Right and History, 49, 60, 166, 198, 205
"Notes on Carl Schmitt's *Concept of the Political*," 101
"Notes on Maimonides' *Book of Knowledge*," 45
"Notes on Maimonides' *Treatise on the Art of Logic*," 45–46
"Notes on Maimonides' *Letter on Astrology*," 46
"On Abravanel's Philosophical Tendency and Political Teaching," 44
Persecution and the Art of Writing, xxix, 33, 45, 136, 138, 171, 203
"The Place of the Doctrine of Providence According to Maimonides," 44
"Progress or Return?," 81
"Restatement of Xenophon's *Hiero*," 163
"Some Remarks on the Political Science of Maimonides and Farabi," 44, 173

Strauss (*continued*)
  Spinoza's Critique of Religion, 36, 44, 51, 108, 136, 138, 171
  Studies in Platonic Political Philosophy, 51, 182
  "What Is Political Philosophy?," 71–73, 76–78, 87, 89–132, 135, 139–140, 151, 166, 168, 185, 191–193
  "Why We Remain Jews," 19, 22–23, 99–100
Straussianism, xxii
  East Coast, xxii
  West Coast, xxii
  Midwest, 166
Synchronic approach, xxiv–xxv, 50. *See also* Diachronic approach

Taubes, Jacob, 102, 106, 196
Tertullian, xxvi, 5–7, 10–11, 15, 169, 171
Theological-Political Problem, xx–xxi, xxiii–xxiv, xxvi–xxvii, 13, 17–20, 22, 24, 31–32, 34, 37, 44, 50–51, 55, 63, 69–71, 76, 78, 91, 99, 103, 111, 113, 119–120, 123, 130, 135, 137, 139, 154, 163, 166–167, 173–174, 178, 182, 204
Torah, 40, 53, 60, 69, 80–81, 97, 118, 131

Urbach, Ephraim, 78
Urban, Martina, 36, 178, 179

Vatter, Miguel, xxix, 137–138, 155, 158–161, 201, 205
Velkley, Richard, 52, 90, 169, 174–175, 182–183, 189, 196, 198

Weber, Max, 13–14, 36, 60
  Weberian, 13, 15, 164
Whitehead, Alfred North, 11, 197
Wissenschaft des Judentums, 18, 35, 37, 112
Wolfson, Harry Austryn, xxvii, 35, 37–39, 42–43, 49, 57, 178–179, 186

Xenophon xxi, 48, 94, 163, 166, 198

Zetesis, Zetetic, 15, 52, 54–55, 59, 94, 96, 119, 152, 174
Zionism, xxi, 19–20, 23–24, 29, 66–67, 70, 108, 177
  Cultural, 29, 108
  Political, 17–18, 23, 67, 80, 84, 99–100, 118
  Religious, 99, 108
Zuckert, Michael, 160, 166, 205
Zunz, Leopold, 35–36, 178